Jazz Child

Studies in Jazz

The Institute of Jazz Studies
Rutgers—The State University of New Jersey
General Editors: Dan Morgenstern and Edward Berger

1. BENNY CARTER: A Life in American Music, *by Morroe Berger, Edward Berger, and James Patrick, 2 vols., 1982*
2. ART TATUM: A Guide to His Recorded Music, *by Arnold Laubich and Ray Spencer, 1982*
3. ERROLL GARNER: The Most Happy Piano, *by James M. Doran, 1985*
4. JAMES P. JOHNSON: A Case of Mistaken Identity, *by Scott E. Brown;* Discography 1917–1950, *by Robert Hilbert, 1986*
5. PEE WEE ERWIN: This Horn for Hire, *as told to Warren W. Vaché Sr., 1987*
6. BENNY GOODMAN: Listen to His Legacy, *by D. Russell Connor, 1988*
7. ELLINGTONIA: The Recorded Music of Duke Ellington and His Sidemen, *by W. E. Timner, 1988; 4th ed., 1996*
8. THE GLENN MILLER ARMY AIR FORCE BAND: Sustineo Alas / I Sustain the Wings, *by Edward F. Polic;* Foreword *by George T. Simon, 1989*
9. SWING LEGACY, *by Chip Deffaa, 1989*
10. REMINISCING IN TEMPO: The Life and Times of a Jazz Hustler, *by Teddy Reig, with Edward Berger, 1990*
11. IN THE MAINSTREAM: 18 Portraits in Jazz, *by Chip Deffaa, 1992*
12. BUDDY DeFRANCO: A Biographical Portrait and Discography, *by John Kuehn and Arne Astrup, 1993*
13. PEE WEE SPEAKS: A Discography of Pee Wee Russell, *by Robert Hilbert, with David Niven, 1992*
14. SYLVESTER AHOLA: The Gloucester Gabriel, *by Dick Hill, 1993*
15. THE POLICE CARD DISCORD, *by Maxwell T. Cohen, 1993*
16. TRADITIONALISTS AND REVIVALISTS IN JAZZ, *by Chip Deffaa, 1993*
17. BASSICALLY SPEAKING: An Oral History of George Duvivier, *by Edward Berger;* Musical Analysis *by David Chevan, 1993*
18. TRAM: The Frank Trumbauer Story, *by Philip R. Evans and Larry F. Kiner, with William Trumbauer, 1994*
19. TOMMY DORSEY: On the Side, *by Robert L. Stockdale, 1995*
20. JOHN COLTRANE: A Discography and Musical Biography, *by Yasuhiro Fujioka, with Lewis Porter and Yoh-ichi Hamada, 1995*
21. RED HEAD: A Chronological Survey of "Red" Nichols and His Five Pennies, *by Stephen M. Stroff, 1996*
22. THE RED NICHOLS STORY: After Intermission 1942–1965, *by Philip R. Evans, Stanley Hester, Stephen Hester, and Linda Evans, 1997*
23. BENNY GOODMAN: Wrappin' It Up, *by D. Russell Connor, 1996*

24. CHARLIE PARKER AND THEMATIC IMPROVISATION, *by Henry Martin, 1996*
25. BACK BEATS AND RIM SHOTS: The Johnny Blowers Story, *by Warren W. Vaché Sr., 1997*
26. DUKE ELLINGTON: A Listener's Guide, *by Eddie Lambert, 1998*
27. SERGE CHALOFF: A Musical Biography and Discography, *by Vladimir Simosko, 1998*
28. HOT JAZZ: From Harlem to Storyville, *by David Griffiths, 1998*
29. ARTIE SHAW: A Musical Biography and Discography, *by Vladimir Simosko, 2000*
30. JIMMY DORSEY: A Study in Contrasts, *by Robert L. Stockdale, 1998*
31. STRIDE!: Fats, Jimmy, Lion, Lamb and All the Other Ticklers, *by John L. Fell and Terkild Vinding, 1999*
32. GIANT STRIDES: The Legacy of Dick Wellstood, *by Edward N. Meyer, 1999*
33. JAZZ GENTRY: Aristocrats of the Music World, *by Warren W. Vaché Sr., 1999*
34. THE UNSUNG SONGWRITERS: America's Masters of Melody, *by Warren W. Vaché Sr., 2000*
35. THE MUSICAL WORLD OF J. J. JOHNSON, *by Joshua Berrett and Louis G. Bourgois III, 1999*
36. THE LADIES WHO SING WITH THE BAND, *by Betty Bennett, 2000*
37. AN UNSUNG CAT: The Life and Music of Warne Marsh, *by Safford Chamberlain, 2000*
38. JAZZ IN NEW ORLEANS: The Postwar Years Through 1970, *by Charles Suhor, 2001*
39. THE YOUNG LOUIS ARMSTRONG ON RECORDS: A Critical Survey of the Early Recordings, 1923–1928, *by Edward Brooks, 2002*
40. BENNY CARTER: A Life in American Music, Second Edition, *by Morroe Berger, Edward Berger, and James Patrick, 2 vols., 2002*
41. CHORD CHANGES ON THE CHALKBOARD: How Public School Teachers Shaped Jazz and the Music of New Orleans, *by Al Kennedy*, Foreword *by Ellis Marsalis Jr., 2002*
42. CONTEMPORARY CAT: Terence Blanchard with Special Guests, *by Anthony Magro, 2002*
43. PAUL WHITEMAN: Pioneer in American Music, Volume I: 1890–1930, *by Don Rayno, 2003*
44. GOOD VIBES: A Life in Jazz, *by Terry Gibbs with Cary Ginell, 2003*
45. TOM TALBERT—HIS LIFE AND TIMES: Voices from a Vanished World of Jazz, *by Bruce Talbot, 2004*
46. SITTIN' IN WITH CHRIS GRIFFIN: A Reminiscence of Radio and Recording's Golden Years, *by Warren W. Vaché, 2005*
47. FIFTIES JAZZ TALK: An Oral Retrospective, *by Gordon Jack, 2004*

48. FLORENCE MILLS: Harlem Jazz Queen, *by Bill Egan, 2004*
49. SWING ERA SCRAPBOOK: The Teenage Diaries and Radio Logs of Bob Inman, 1936–1938, *by Ken Vail, 2005*
50. FATS WALLER ON THE AIR: The Radio Broadcasts and Discography, *by Stephen Taylor, 2006*
51. ALL OF ME: The Complete Discography of Louis Armstrong, *by Jos Willems, 2006*
52. MUSIC AND THE CREATIVE SPIRIT: Innovators in Jazz, Improvisation, and the Avant Garde, *by Lloyd Peterson, 2006*
53. THE STORY OF FAKE BOOKS: Bootlegging Songs to Musicians, *by Barry Kernfeld, 2006*
54. ELLINGTONIA: The Recorded Music of Duke Ellington and His Sidemen, 5th edition, *by W. E. Timner, 2007*
55. JAZZ FICTION: A History and Comprehensive Reader's Guide, *by David Rife, 2007*
56. MISSION IMPOSSIBLE: My Life In Music, *by Lalo Schifrin, edited by Richard H. Palmer, 2008*
57. THE CONTRADICTIONS OF JAZZ, *by Paul Rinzler, 2008*
58. EARLY TWENTIETH-CENTURY BRASS IDIOMS: Art, Jazz, and Other Popular Traditions, *edited by Howard T. Weiner, 2008*
59. THE MUSIC AND LIFE OF THEODORE "FATS" NAVARRO: Infatuation, *by Leif Bo Petersen and Theo Rehak, 2009*
60. WHERE THE DARK AND THE LIGHT FOLKS MEET: Race and the Mythology, Politics, and Business of Jazz, *by Randall Sandke, 2010*
61. JAZZ BOOKS IN THE 1990S: An Annotated Bibliography, *by Janice Leslie Hochstat Greenberg, 2010*
62. BENNY GOODMAN: A Supplemental Discography, *by David Jessup, 2010*
63. THE LIFE AND MUSIC OF KENNY DAVERN: Just Four Bars, *by Edward N. Meyer, 2010*
64. MR. TRUMPET: The Trials, Tribulations, and Triumph of Bunny Berigan, *by Michael P. Zirpolo, 2011*
65. HARLEM JAZZ ADVENTURES: A European Baron's Memoir, 1934–1969, *by Timme Rosenkrantz, adapted and edited by Fradley Hamilton Garner, 2012*
66. WHAT IT IS: The Life of a Jazz Artist, *by Dave Liebman in conversation with Lewis Porter, 2012*
67. BORN TO PLAY: The Ruby Braff Discography and Directory of Performances, *by Thomas P. Hustad, 2012*
68. THE LAST BALLADEER: The Johnny Hartman Story, *by Gregg Akkerman, 2012*
69. PEPPER ADAMS' JOY ROAD: An Annotated Discography, *by Gary Carner, 2012*
70. JAZZ CHILD: A Portrait of Sheila Jordan, *by Ellen Johnson, 2014*

Jazz Child

A Portrait of Sheila Jordan

Ellen Johnson

ROWMAN & LITTLEFIELD
Lanham • Boulder • New York • London

Published by Rowman & Littlefield
A wholly owned subsidiary of The Rowman & Littlefield Publishing Group, Inc.
4501 Forbes Boulevard, Suite 200, Lanham, Maryland 20706
www.rowman.com

16 Carlisle Street, London W1D 3 BT, United Kingdom

British Library Cataloguing in Publication Information Available

Library of Congress Cataloging-in-Publication Data

Johnson, Ellen, 1954–
Jazz child : a portrait of Sheila Jordan / Ellen Johnson.
pages cm. — (Studies in jazz)
Includes bibliographical references and index.
ISBN 978-0-8108-8836-4 (hardcover : alk. paper) — ISBN 978-0-8108-8837-1 (ebook)
1. Jordan, Sheila. 2. Women jazz singers—United States—Biography. I. Title.
ML420.J7775J64 2014
782.42165092—dc23
[B] 2014012541

∞™ The paper used in this publication meets the minimum requirements of American National Standard for Information Sciences—Permanence of Paper for Printed Library Materials, ANSI/NISO Z39.48-1992.

Printed in the United States of America

To Sheila Jordan for trusting me to be the voice of her story; to my husband, Jeff, for his constant love and belief in everything I do; to Halona for keeping me company no matter how long I stayed up to write; and to those courageous individuals who continue to innovate, inspire, and advocate for the rights of all life.

I would like to share this dedication with Sheila Jordan, who would like to recognize first and foremost "Bird" (Charlie Parker), who was her spiritual big brother and musical guru; George Russell for believing in her music; Dr. Billy Taylor, who always remained in her corner; Dr. Fred Tillis for his never-ending support; Ed Summerlin, John Lewis, and Janet Steele for encouraging her to start a vocal workshop; her loving daughter, Tracey; and the wonderful instrumentalists and singers who continue to keep the message of jazz alive.

Contents

Foreword

Sheila Jordan's been in my life since the early '60s. I first remember her from the early years of that remarkable decade as a unique Greenwich Village lady. But two close friends—the great jazz composer/arranger George Russell and the eccentric but immensely gifted avant-garde composer John Benson Brooks—introduced me to another, very different aspect of Sheila's extraordinary qualities, her singing.

It was a memorable musical era, with adventurous jazz of every imaginable style being explored all over New York City (and beyond) by players young and old, new and established (think Miles Davis, John Coltrane, Cecil Taylor, Don Ellis, and Gary McFarland, among many others). And Sheila, in her own inimitable vocal fashion, was just as creatively exploratory as the instrumentalists.

Persuasively urged by Brooks and Russell to hear Sheila in action, I checked her out at Page Three, a Village club near my apartment on Christopher Street. To say that what I heard was surprising doesn't really do justice to Sheila's level of creativity at that stage in her career. There was, after all, a lot happening in the jazz vocal world at that time: singers whose styles were desperately eager to imitate Sarah Vaughan, Billie Holiday, and Carmen McRae; others struggling their way through the high-speed lyrics of vocalese; and a few who were attempting to imitate the complexities of the instrumental avant-garde.

Sheila did little of that. She didn't have to. She had already found her own compelling expressiveness, gradually exploring the early stages of a personal style that would continue to grow and develop over the next five decades. And when she did take on challenges such as vocalese, she immediately seized the style and made it her own. As recently as 2012, Sheila's performances in Los Angeles included extraordinary examples of her continuing ability to spontaneously create inventive displays of vocalese that included on-the-spot blends of crafted, rhyming lyrics and captivating melody making.

As the '60s unfolded, so too did Sheila's rapidly burgeoning career. In 1962, she recorded a version of "You Are My Sunshine" with George Russell in a performance that resulted in an incomparable version of the classic country song. Later that year her career took a leap into the future with the recording of her first album, *A Portrait of Sheila*, released on Blue Note in 1963. It was the beginning of a Jordan discography of dozens of recordings. Despite the occasional distractions of some health problems, she never stopped embracing her music. At eighty-five, still very much at the peak of her powers, she continued to issue new albums and make memorable live performances.

In 2011, reviewing her performance at L.A.'s jazz club Vitello's for my *International Review of Music*, I noted that "everything she sang sounded new again. More than many performing artists, she lays her life on the line with everything she sings." Everything I wrote in that review is still on target, continuing to express my great admiration for the pleasures of her vocal art.

My friendship with Sheila, starting in the early '60s, has continued, full-fledged, into the present, and that friendship has been deeply embedded in the many articles and profiles I've written about her over the years. In 1963 I recorded a long, illuminating conversation with her that wound up in the pages of *DownBeat*. Since then I've written about her in the *New York Times*, the *Los Angeles Times*, the *International Review of Music*, and more.

Along the way, we found a creative musical linkage, as well. Late in the '60s, Sheila often performed with a group I led with saxophonist Ed Summerlin. And she occasionally recorded demos of my songs—often bringing them vividly to life with her inimitable interpretations.

That's a quality that's ever present in Sheila's personal worldview. As the readers of this fascinating story will discover, the richly colorful descriptions of the deep complexities of her life and music are told with the same remarkable creative honesty that is inherent to her music.

Read on, and discover the seemingly unlimited fascinations of Sheila Jordan, her complex life history, her ever-present sense of humor, and the stories behind her irresistible music.

Don Heckman
The International Review of Music

Preface

"It's the love I have when I'm singing for you,
Oh the spirit of the music sets me free."

—Sheila Jordan from "The Crossing"

I was dining with Sheila Jordan after one of her performances on the West Coast in 2005, and she mentioned that someone suggested she should have a book written about her life story. Since she was one of the last vocal icons of the early jazz era, I encouraged her to pursue the book. I felt, as I still do, that it was significant for her stories to be passed down to future generations. Never in my wildest dreams did I imagine that I would be the author of her biography. Whenever I brought her to the Los Angeles area for performances and workshops Sheila would stay at my home, and it was during those times that we revisited the concept of her biography. A few years prior I had written an article about her for a magazine, and so I facetiously offered to write the book myself. My response came more out of frustration in wanting to get the book off the ground than being serious about being the author. Oddly enough, the idea of my writing the biography took wings, and I was delighted when Sheila anointed me with the endeavor.

Since I'd never written a biography, let alone a book, I was completely intimidated by the thought of the many jazz journalists, some of whom are friends and colleagues, who could accomplish this task far better than I. So one can imagine that the responsibility of relating the experiences of this remarkable woman was an intense weight on my shoulders—at times so much so that I almost gave up. However, the story was too important to tell, and as a woman, vocalist, and educator myself I sensed that Sheila had somehow intuitively chosen me as her spokesperson. And certainly I didn't want to let her down. When contemplating how to go about telling this story, I decided that the best way was to keep the spirit of Sheila's voice within the context of the book. My intention was to relate the multitude of intriguing aspects of Sheila's life without becoming overly academic or impersonal. I wanted this book to touch a common thread in people of all genders, ages, and cultures. If Sheila is the "messenger" of the music, as she often says, then I could only hope to be the lens through which to observe her life by way of her words, interviews with others who knew her, and my own observations.

Although Sheila Jordan is not a household name, nor did she garner the incredible fame of Ella Fitzgerald, she auspiciously helped blaze a path for women in music during a suppressed era: the late 1940s through the 1950s. During those times a single mother struggling for a career in music was frowned upon, but Sheila never let that stop her from reaching her dreams. With a unique voice and musical point of view she found herself associating throughout her life with some of the most innovative artists of our time: Charlie Parker, George Russell, Lennie Tristano, Sonny Rollins, George Gruntz, Mark Murphy, Lee Konitz, Steve Kuhn, Shirley Horn, and countless others. In fact, one of the most enjoyable parts about writing this biography was being able to talk with so many amazing musicians and friends of Sheila's who took me by the hand and walked me through their memories. Each interview had its own fascinating story and sentiment, which enriched my own perspective in profound ways. Not to mention the many hours of interviews with Sheila, which bridged my academic understanding of jazz history by giving me insight into one of the most remarkable eras in jazz history, a time that has continued to inspire innumerable vocalists and instrumentalists to this day. I was admitted to this special jazz "club" to share the language, thoughts, and hardships of a culture that would dominate the American musical landscape and become the impetus for my own life.

Through these pages I have come to know Sheila as an inspiration to everyone she meets. She is not only a jazz singer but also a loving mother, an advocate for the oppressed, an ambassador of peace, a joyful jester, a compassionate voice, and my friend. I am certain that after you read these pages you will understand her motivation for being the messenger of the music. I hope that you will seek out the message she shares by listening to her music so that you can experience a visceral reaction to a woman who has lived the life of a true jazz artist.

Acknowledgments

Often a thank-you doesn't come close to acknowledging the invaluable help that constitutes such a project of this magnitude. This story could not have been written without the help and generosity of so many individuals and organizations. Throughout the world Sheila Jordan is loved and admired, so there were many people who offered information and photos for this book, frequently without my asking. Sheila and I owe them our gratitude in allowing us to share their memories and information. Most likely I will neglect to mention someone's contribution and kindness, and for that I apologize profusely in advance.

My deepest heartfelt thank-you to my husband, Jeff Foster, who provided constant support by assisting in the final preparation of the photographs—but more importantly for his belief in my abilities, practical suggestions, and sense of humor, which kept me from pulling the covers over my head and giving up. My gratitude to my family, dear friends, and even social media friends who were my continuous love and support and never let me give up on what appeared to be an overwhelming endeavor. To Halona, my faithful dog, who stayed by my side as I was writing, reminding me to take breaks and give her treats. To Mysty, the wonder horse, who kept me grounded by reminding me what the important things in life are, specifically being tuned in at all times to nature. And to my insane passion for music and how it affects our lives in such profound ways, which has been the driving force throughout my life.

Sheila and I started this book sometime in 2006, and we both have to thank Monica Faulkner and Tessa Souter for their encouragement about the necessity of this story. However, without my longtime friend and musical partner Rick Helzer, this book might not have come to fruition as a published work. Because of his suggestion, I contacted Gregg Akkerman, who had just completed *The Last Balladeer: The Johnny Hartman Story* for Scarecrow Press. Gregg thankfully introduced me to Bennett Graff, senior acquisitions editor at Rowman & Littlefield (formerly Scarecrow Press), who without hesitation took this project under his wing. I was greatly impressed with him because he actually knew who Sheila Jordan was and understood the importance of telling her story. Bennett immediately went to bat for this project, being beyond patient with some unexpected delays along the way and generously took all my opinions into consideration. I am forever grateful to Bennett, Monica Savaglia, and Rowman & Littlefield for allowing Sheila's story to have a literary place in history along with her fellow jazz musicians.

Don Heckman graciously supplied a compelling foreword for this story, which meant so much to both Sheila and me because he has followed her career from New York until the present. I'll always think of "Baltimore Oriole" as Don's song; Sheila sings it for him every time he is in the audience when she performs on the West Coast.

A huge debt of gratitude goes to Sonia Nordenson, who brought my sample chapters to life with her wisdom and editorial skills. I'm not sure I could have made it to a publisher without her inspiration. It was such a pleasure to work with her in the beginning stages; she truly understood my direction and shared a love for the music. More gratitude for help in the early stages of the book goes to jazz journalist Howard Mandel and best-selling book editor Maureen O'Brien. They both gave me additional encouragement by looking over parts of the manuscript and offering beneficial suggestions. I also appreciate the professionalism of Grace Kono-Wells and her staff at Keystrokes, who saved me thousands of hours of typing transcriptions that were critical to the completion of the manuscript.

I was deeply moved at the many musicians, music professionals, and friends and family of Sheila's who provided important details or shared precious memories. I had some fascinating conversations that enlightened me about jazz history and met some remarkable people in the process. Those include Arild Andersen, Laurie Antonioli, Theo Bleckmann, Willie Bolar, Cameron Brown, Kenny Burrell, Jay Clayton, Len Dobbins, Billy Drummond, Kurt Elling, David Finck, Frank Foster, Carol Fredette, Ray Gallon, George Gruntz, Tracey Jordan, Jenny Devries (King), Coryelle Kramer, Stephan Kramer, Steve Kuhn, Jean-Pierre Leduc, Andy Luparello, Leroy Mitchell, Ra-Kalam (Bob Moses), Mark Murphy, Alan Pasqua, Sonny Rollins, Roswell Rudd, Harvie S, Tessa Souter, Tierney Sutton, Steve Swallow, Dr. Fred Tillis, Eugene Uman, and Attilio Zanchi. Sheila and I were deeply disappointed that we were not able to include George Russell or Dr. Billy Taylor, both prominent figures in Sheila's life; they both passed away prior to arranging interviews. I apologize to those people I never got to interview due to time, distance, or lack of contact information, but I have made an effort to represent them within these pages. It's impossible to include all of the many people and experiences in Sheila's life and career, so I did my best to represent those who Sheila felt were most important or who could be remembered.

Our deepest gratitude to all the photographers who donated wonderful images: Ed Cohen, Jim Gale, Jeff Foster, Juan Carlos Hernandez, Randi Hultin, Ed Ianni, Hans Kumpf, Chris Ramirez, Mitchell Seidel, Bill Sitler, Guy Smith, Tessa Souter, Michael G. Stewart, Ziggy Willmann, and especially Brian McMillen for supplying the perfect cover photo. To Don Was at Blue Note and the Universal Music Group for allowing us to use the album cover to *Portrait of Sheila*, Don Sickler at Second Floor Music for the lead sheets to Sheila's songs and lyrics, and Joe and Barney Fields at HighNote Records for the CD/album covers.

Special people give their time for others without any motivation or reward, and I would like to recognize those who helped make my job easier. First, Coryelle Kramer, for her tireless work collecting all of Sheila's old family photos that were so important to the visual aspect of this story. Second, Valerie Tichacek, who has been Sheila's webmaster and constant support for many years, and who generously helped me whenever I asked; and third, Peter Grosett, who volunteered to assist me with the final format of the discography and other organizational aspects of this book. Others who were helpful in supporting this project were Laurie Antonioli, the Jazzschool, Cade Bursell, Jean-Pierre Leduc, Tracey Jordan, Jay Clayton, Kirk Silsbee, Adrian Mendoza, Elizabeth Auclair (NEA), George Gruntz, Scott Yanow, Timothy Yan, Jeff Weber, and the many jazz journalists and writers whose reviews or comments have been quoted.

Thanks to Bill Harrison, who gave me my first introduction to Sheila Jordan through her bass and voice recordings in the 1970s, when I was a young singer interested in exploring the bass and voice format. She quickly became my mentor even though we never met until almost twenty-five years later.

Because the majority of information in this book is from the source, either Sheila or other people I interviewed, there may be discrepancies and inaccuracies. Along with a great deal of information available is the opportunity for misinformation and I humbly take sole responsibility for any mistakes and urge readers who have corrections to contact me through the publisher.

And finally, Sheila asked that I add this for her: First and foremost, my deepest gratitude goes out to Ellen Johnson for spending all of her time and energy writing my life story and to all the fantastic musicians, students, fans, and friends who kept urging me to put my stories in writing.

• 1 •

God Blessed the Child

"At times I wonder where my life would be if I'd never heard the music of Bird back when I was just a kid."

—Sheila Jordan's lyrics to "Quasimodo," by Charlie Parker

Sheila Jordan's life story is a series of triumphs over odds that were stacked against her from the time she was born: abandoned by her father, growing up with her grandparents in a poor coal mining town in Pennsylvania, seduced by alcoholism and drugs, battling racism, and simply being a woman, a woman whose dream was to become a jazz singer. Jordan attributes her survival to the music of jazz and the person whose music she declares "saved" her life, Charlie "Yardbird" Parker, who bestowed his blessings of bebop on a young, struggling girl living in Detroit in the late 1940s. When Jordan made her first recording, "You Are My Sunshine," with composer George Russell, it was more than a song she was singing. It was a haunting memory of her life and a significant part of what would mold the self-reliant woman who had emerged from a childhood of pain and poverty. Clearly, when Jordan sings that song, it is not meant for a particular person but for her one and only love—jazz.

Jazz has remained the sunshine of Jordan's life, shedding light on the path she was destined to walk and supporting her all along the way. She often says to young singers, "be good to the music and the music will be good to you." And so it has been with Jordan, who has found her purpose in a life that has spanned seven decades. She spent years of feisty ambition to examine the music inside her soul and forged ahead in step with the many innovators of her time, ultimately finding her own point of view. From being a singer who knew all the "Bird" lines to having the courage to attempt a duo with an instrument few singers would even consider, the bass, Jordan shaped the course of her career at an early age as a pioneer who was not afraid to tread new waters. In fact, it is this trait that makes her so beloved to instrumentalists and vocalists alike.

Musically she is recognized not only as an exceptional singer but also as the prime innovator of bass and voice duets, a style that she developed and pursued in spite of unwarranted criticism. As a result, she maintains a body of work with bass virtuosos Harvie S (Swartz) and Cameron Brown that continues to set the bar for other vocalists. Jordan was gently nudged into her next big challenge as a jazz educator to create one of the first solo vocal jazz programs at City College of New York (CCNY). With the achievements of that program, she began teaching workshops and creating jazz vocal programs both nationally and internationally. This was not a simple assignment in those days, since the majority of college and university vocal music programs taught classical repertoire exclusively and found singing any type of popular music blasphemous at best. Nonetheless, Jordan's passion for jazz and her own musical mentors had prepared her for this moment. She not only met the challenge but also fearlessly influenced younger singers who continue to follow in her footsteps to this day. Many of us have been touched by her generosity of spirit as she respectfully and without hesitation passes down the lessons from her mentors. Jordan embraced teaching as a way to keep their memories alive and to make sure their insights were remembered accurately. Jazz education delivered from the source or the architects of the music guarantees a soulful connection to the next generations of musicians.

Jordan also reminds us that we should be true to ourselves first and let the rest of life catch up to our beliefs. Maybe that explains why it took so long to appreciate her artistry or why she never became famous. Jordan has always propelled herself forward through her difficult experiences, transforming them into works of depth and beauty. More importantly she never lost her faith or succumbed to bitterness. Perhaps it speaks to the consciousness of artists when they are able to mold the entirety of their emotional experiences, negative or positive, into sculpted works of art. These works are mastered by dedication and translated to the masses as a confirmation of the oneness of existence. This transcendence can be witnessed each time Jordan performs. When Jordan first takes the stage you see a diminutive woman with a voice some have criticized for lacking proportion—surely their own misfortune for disregarding the power of understatement. Then the room is filled with a special kind of nuance and a voice that takes us on a heart-stirring ride. It is then that we experience the strength of her delivery and the mastery of her expression. Her use of space, inflection, and gentle dynamics makes her a formidable songbird.

Jordan's career fully bloomed during her late fifties and continues well into her eighties. As an octogenarian and a highly respected jazz elder, she continues to travel around the world gaining new fans by performing consistently at jazz festivals, concerts, and venues. In 2012 Jordan reached another milestone in her career by being awarded the prestigious NEA Jazz Masters award along with instrumentalists Jack DeJohnette, Von Freeman, Charlie Haden, and Jimmy Owens. She is in the true sense of the word a professional and brings the highest standards to every performance she gives, leaving not only the audience but the musicians standing in awe of her mastery. Recognition by vocalists and instrumentalists of all ages, as a result of her mentorship, provides further testament to her dedication to the music that she declares saved her life.

And clearly one cannot separate the musician from the woman. Jordan's Cherokee roots speak to her understanding of nature and the community of mankind, which she has demonstrated throughout her life in both serious and amusing ways. Compassion to fight for injustice has always been her signature as she repeatedly stood up for her brothers and sisters wrongly treated by racism. Her steadfast belief in equality took her into dangerous situations where she often endured brutal altercations of her own. She boldly provoked an unjust society by marrying an African American man and bringing a biracial daughter into a bigoted civilization, leading the way for others and inspiring the change she awaited. One must not forget her maternal instincts either. Jordan is a mother who deeply loves her only child, Tracey, and so protected her from the hostile and cruel afflictions of an inequitable nation. In doing so she found herself ostracized and criticized, yet she never considered that there was any other choice, because she knew in her heart it was just.

She bares her own physical and emotional battle scars as a result, wearing them proudly in demonstration of her valued convictions. She is fearless in her resolve, never taking the road of least resistance but always defending the rights of others. Lest one be concerned she will have too far to fall from this pedestal of heroic deeds, be reassured that it is due to the fact that Jordan shows her weaknesses that she always has her feet securely planted on the ground. She freely admits her own frailties and recognizes the many times that she lost her way and succumbed to human vices. She makes no excuses for her dance with the demons that drove her to the excesses of alcohol and drug abuse. Yet, because of those dark days Jordan can relate to both sides of the human condition, making her a champion for those who seek another route, and she never fails to help a hitchhiker on the road to recovery through her music and words.

Perhaps this dichotomy of dark and light, a Taoist principle of dynamic balance, accounts for her intimacy with nature and the fact that her second home is nestled on six acres in upstate New York. Her home shares an inexplicable kind of musical experience—the natural ambient sounds and those of her beloved birds, frogs, and cows compelling Jordan to delight in a myriad of stories both humorous and mystical. As Lara Pellegrinelli writes in *JazzTimes*:

> It may not surprise some that so vivid a musical imagination finds parallels in her everyday life. A personal tour of her tranquil domicile, for example, uncovers spirits besides Parker. She bypasses plaques and awards to point out artwork: a dignified engraving of a Native American that reflects part of her ethnic heritage plus a wide-mouthed, almost operatic-looking bust of Michael Jordan. She kids he's no relation. Her houseplants have names like Paris and Jewel with Tiny the tree just outside. Buddy the car resides in the garage. She communes with fish in her pond and the woods themselves. Local cows, too, who apparently enjoy "Scrapple from the Apple." ("How stupid could they be? I don't see horses come over when I run bebop changes.")[1]

Perhaps in some profound way it is the music that has kept her spirit free. From the moment she uttered her first sound as a baby to each performance that feels like the last, to Jordan it was the music that helped her endure her childhood, find purpose, commit to recovery, and find meaning in her advanced years. Music, specifically jazz, has been her loving partner, and as she says, "it never let me down." Appropriately enough it was Billie Holiday, one of Jordan's favorite vocalists, who sang "God Bless the Child," a symbolic reflection on Jordan's life with the poignant lyrics, "the strong get more and the weak ones fade." Jordan found her "own" way and God has truly blessed this jazz child, and for that matter anyone who has had the good fortune of being touched by her music. As jazz journalist John Fordham succinctly put it, "Quiet please, unique expert at work."[2]

• 2 •

Little Song

"My mother said when I first came out of her womb I didn't cry, I sang."

—Sheila Jordan

Sheila Jeanette Dawson (referred to throughout this book as Jordan, her married name) was born on November 18, 1928, in Detroit, Michigan, to a seventeen-year-old General Motors factory worker, Margaret "Maggie" Helen Hull. Her arrival into the world took place on a Murphy bed in a furnished room, with her father and a local doctor attending her mother. Jordan had very little contact with her father, Donald Mackenzie Dawson, for most of her life. He remarried after Jordan was born and had five more children, with whom she would reunite in later years. Maggie had minimal resources for raising Sheila and was distracted by her own demons, which included alcohol and the deleterious effects of her choices in male partners. When Jordan was a few months old, she went to live with her grandfather Walter Hull and grandmother Irene Hull in Summerhill, Pennsylvania, a borough in Cambria County located in the Laurel Highlands of the Allegheny Mountains.

Jordan's father left Maggie to raise the child alone; since she had to work full-time, she could not care for her, so Jordan went from being an only child to being the tenth child among siblings who were actually her aunts and uncles. In many ways, Jordan shared a similar beginning with her grandmother, who had been an abandoned child. Grandmother Irene's biological mother, whose last name was Hoover, had left her baby daughter on the doorstep of a rather well-to-do family. No doubt Jordan's great-grandmother had assumed that the family could offer Irene a much better life. The family happily brought the unexpected child, renamed Irene, into their family but were bitterly disappointed when in her early teens she married Walter Earl Hull,

Jordan's grandfather. Perhaps they had surmised that Hull would not become the successful son-in-law they had sought for their adopted daughter.

For the first fourteen years of Jordan's life, she lived in her grandparents' home with occasional visits from her estranged mother. Eventually, around the age of seven, she began spending several weeks in Detroit each summer with her mother, Maggie. From her birth until she was in high school, Jordan grew up with her uncles Harry, Earl, Delbert, Lester (nicknamed "Bunky"), and Jackie, as well as her aunt Esther. Her other two aunts, Henrietta and Rowena (nicknamed "Bobbie"), along with Jordan's mother, lived and worked in the factories and beer gardens of Detroit. The family actually had eleven children, but tragically one girl was stillborn and a boy named Tommy died at two years of age when he fell down a staircase. It was her aunt Esther, six years her senior, who became her surrogate mother, taking baby Jordan under her wing and treating her like a "little doll."

Further memories of abandonment for Jordan occurred again at the age of two, when her aunt Bobbie took her to visit her father upon his request. By that time her father had remarried and he and his second wife, Rita, were living in Toledo, Ohio. For some reason he took his daughter, Sheila, to a nearby Catholic orphanage to be adopted. Evidently there was a wealthy couple from Canada that had inquired about her while she was at the orphanage, and they were prepared to file adoption papers with her father's approval. According to Jordan, "I had been living at the orphanage for a little while and one day I was playing with these kids. We were sliding down the brass beds they had for us just having some fun. Suddenly a nun came into the room with her gown flying and I remember it frightened me. She took my hand and I thought she was going to beat me. But instead she took me to my Aunt Bobbie, who came to get me out of the orphanage." Aunt Bobbie had no idea that her father had planned to take her to the orphanage, so as soon as she found out what happened she immediately rushed to get Jordan out.

This circumstance would affect Jordan in a traumatic way for most of her life, only finding resolution when she joined the recovery "program" in later years: "My father was just a factory worker who never knew how to read or write. In retrospect I believe that he wanted me to have a better life than living in poverty with my grandparents or with my alcoholic mother. I'll never know for sure why he made that decision but either he was convinced that he couldn't take care of me himself or he didn't want me for other reasons. Fortunately after many years and with the help of the program I was able to work through my anger and emotional issues to finally forgive him."

Life was difficult growing up in Cambria County near the coal mining towns of South Fork, Wilmore, and Ehrenfeld, or as the locals called it, "Scoopy Town." During the active decades, Cambria County produced over sixteen million tons of coal annually until the Great Depression severely affected the area, making way for the smaller surviving companies to consolidate with larger companies. The community had their share of hardship when miners were either killed or trapped by mine explosions. There were so many deaths that the funeral parlor couldn't handle the number of bodies, nor could the locals afford the burial services. The custom was to hang a wreath on the door when a wake was in session, and Jordan could recognize the tragedy of her neighbors by merely walking down the streets: "There was one terrible mine explosion in Wilmore where so many young men were killed that every other door had a wreath on it. The memory of the miners with coal dust embedded in their eyes stayed with me and whenever I saw women with eyeliner I always thought of the miners." Although her uncles Earl and Harry worked in the coal mines for a brief time, the Hull family was spared the grief of loss that so many others in the town had experienced. Instead, her uncles joined the Civilian Conservation Corps (CCC), which was a U.S. government public work relief program in operation from 1933 to 1942. The CCC was a part of President Roosevelt's "New Deal" during the Great Depression era. It provided jobs for unemployed single men between the ages of eighteen and twenty-five, as well as shelter, clothing, and food along with a small wage they were required to send home to their families.

Another factor that made life difficult for Jordan was constant ridicule about being one of the poorest families in the town. The treatment of the entire Hull family, ostracized by the community because of their impoverished status, created an enormous impact on the perspective that Jordan would carry with her throughout her lifetime. She describes the severity of the situation this way: "We had an outhouse and no water in the house. The pump was outside and we heated the house with wood and coal. In the wintertime all of us would sleep in one bedroom without any sheets or pillowcases on our beds; we just had blankets. You couldn't sleep on the other side of the house in the winter because it was too cold." When Jordan was in the fourth grade, she was completely humiliated one day when her teacher asked her to go get a book from the bookcase. As she leaned over her little behind was exposed to the entire class because of her torn underwear. The class laughed and the teacher sent her home with a note to her grandmother requesting that she not return until she had a new pair of underwear.

Although Jordan remembers grandfather Hull as basically a good man, his addiction to alcohol made his financial obligations a problem. He continuously squandered his house-painter wages on alcohol, leaving the family dependent on welfare assistance. On a regular basis, he would take his paycheck and head down to the local beer gardens, his favorite being McCalls and a private club called The Bunt. According to Jordan, "My grandfather got very drunk and wouldn't want to come home, so my grandmother always made me go to the beer gardens to get him. I'd be with him as he was staggering down the street for everybody to see, singing at the top of his lungs. It was very embarrassing." Although his nickname was "Happy Hull" when he was drunk, Jordan remembers his personality changed to a gruff disposition when he was sober. Grandmother Irene didn't start drinking until Jordan was about ten years old, and Jordan recalls, "I always knew when she was drunk because she would slobber all over me and that made me uncomfortable." The alcoholic behavior of her grandparents and mother triggered habits that Jordan would have to contend with in later years. Another unfavorable circumstance was that neither grandparent demonstrated much affection to the young Jordan. "My grandfather didn't talk much, never hugged you and never told you he loved you. There was never any physical contact, but that's the way he was. My grandmother would pat you on the head every once in a while, but she would never kiss you. I know they tried to do their best. We even went to Catholic Church every Sunday even though my grandfather disapproved of organized religion."

Jordan's early exposure to music came from her grandmother, who had learned the piano when she was young and played from time to time an old upright that had been given to the family. Although this might have had some influence, Jordan remembers that she was drawn to music even when she first began to talk. She found pleasure and satisfaction in making up songs that she could sing to herself. Jordan remembers, "My grandfather used to call me 'little song' because I was always singing." Besides being enjoyable, singing became an essential part of her survival. She felt that it helped her get through the rough and sad times of her childhood. Music was her escape, confidant, and partner, and it gave her hope. Jordan offers a compelling example of the strength music provided her as a child: "When I was very young I was terrified of graveyards. Dead people scared me as they do most kids. So when my grandmother would send me to the store and I had to pass the graveyard I would just sing and then I was okay." On the occasion when her mother or her aunts from Detroit were visiting, the family would go to the beer garden outside of Summerhill to drink and hear live music. They would take Jordan with them and make her sing for people because when she was finished people would throw money on the dance floor. Jordan remembers, "My grandmother always told me not to pick up the money until I was finished singing. I still carry that thought with me today whenever I sing or make a mistake. I tell myself just keep going and it will all work out." Growing up among the coal miners, Jordan was first introduced to the 1939 American popular music song by Jimmie Davis and Charles Mitchell, "You Are My Sunshine," which eventually became the first song she ever recorded. The coal miners would have a few beers and sing this song together after they had paid their food bill at the company store. "You are my sunshine, my only sunshine, you make me happy when skies are grey," etc. The song holds special meaning for Jordan to this day.

Jordan enjoyed listening to the radio but quite often she had to listen at the homes of her friends when her grandparents didn't have enough money to pay the electric bill. One of her favorite shows was *Your Hit Parade*, which featured the top songs of the week. *Your Hit Parade* actually referred to a list of compositions published as sheet music for purchase, recorded by different artists of the day, and promoted through airtime on commercial stations. According to Jordan, "It was easy for me to sing and I was able to memorize tunes immediately after hearing them. Even in grade school, they used to have me sing for the PTA meetings and any kind of special event. It was hard for me because the other kids would get jealous, try to imitate me and make fun of my singing." It was torture for Jordan, being taunted not only for being poor but for the very thing that brought her so much enjoyment, singing. Even one of her uncles who constantly teased her about her singing later admitted that he did so because he was jealous. Jordan's mother helped pay for a few piano lessons from her great-aunt Alma, who lived nearby in South Fork. However, it was impossible for her to meet Aunt Alma's very strict and rough demands because her tiny hands had difficulty reaching the piano keys. "When my hands couldn't do what she asked," comments Jordan, "she'd whack my hands with a ruler, which frightened and hurt me so I didn't go back."

During her formative years, between 1936 and 1941, Jordan sang for *Uncle Nick's Amateur Hour* in Detroit and other amateur-hour radio shows with contests in the nearby towns of Altoona and Johnstown. Jordan sang the hit songs of the day such as "I'll Never Smile Again" (Ruth Lowe, 1939), "He Wears a Pair of Silver Wings" (Eric Maschwitz and Michael Carr, 1940), "I'll Be Seeing You" (Sammy Fain and Irving Kahal, 1938), and others. At eight years of age, she came in second place singing at one of the radio shows, but unfortunately it was only the first-place winner who received any monetary award. What Jordan did receive, oddly enough, was a marriage proposal in a letter from a man who had listened to the show. Evidently, because of the maturity of her singing he thought she was a grown woman. Her grandmother wrote the man back explaining that she was only eight years old and not available for marriage for at least another ten to fifteen years.

Jordan loved to make up songs, which was one of the ways she could escape and cope with the difficult situations in her life. While in the seventh grade, she directed her own play that she made up for the kids in her class using the hit songs of the day. It was another opportunity to forget her woes, and she used her imagination to choreograph dances and arrange songs. She seemed to be a natural at doing this and the play was a success. She even won a medal from the Knights of Columbus, the world's largest Catholic fraternal service organization, which enabled her to build some much-needed confidence in her artistic abilities.

Although Jordan's mother, Maggie, was not with her on a regular basis, she did make occasional trips from Detroit to see her daughter in Pennsylvania. Jordan also spent time with her mother in Detroit during her summer breaks from school from about 1939 to 1942.

> I loved my mother and thought she was so beautiful. She was always very sweet to me and quite affectionate. There was one occasion when she came to visit I didn't realize she was going to be leaving so soon because she didn't tell me. When I discovered she was gone, I was really upset and then I found her moccasins under the bed. I took them to bed with me and hugged them all night. My grandmother used to tell that story to everyone about the night "Jeannie was hugging those shoes like it was a real person." To me they represented my mother and so they were the closest thing to my mother being with me.

Jordan's mother had a few risqué common-law relationships and she was married approximately four times. Jordan remembers a few of these relationships that were active during her summer visits to Detroit. One of them was a gangster named Johnny Godleski, who was associated with one of America's most notorious criminal groups, the Purple Gang from the Lower East Side of Detroit. The FBI had reported them as a group engaged in criminal activities that included bootlegging, shakedowns, theft, and a number of illegal pursuits including brutal murders. Johnny owned a tavern with his brother-in-law, Jimmy, as a front for their illegal operations. On one particular visit, Jordan recalls sleeping in the bedroom above the tavern. At one point she heard the bedroom window open and saw a man climb in with a handkerchief around his face. Jordan instantly recognized the face; it was her Uncle Jimmy, and so she innocently said hello to him. Unbeknownst to her at the time, Johnny was keeping some stolen fur coats in the bedroom. Uncle Jimmy had sneaked in the window in order to steal the coats from her current stepfather, Johnny. The next day her mother and Johnny asked the young Jordan if she had seen anyone take the coats. Jordan naïvely replied, "Yes, Uncle Jimmy took the coats." She never realized until much later what the situation was, and wonders to this day whether, had she not been a child, the incident might have resulted in her death.

Around 1941 Jordan entered South Fork High School in Cambria County, where she met a teacher, Mr. Rusher, who would be instrumental in changing her life. Jordan's experience with her great-aunt Alma had crushed her spirit for playing the piano, and although Mr. Rusher tried to give her piano lessons, he observed that she was fearful and instead encouraged her to sing. His getting her to sing in a school musical show was a turning point in her life. Rusher was wise enough to take it slowly with Jordan by first having her sing with another girl and finally convincing her to sing solo on the song "My Ideal" (music by Richard A. Whiting and lyrics by Leo Robin for the 1930 Paramount Pictures talkie entitled *Playboy of Paris*). The success of singing confidently in front of her classmates paved the way for future experiences and Jordan gives him credit: "I have Mr. Rusher to thank for encouraging me because I could have carried that fear the rest of my life and never opened my mouth to sing."

During this time Jordan's mother was having an affair with one of the men in a town near Jordan's grandparents so she came by to visit more often. The idea of Maggie having an affair annoyed and upset her grandfather to such a degree that he finally told his daughter that he no longer wanted Jordan to live with them. "On that day my grandfather and grandmother were drinking with my mother, which they often did. They got into a nasty fight and my grandfather told my mother to get out and take your kid with you. I was fourteen years old at the time and once again I felt really unwanted." This would prove to be an ongoing pattern in Jordan's life as she struggled with monogamous relationships. At the time, young Jordan was off to her next adventure in Detroit, where she would find the true love of her life, jazz.

• *3* •

Detroit Days

Jazz child, jazz child,
in Cuban heeled shoes
belonging to her sister
in a soft shade of blue.
Strutting down the street
on her wobbly feet.

Lips so red,
Smeared over the line,
Eyebrows arched with a dark brown line.
Hair she curled so long, so tight.
"Chile, why aren't you home this night?"

I'm going to the Club Sudan
to hear the music of my magic man.
They call him Bird, cause he plays so sweet,
Goes to my head, my heart, my feet.

I think, I look at least sixteen,
And maybe if I act like class,
they won't look too close
and let me pass
Then I could sit with him right near,
and hear him play,
the music sad, the music gay,
that makes my lonely life less gray.

Jazz child, jazz child,
you can't come in here.
Go home to your mama,
come back in a year.

She hurries down the alley
and sits by the door,
straightens her skirt
which brushes the floor.
She hears him start—
the music soars and roars
and twists and bends—
she prays that it will never end.
This is what she came to hear.
This is the music she holds dear.
Music to make for her a life and
Take her far away from here.

Jazz child, jazz child,
sits a long while—
a little lonely gifted child,
storing sounds she heard to sing
and lyrics to bring—
to her instrument, her voice,
for Bebop is her God of choice.

—Marria Elizabeth Banks
(part of the liner notes on
the recording *Jazz Child*)

Jordan returned to her birthplace during a time when Detroit's economy was booming, creating an increasingly diverse population that led to altercations between blacks and whites. As segregation became illegal, the white community felt resentful, which created a hostile environment for racial interactions. It was 1942 and Jordan had recently transferred from the high school in Summerhill to Cass Technical High School and again switched after her first year to Commerce High School, a clerical trade school, directly next door. Both schools were integrated and Jordan found herself mixing with ethnic groups primarily because she understood the feeling of discrimination after her experiences in Summerhill. "It was easy for me to identify with African American people because I had been so tormented by white kids when I was younger. So I just felt more comfortable with African American kids and trusted them more." Her mother was still drinking quite heavily and was now married to a professional gambler. He was just another in a string of abusive relationships for Maggie. "My mother was always very sweet but she had a lot of relationships that were very sick. She had very low self-esteem and being the alcoholic that she was I saw a lot of stuff growing up when I was with her, like beatings, and it was horrible. And I thought I would never go with men like that the same way I said I would never drink. I think all of that carried over to me because I ended up attracting abusive relationships in my own life."

This time the abuse had ramifications for young Jordan, who was already struggling to get her footing in this new location. Jordan remembers distinctly that her stepfather would molest her when her mother was gone or passed out drunk. Although she was afraid to tell anyone, she mustered the courage to tell her mother and grandmother, who eventually confronted him. Ultimately nothing was resolved; her stepfather denied the charges, instead accusing Jordan of imagining the incidents. As much as Jordan loved her mother, living under these conditions was distressing and she counted the days until she could leave. Transferring to Commerce High School turned out to be beneficial for her in that she could achieve financial independence. Since it was primarily a business-oriented school, it provided the necessary skills of the day for a woman seeking to find employment. At the school she learned the typical skills for career women of that era, which included typing, filing, and shorthand; these skills contributed to her survival and success in future years.

Jordan was a sophomore in high school when she found her musical guru, Charlie Parker. Jordan affectionately recalls, "I always sang but I didn't know what kind of music I wanted to sing until that unforgettable day I went to the hamburger joint across the street from my high school. I was looking through the selections of songs when I saw a tune called "Now's the Time" by Charlie Parker and his Reboppers. I thought it looked interesting so I put my nickel in the jukebox and after the first four notes I was hooked. I got goose bumps and I instantly knew that was the music I had been waiting to hear and would dedicate my life to singing." Charlie "Yardbird" Parker became the guiding light Jordan had been waiting for; now she understood her life's mission. Her first instinct was to find more of this music known as bebop or bop for short. The music was progressive and modern, moving away from the swing big bands and centering on smaller combos whose musicians were being influenced by the creators of bop, including Parker, Dizzy Gillespie, Thelonious Monk, Bud Powell, Kenny Clarke, Max Roach, and older influences such as Coleman Hawkins and Lester Young. Since the music was primarily being introduced by black musicians, it was mostly heard at black clubs or on 78 RPM recordings. Jordan had limited funds, so she decided to buy Parker recordings instead of vocalist recordings and began learning the tunes. "I would listen to the records over and over and try to sing with Bird and all the musicians on the record. So many of the songs were based on the standards and I could always hear the new bebop melodies the musicians were playing. There were a lot of them—Gershwin's 'I Got Rhythm' is a good example since there were so many tunes based on that song and what the musicians called 'rhythm changes.' I just learned by ear."

Fortunately for Jordan, Detroit was quickly becoming a Midwest hot spot during the birth of bebop. There were young players eager to learn the new sounds and plenty of seasoned players performing around town who helped to create a new generation of jazz. Detroit became part of the circuit for visiting bands in Paradise Valley and other areas, bringing in early bebop pioneers who discovered talent and often left town with them. "I think Detroit was an incubator for introducing jazz musicians," comments Detroit jazz historian Willie Bolar, "and I'm telling you, it was a really tight scene." Eventually Jordan began seeking out the jazz clubs that were presenting this exciting new music, but they were primarily in black neighborhoods. Jordan was already being ostracized for spending time with her black friends at school so it didn't bother her to consider going to these places, even if it was highly frowned upon in the white community. However, the majority of the clubs were not open to minors, so Jordan either found places where they didn't serve alcohol or occasionally resorted to fake ID. "I started hanging out with this girl I met in high school, Jackie Burkhoff, and we used to go to the jazz clubs like the Club Sudan [located in Paradise Valley in the basement of the Norwood Hotel] where teenagers could hear this music because there was no alcohol served. It was actually owned by a white couple from Canada, which was unusual at that time, but I think they were more open to interracial mixing. That's how I found Tommy, Barry, and Kenny."

Tommy Flanagan, Barry Harris, Kenny Burrell, and all the other young musicians were working on their jazz chops at the rooms that either didn't serve alcohol or would hold underage jam sessions. The Club Sudan was known for having Monday night after-hour sessions promoted by disc jockey Bill Randle, who also had a jazz program on WJLB. According to Bolar,

> Bill Randle was promoting these Monday night sessions and everybody who was anybody or wanted to try to be somebody would make these sessions. He had all of the best musicians, black and mostly black trying to play the music at that time. There was an old trumpet player named Doug Mettome. Doug used to be in Detroit a lot during that time and he would play. Warren Hickey, Coco Winfred, Willie Anderson, and Paul Foster. These were stellar musicians. So Bill Randle to me was one of the spearheads of introducing new music in Detroit.

The Detroit modern jazz scene was hip and happening as Burrell recalls, "especially among the younger guys who were the same age as Sheila and me. There were a lot of jam sessions going on and rehearsals. . . . Those rehearsals and jam sessions were at various places including clubs like the Blue Bird Inn, Klein's, and especially at the West End Hotel. So it was a very invigorating and informative educational situation and we all benefited." Besides the tremendous influence of these first-rate musicians, Jordan found an opportunity to work on her own skills and sing the music that so moved her after meeting two talented African American vocalists, Leroy Mitchell and Skeeter Spight. According to Mitchell,

> I first met Sheila at a club called the Twelve Horsemen with another musician, Ulysses "Skeeter" Spight. We were scatting along at our table to one of the tunes the band was playing and we notice this white girl scatting too. Since we were both black men and not used to seeing white girls singing jazz we were kind of surprised. Then throughout the evening every time we starting scatting she would scat along with us. So when we were all getting ready to leave we asked her which way she was going and she said she was taking the Woodward bus line. So we all walked together and got to know each other. Then we saw her again at the Blue Bird and eventually we all started singing together.

The Blue Bird Inn was a black-owned, working-class bar in the heart of the West Side black community where six nights a week the house band would play "Modern Jazz."[1] With the presentation of this new music, the Blue Bird appealed to the younger set and became recognized for hosting such acclaimed musicians as Charlie Parker, Sonny Stitt, Milt Jackson, Thad Jones, Billy Mitchell, Frank Foster, and Elvin Jones. Flanagan says, "I never saw a place like it even in New York. It had a neighborhood atmosphere and all the support a jazz club needed. Everyone who loved jazz in Detroit came, and it was a very inspired group that played there."[2] The instant Jordan heard Spight and Mitchell bopping, she knew it was what she wanted to do. All Spight and Mitchell had to do was name a Bird tune and she would sing the line with them, which they found remarkable. Due to Jordan's painful memories of being ridiculed as a child she used her middle name: "I hated the name Sheila because I got teased so much as kid. They'd call me Sheba, queen of the jungle and all kinds of weird things because they thought I had a strange name. So I went by my middle name, Jeanette, which turned into Jeannie and then I was known as Jeannie Dawson." Eventually the three singers formed a vocal group called Skeeter, Mitch, and Jean that was similar to the famous group Lambert, Hendricks and Ross, singing vocalese and scatting. "Oh yeah, Jon Hendricks, he's great, he's very great," recalls Mitchell, "But we did some stuff beyond what they were doing at one time. And I wrote most of the stuff we did, I wrote it out. One tune we did, we got a big kick doing. It was called "Hop, Skip and Bop." That was one of our favorite tunes. And Sheila did a counterpoint with us on 'Oh Henry.' It had two melodies. It was written by Gil Fuller. That was another favorite tune."

According to Mitchell, "We had a trumpet player, Theophus; Cokey Winfred on alto sax with Barry Harris or Tommy Flanagan on piano, Doug Watkins or Paul Chambers on bass, and Pat Mento on drums. And then the three of us singing and scatting. We used to practice at Pat's house." They also often went to their friend Virginia Cox's house to rehearse. Although Cox wasn't a musician, as a visual artist and painter she had a keen understanding of progressive thinking and was interested in all modern forms of art. Jordan's group of musicians would often hang out for hours at her place, playing and singing bebop and listening to bebop recordings. On a documentary Cox was quoted as saying, "They made me sick with that bebop stuff," which Jordan found amusing. Besides singing standards, the group, especially Spight and Mitchell, wrote lyrics to many of the Parker tunes such as "Little Willie Leaps," "Barbados," and "Confirmation," the latter of which was written about Jordan. *"Casting a line to you while the moon was shining bright, yes one night (just like) the time I first saw you. You set my soul on fire, My hopes were higher 'cause I had you and you had me too."* They also sang bebop tunes such as John Lewis's "Bobbin' with Robin" and the tune Mitchell wrote for Parker, "Parker's Refrain." Bolar remembers sessions where the group sang together and one in particular that he recorded and has to this day. "It was at Barry Harris's mother's house, which was on Russell Street on the East Side. In fact, there was a trumpet player named Clare Rockamore. You know, he's gone now, but I can tell you this. One time, Donald Byrd wouldn't even take his horn out in his presence. But at this particular session, it was Clare Rockamore, Sheila Jordan, Mitchell, Paul Chambers, Doug Watkins, all of them were around, Sonny Red. You know, they're all on this tape. Now that's one of my really higher tapes that I really, really love."

There appeared to be an explosion of jazz venues during the late '40s and early '50s, and many of them focused on cultivating young talent who were interested in a modern sound. "At that time, Sheila became a part of our younger musicians' jazz scene in Detroit," says Burrell. "We were all really excited about the music and trying to learn all we could. We were really enthralled with the new developments called bebop at the time. It was very exciting and we all tried to learn and grow to the best of our ability." Burrell goes on to identify the group that all hung out together.

> And there was a pretty sizable group of people. . . . There was myself and Tommy Flanagan, and a drummer named Leon Rice, Curtis Fuller, Donald Byrd, Frank Foster, and a little bit older but still part of that group was Billy Mitchell, Edwin Davis, Cokey Winfred, Warren Hickey—these were kind of the older guys. And the other older guys who were certainly influential and somewhat, maybe not exactly as eager as we were would be the great pianist by the name of Willie Anderson and my brother, Billy, who played guitar and also played bass. Then coming up under us for the next generation following would be Barry Harris and Harold McKinney, Bernard McKinney, Sunny Red, Paul Chambers, Joe Henderson, and my friend Hindal Butts. And Pepper Adams, of course, and later Yusef Lateef, but Pepper Adams was part of that same group, same age and so forth as Sheila.

The bebop modern jazz movement had taken hold with the young musicians, and it was Charlie Parker who became the main spokesman of this new music. According to Burrell,

> And so, this new music had its leaders and the leaders were Charlie Parker, Dizzy Gillespie, Thelonious Monk, Bud Powell, and then Miles Davis, people like that. However, all of the musicians involved looked to Charlie Parker as the voice, the main voice, of this new music. In other words, as to quote Dizzy Gillespie, Dizzy Gillespie said, "Monk and I," speaking of Thelonious Monk, "have the ideas but Charlie Parker delivers the ideas." He put it a different way. He said, "Bird showed us how to play them." So the point is they were all happy with Charlie Parker's voice, his melodic sense, and his delivery of this new sound more than anyone and we were as well. No disrespect for anyone else, it was just that he was the stellar voice of that movement. And we all knew that and that's why he connected to us.

Jordan remembers that the first time she heard Parker in a live performance was at Jazz at the Philharmonic. "It was incredible. I knew in that moment that I was right; this is the music for me. This is the music I want to dedicate my life to because it frees me. It helps me. Bird was my savior and I have him to thank." Eventually Parker started to come to Detroit on a regular basis, performing at venues such as El Sino, Graystone Ballroom, Madison Ballroom, and the Crystal Show Bar. The Parker Quintet's stay at the El Sino was also memorable because some classic recordings took place. On December 21, 1947, the group recorded four sides for Savoy Records.[3] The younger musicians were passionate about the music of Parker and would find ways to hear him even though they were not allowed in the clubs because they were underage.

> We used to stand in the alley [recalls Burrell]. It was a club called the El Sino and we would listen to Charlie Parker. Most of the time when he had a group, the group that came to Detroit was Miles Davis on trumpet, Duke Jordan on piano, Tommy Potter on bass, and Max Roach on drums. It was a pretty hip group and we certainly wanted to hear everything they had to do. So we couldn't get in most of the time. Tommy and I finally painted some moustaches on and we got in for a little while but then they kicked us back out.

Jordan tells a similar story:

> Since I knew I couldn't get in because I was underage, I forged my mother's birth certificate. I tried to look older so I put on some red lipstick and wore my mother's clothes, a hat with a veil and high-heeled shoes that killed my feet and I was smoking a Lucky Strike cigarette. I was desperate to get in the door to hear Bird. In fact, Bird was by the door and heard what was going on. The club owner looked at me and said "hey little white girl, you better go home and do your homework or you're going to get me in a whole lot of trouble." I was determined to hear Bird so I went around back to the alley and I sat on the garbage cans hoping to hear him play.

> Bird knew I was out there so he opened up the back door and he played his heart out for me. That's the kind of generous person he was. He loved the music and he wanted to share it with us. Oh what a treat for a teenage kid who loved jazz.

One of Parker's most dedicated fans was Jordan, who knew all of his songs. "I remember the first time Bird heard me sing," beamed Jordan, "I sang one of Bird's songs. I sang the song in Charlie Parker's ear and he said to me, 'You have million-dollar ears, kid.' I didn't even know what that meant at the time. All I could think is, the first time I sang for The Bird was right in his ear." At that time Sheila was singing regularly with Skeeter and Mitch and at every opportunity they would sit in with the local group of musicians and their friends. Any time major jazz artists would come through town, such as Dizzy Gillespie or Charlie Parker, the three would ask if they could sit in and generally the musicians would let them. Parker would not forget these loyal Detroit fans as they went to see him every time he came to Detroit, sitting right in the front. Quite often they would dance to the music but mostly they took in Bird's solos and were in awe of this genius of jazz. Mitchell recounts,

> Every time Diz [Dizzy Gilespie] came, me and Skeeter sang with the band. Diz said the people in Detroit did more dancing to bebop than anywhere else they went in the United States. And Charlie Parker said the same thing. He liked to come to Detroit because we danced. You can't beat Detroit—I used to be one of the best dancers in the city, but you couldn't beat Detroit bands. I'm talking about social dancing. We danced to everything because every time Charlie Parker came here, we danced! And Charlie Parker used to play something and say just let them dance.

Bebop style also influenced the Beat Generation, whose spoken-word style drew on African American "jive" dialog and jazz rhythms, and whose poets often employed jazz musicians to accompany them.[4] The beboppers had developed their own lifestyle, a way of communicating and a counterculture that was rebelling against the mainstream values. Jordan and her friends were immersed into this jazz society, and Mitchell concurs:

> I was married at the time and I remember the first time my wife met Sheila. It was at the Blue Bird. I think Sheila was already there and we went in and I said, "Oh, that's Sheila." And I sat down beside her and she started talking and when she got up and left, my wife said, "I don't understand a word she's saying." [Mitchell laughs.] Sheila was so hip. You understand what I'm saying? I understood everything she was saying. She was talking about gigs and all that stuff and I'm going to split and all that stuff. We had our own language. It's been adopted now. When we were singing together

> nobody used the term "gig" but beboppers. Gig originated with bebop. Now all the musicians use it. Even some symphonic musicians use the word "gig." But at that time, beboppers used gig and we used split. We didn't say we're going to go—you got ready to go, and then you said, "Well, I got to split." That means I'm getting ready to go. And there were a whole lot of terms we used that were only used among beboppers. And it's a shame that people don't know that but it's the truth.

It was not uncommon for singers to write lyrics to the instrumental tunes they wanted to sing, and Jordan was no exception. She wrote lyrics to the Monk ballad composition, "'Round Midnight," and would sing it every once in a while. On one occasion Parker's pianist, Duke Jordan, decided to stay in Detroit for a few weeks. Jordan recalls that Duke was flirting with her when they first met and she felt flattered that Parker's piano player would be interested in her and find her attractive. But instead, the two became friends and wouldn't reunite romantically until later when she relocated to New York. "Duke had said to me that if I should come to New York I should look him up. And so I told him I would but I was really thinking, great, he'll be playing with Bird and I'll get to hear and meet Bird again." While Duke was in town, Jordan went to the Club Sudan where he was working a gig and sat in with him with Spight and Mitchell. Afterward Spight and Mitchell encouraged Duke to let Jordan sing her original lyrics to "'Round Midnight," which she did. Sheila remembers, "Duke was yelling, 'Jesus, man, this chick is singing on the changes. I've never heard this. What's going on? This chick is singing on the chord changes.' I had no clue what he meant and I thought I was doing something wrong. Instead he was amazed that I was actually singing on the *chord changes*."

As Jordan thrived in the jazz scene, she was continuously grappling with the prejudiced attitudes within the white community and her own personal struggles. She could no longer hang out with her jazz club buddy, Burkhoff, after her parents discovered the girls had been visiting the black jazz clubs. Burkhoff, being of Turkish ancestry with dark olive skin, became concerned about her own safety since she was often mistaken for being black. The police were constantly pulling over whites and blacks for mixing, so it wasn't unusual for the two girls to run into the same situation when they hung out together. It was worse for Jordan; she found herself endlessly being accosted by the police for being with black musicians, and she remembers at least forty or more occasions of being harassed during the time she lived in Detroit. It became even more difficult when she starting hanging out with Mitch and Skeeter. Because she was a single white woman singing with two black men, the all-white audiences would walk out in disgust. However, that never stopped Jordan from following her muse and she braved the danger and ridicule to be around the people she adored. Prior to meeting Spight and Mitchell, Jordan had started drinking with her high school friends at parties or whenever there was alcohol around. Skeeter and Mitch insisted that if she was going to sing with them she would have to stop drinking, and she did. It was her desire not to fall into the same pattern she had witnessed in her mother and other members of her family; because her will to sing was stronger it was easy at that point in her life to walk away from drinking. It wasn't until later that she would fall prey to the seductive charm of drinking again, but for now music had outwitted her demons.

Around 1947 Jordan had found her first typing job working for the Charles A. Strelinger Company located at 43 East Larned Street, which sold machinery, tools, and factory supplies. Jordan finally left her mother's residence and went to live at the Evangeline Home, a type of boardinghouse for young working women. Her Aunt Esther found out that Jordan was living in the Evangeline Home and thought it was terrible that her niece was living apart from her family, so she invited Jordan to rent a room at her home. Jordan was still frequenting the jazz clubs and by this time had found another friend to join her, a twenty-two-year-old young white man named Carl whom she met at the Club Sudan. One of the advantages of hanging out at the clubs with Carl was that she was able to avoid being pulled over by the police. But Carl became ill and it was then that she encountered her longtime friend, Jenny Devries (who later married and changed her name to Jenny King). Jordan and King (Devries) met through a mutual friend, Delphine, who worked with Jordan at the Strelinger Company. Delphine thought the two would be a good match since they both loved the music of Parker. The two discovered they were quite different from their other white friends and it was a connection they would share for many years as a result of their musical bond. "I guess we thought differently than most people, we were the dreamers," remembers King. Jordan couldn't seem to avoid racism on all fronts, and when her Uncle Jack discovered that she was hanging out with black musicians, she was asked to leave her Aunt Esther's house. "She ended up moving in my house with my mother and me," says King. "She was very independent and paid rent to my mother for the room. When we would come back from a gig on the weekends, I remember we would go into the refrigerator and fix a B.LT. We always had a good time listening to the music together." Jordan and King enjoyed going to the Bluebird Inn because all the locals would be there and eventually that's where Jordan met her first love.

In 1949, a handsome young African American tenor saxophonist, Frank Foster, left the slim pickings of the jazz scene in Cincinnati to join the thriving Detroit jazz community. Says Foster, "I even braved the horrible weather. I didn't have a hat or a decent overcoat but I braved it just to be there because

I was so excited about living in the Detroit jazz scene. It probably wasn't as hip as New York, but to me it was everything that they said New York was. I first met Tommy Flanagan, Kenny Burrell, and a number of others. I was just so excited to be there." He was also introduced to Jordan through Willie Bolar at the Blue Bird Inn, and as King put it, "they immediately had eyes for each other." Foster and Jordan had a tempestuous relationship in the beginning stages but things became exclusive when Jordan returned from a short trip to New York in 1950. Foster fondly remembers,

> I recall the very moment I fell in love with her. My friend Ernest Blake was going with a friend of hers, Jenny Devries. We had a foursome, and we went to Belle Isle. Ernest had a car, and he drove us all out to Belle Isle, and while we were lying on the grass I knew it was a special moment, and that's the very moment I fell in love with Jeannie [Jordan]. Before then I had to give her a hard time, being elusive because of these other women I was involved with. But at that moment I just fell desperately in love with her. She was the most exciting woman I'd ever met and as thrilling to make love to as she was to hear sing.

As magical as that moment was for Foster and Jordan, they were quickly reminded of reality when on the way back they were pulled over by the police and berated once again for "race mixing."

In those days, interactions between white women and black men were considered taboo and blasphemous in both cultures. Segregation was the rule and the police were known to be quite racist and threatening. Foster remembers, "I'd been stopped on the street on more than one occasion. For interracial couples in Detroit at that time, it was very hard. The police wouldn't think anything of stopping somebody just because they were interracial. I always had to be on my guard because I was black and she was white." Foster demonstrated more of a commitment to the on-and-off relationship by inviting Jordan to move into his place on John R and Owen Streets, about a block from Woodward Avenue, the dividing line of the black and white neighborhoods. In the short time that Jordan and Foster spent time together they became very close and understood each other's passion for music. According to Foster,

> We used to be on the bandstand and if we saw a singer come up we used to say, "Oh, shit, here he comes," or "here she comes." But it wasn't that way with Sheila. When you saw her coming, you were immediately delighted to see her, because you knew she was going to do something to excite you, musically. She has a tremendous ear and an exciting style of singing. She didn't just sing a simple melody; she knew how to embellish upon the melody in a way that would excite the listener. I haven't heard anybody in years that attracted my attention the way she did back then.

> She was, what you call, a tone natural. Like her theoretical knowledge of music wasn't much, but that didn't matter. The way she sang, it sounded as if she knew everything there was to know. And it was natural, it wasn't mechanical or clinical. I thought she was great, had a great ear, great voice. I never thought that she got her just ratings or, you know, I never thought she got the raves that she should've gotten, because compared to so many other singers she was head and shoulders above all of them.

In the spring of 1951 Foster was drafted into the U.S. Army, where he served in Korea with the 7th Infantry Division. Jordan moved to New York, thinking that the racial climate would be better and to follow her musical mentor, Parker. "As much as I loved Tommy, Barry, and Kenny, I just needed to get out of Detroit. I couldn't take the racial prejudice and I thought New York would be better." Although Jordan and Foster had a strong love for each other, the distance between them ended up being the cause of their separation. Sheila admits, "My first true love was Frank and he was a gem. He was such a beautiful, caring guy. Of course we fought at times but most of it was over the racial prejudice because we really had to struggle. A lot of people thought Frank and I would end up together but he went away to the Korean War and I moved to New York City and we just sort of drifted apart. He was my one special guy because he always treated me right."

As much as she knew she would miss her friends, she believed that New York City would provide the freedom to express herself as a person and artist. So around 1952, when Jordan was about twenty-four, she left Detroit behind for the Big Apple. New York became her home; to this day she shares time between the heart of the city and the upstate countryside. Foster wouldn't see Jordan again until he got out of the army in 1953, and by that time Jordan was living in New York. According to Foster,

> Well she was very much on the scene because she took me out on one of the most exciting nights in my life on July 27, 1953. I was getting ready to join the Count Basie Orchestra and she took me to Birdland, and I sat in with Charlie Parker. She knew him personally and she persuaded him to allow me to sit in. Charlie Parker even told Sheila, "that soldier boy sure can play." Then she took me to another place called the Open Door where Thelonious Monk was playing. Boy, what a night. That was like being in heaven.

• 4 •

A Helluva Town

1950–1980

"I went to New York so I could be closer to the music of Bird."

—Sheila Jordan

When Jordan stepped off the train in New York, she was entering the nucleus of a creative and expansive artistic scene. Charlie Parker and the generation of bop musicians were infecting jazz with a new language that Jordan had already embraced. She immediately jumped into the scene and rented a room in a house by Gramercy Park in the same building as her Detroit friends, Jenny King (Devries) and Virginia Cox. Says King, "Virginia and I got a pad in Gramercy Park which was a beautiful area. Our apartment was a great big room with a kitchenette and a little bathroom. When Sheila came to New York she took the apartment across from us." Jordan then found employment as a temp until she got a steady job in the typing pool with a top Madison Avenue advertising agency, Dancer-Fitzgerald-Sample. The excellent typing skills she developed at Commerce High School and at her job at Strelinger's in Detroit came in handy to maintain steady employment.

On the weekends, she would go to the jazz clubs on Fifty-Second Street and after-hours sessions at Minton's Playhouse in Harlem that often went all night long. The jazz jams were a meeting place for renowned and upcoming instrumentalists and singers, so it was beneficial for Jordan because she met serious jazz musicians and fans. "That was like going to church for me," says Jordan. "I started getting calls from a lot of the musicians back in Detroit to find out about the New York scene and I told them it was great. There were clubs in the Village, little jazz clubs and then there was Fifty-Second Street where I hung out when I first moved to New York. There were clubs like the Downbeat Club and the Three Deuces and I would see Dizzy, Bird, Fats Navarro, Lester Young, Billie Holiday, Monk, Max Roach, Roy Haynes,

Kenny Durham, and all the great beboppers. That's what I lived for, bebop." It was at one of the after-hours sessions at Minton's that Jordan would meet a lifelong friend and supporter, pianist Billy Taylor. Jordan fondly remembers, "Billy stood out from the rest as he always was dressed fine. He was a good friend to me through the years and always believed in me. He supported me in all areas of my career and he was a wonderful musician. I just adored him." Jordan always embraced the opportunities, in New York and Detroit, to hear the innovators and virtuosos of jazz; they were the modern-day equivalent of master classes. Jordan attended these sessions on a regular basis, soaking in the rich and visceral experiences that remain with her today.

Of course, Jordan went to hear her guru, Parker, whenever she could. "I told Bird I moved from Detroit to New York because I needed to hear his music. Bird just laughed, he had such a fantastic laugh." Duke Jordan was also on the bandstand on these occasions, so the two reconnected and started a kindling romance. "Duke remembered me from Detroit and told me that he always had big eyes for me. Of course I was flattered and found him attractive too. He was the second love of my life after Frank Foster." The two started hanging out and eventually decided to move in together. Finding a place for a biracial couple to cohabit was not easy in those days, but they eventually were able to rent a room next door to another biracial couple in Brooklyn. "Max Roach used to live near us in Brooklyn. J. J. Johnson and Miles all lived in Brooklyn at one point too. Max already knew me from when I was hanging out in the clubs in Detroit. I saw Max a lot when I was living in Brooklyn with Duke so we became very good friends." Jordan was working her day job in the city, and when she came home at night she would quite often find Duke slumped over and unaware. "So he was nodding out and that scared me. I had never seen him like that before and I had no clue what heroin was about." Eventually Jordan discovered that Duke was a heroin junkie, something that Jordan was naïve about at that point. She would realize the repercussions it would have on her relationship with Duke as time went on.

But in the meantime, Jordan was eager to learn as much as she could about music to help with her singing. Charles Mingus originally encouraged her to study with Lennie Tristano, a renowned jazz pianist and teacher of jazz improvisation. He emerged as an original voice in the New York jazz scene in the 1940s; during this period, a time of growing awareness of historical evolution in jazz, he was considered a prime representative of "progressive jazz" by many critics and musicians.[1] "Max also told me about Lennie, and it was Mingus who took me up to his place because they both knew I was looking for a teacher. I studied with Lennie for a couple of years," says Jordan. In retrospect, it may seem odd that Mingus and Max Roach, virtually alone among black musicians, were for a short while quite enamored of Tristano's approach to jazz, which restricted the rhythmic contribution of bass and drums (as opposed to the improvising soloists) quite severely.[2] However, Tristano was also enamored of Parker, and the two had a kinship that was highlighted by a respect for each other's individual sound. Jordan confirms this and the fact that the two had planned to collaborate on some future music projects, but all was thwarted when Parker died suddenly.

Tristano's studio was located in a loft at 317 East Thirty-Second Street in Manhattan, and on Jordan's first lesson with Tristano he told her he was going to give her a Parker tune to learn. Jordan told him, "I already know them." Jordan describes the first meeting:

> And Lennie said to me, "Oh really? Let's hear you sing one." So I sang "Now's The Time" and he was really impressed that I knew it and could sing it so well. So he said, "What about Lester Young?" I told him I didn't know any Lester Young tunes. So he gave me "Lester Leaps In" to work on. He was kind of surprised that I would know Bird. But then he found out that I'm a Bird freak.

Guitarist Andy Luparello recalls, "Lennie didn't teach us our instrument since he only played the piano. But he taught us music, concentrating on the major harmonic and melodic minor scale, inversions and chordal structures. From there he urged us to improvise around these concepts, me with my guitar and Sheila with her voice. Sheila became quite proficient as well with scat singing."

Jordan had found a safe environment to get over her fears and try out the ideas that she heard in her head. Tristano emphasized the lyrics of the songs, having Jordan speak the lyrics and know what they meant, repeating them over and over. "And I would," says Jordan. "I knew what the lyrics meant but he gave me the confidence to do it and that's what I needed at the time." Luparello talks about the sessions: "Tristano would hold Saturday evening sessions that would go until two or three in the morning. The list of musicians frequenting the sessions would be Don Ferrara [trumpet], Warren Marsh [tenor saxophone], Peter Ind [bass], Al Levitt [drums], Lloyd Lifton [piano], Ted Brown [tenor saxophone], and occasionally Charles Mingus and Lee Konitz would sit in. When Lennie sat in, oh my God, it's the master. Truly he inspired us beyond belief. That's how great he was." Marsh also stated that Tristano fostered his sense of originality: "Now that I look back on my studies with Lennie, though, I have to admit that I came to him with my own feeling for a melody, my own way of playing. What he taught me was that you don't have to imitate your heroes or your idols. You have to accept the responsibility of your own melody."[3] Tristano empowered Jordan to keep her unique sound and pushed her beyond her limits, which only made her more proficient at her craft. "He gave me a lot of encouragement," says Jordan.

> He was really supportive of women musicians and I liked that because he took me seriously. I think he knew that women had a tougher time in the music world and he sincerely wanted to help them. I was one of the first singers he taught so that was new for him too. Bird gave me courage by telling me I was unique in my sound and that I had million-dollar ears, and Lennie went a step further. He used to say that my ears will tell me that it's right and he insisted that I learn the tunes the way they were written before I did anything with them. He told me not to force anything, trust and let it happen.

Jordan and Duke decided to move back to the city since Brooklyn was too far from the clubs, her lessons with Tristano, and her job. Her old friend from Detroit, Virginia Cox, was looking to rent out half of a third-floor loft she was occupying on Twenty-Sixth Street between Seventh and Eighth Avenue. The landlord, Hymie [last name unknown], owned the building and was supportive to visual artists like Cox. He was already renting out spaces to a couple of visual artists living on the second floor as well. Jordan became one of the resident artists as the singer on the third floor. Duke moved in with Jordan initially but was gone for long periods due to his heroin addiction and philandering.

During the early 1950s, lofts were just starting to become popular with artists and musicians. The spaces were just right for large groups of people to bring their instruments and play the music they wanted without having to worry about bothering neighbors or answering to club owners. A variety of musicians could hang out together and experiment with different kinds of musical ideas without interference. For visual artists the high ceilings provided the right situation to hang large paintings and the open areas made it perfect for sculptures. Jordan shared a wall with artist Cox, so the two split the rent and shared a bathroom that was inconveniently located in the hallway. "It was funny," says Jordan. "People used to go into the toilet and shower when I wasn't home and leave me notes on a little stand that I had in there. I remember Mingus and Bird used to leave me notes telling me they stopped by."

Jordan was inspired, because of her studies with Tristano, to invite her fellow musicians to get together for jazz sessions that she hosted at her loft, primarily on weekends. This was before the jazz loft scene had really become popular, so Jordan's place was one of the first to present these kinds of sessions. According to Jordan, "I started inviting the students from Lennie's sessions and anybody who wanted to come and play. It was a hangout for all of us that were just trying to keep the music alive. Everybody in the building was an artist, so if you wanted to have a session, nobody cared." Jordan remembers not only Tristano's students, including Peter Ind, Phyllis Pinkerton, Al Leavitt, and others, but also Thelonious Monk, Arthur Taylor, Mingus, and of course, Parker. "Bird was a constant guest," says Jordan.

> He was always coming up. He'd come up to the loft whether I was having a session or not. It could be anytime of the day or night. I had a lot of sessions up there. I remember so many different people coming up there. I mean, you name it; they were up there at some point. One time I was having a session and I went out for something and when I came back, and I couldn't get in to my own place because it was full of people. I told everyone, "Can I get into my own home, please?" and I laughed, but it was packed.
>
> I had this old upright piano that we used, which was not in very good shape. I would try to keep it tuned and, finally, somebody donated a better upright. So I ended up giving it to Horace Silver. Horace and I went out on a date once and I had a boxer dog at the time that wouldn't let him near me, so I always had to meet him downstairs to have dinner. We became very good friends so when Horace mentioned he didn't have a piano that stuck in my mind. And when I got the better upright I called Horace first and asked him if he wanted that old piano. They had to move it out my loft window and he paid for that and put it in his hotel room. I think Miles Davis wrote one of his compositions on what he called "that old raggedy piano." He talks about it in his book, because he went to Horace's hotel room, and Horace said that the piano took up half the room.

Although Jordan had found great happiness in making the music that moved her and having the opportunity to learn from both mentors, Parker and Tristano, her hopes of finding less racism in New York were disappointed. The sophistication of the city had not overcome the rampant racism that had gripped the majority of the country, and Jordan was once again a witness and participant. Besides being harassed for her mixed company, she had several serious encounters when she socialized with her African American friends. It became clear to her that this would be a continuous battle if she wanted to sustain her mixed-race relationships. Jordan put herself in the heart of race relations by marrying Duke on August 2, 1953. The marriage sealed further controversy for Jordan by not only dealing with more intense racism but also opening a door into the world of drug addiction and abuse. (These topics are discussed in greater length in other chapters.)

Tristano was well aware that Duke was a junkie and heavily addicted to heroin. He expressed to Jordan his dislike for Duke and tried to encourage her to leave him. Jordan confirms, "Lennie told me that I should be careful but I didn't listen. In fact, I was kind of pissed off because he said that and I basically stopped going to him from that point. I felt he was trying to turn me against Duke, and I guess I wasn't ready to see the truth about Duke then. In hindsight he was absolutely right." Jordan finally realized that she had to face the fact that Duke had a very serious problem with heroin addiction. "He used to keep his 'works,' that's what they called the drugs back then, under a loose board on the loft floor. I don't know how I ever lived through that or why I put up with it."

Besides the heroin addiction, Duke was emotionally abusive to Jordan and had numerous affairs with other women where he would be gone for several days at a time. To complicate things further, Jordan became pregnant, and that was too much for Duke to handle.

> When I was pregnant with my daughter one of the women that Duke was seeing on the side came to visit me. She told me that they were seeing each other, which I didn't know about at the time. She said that she thought I should know since I was having a baby. I told her that Duke wasn't giving me any support; all of the money I made went to pay the rent and food. All of Duke's money went to buying heroin. But now I realize she did me the biggest favor in the world because I didn't have to deal with him anymore.

The moral support Jordan did get was from her friends, who came to her rescue when she was struggling to take care of herself. Parker and Jordan became close friends during this time and he looked out for her, especially when he discovered she was pregnant. According to Jordan, "Bird was wonderful to me. He would send a car to pick me up and take me home if he was playing somewhere because he knew I was pregnant. That's the kind of man he was." Parker never got to see Jordan's baby; he unexpectedly passed away on March 12, 1955, creating a lifelong wound for Jordan, who deeply cared for him as if he were her brother.

With the loss of Parker, Jordan found solace in other friends who would lend a hand before, during, and after her pregnancy.

> I must have been about seven or eight months pregnant and I had to go to a doctor's appointment. I had gotten to know Clifford Brown, whom we all called "Brownie," and got him his first apartment in my building when he first arrived from Chicago. We became very good friends and one time he showed up when I was on my way to the doctor. He asked me how I was going to get to the doctor's office and I told him I was taking the subway. He said, "No you won't, I'm going to drive you." So he took me in his car and I told him how sweet that was of him to look out for me. I believe that was the last time I saw him because he died the following year.

When Jordan finally did get labor pains, she took a taxi to the hospital and had her baby, Tracey, on the evening of September 27, 1955. "She was beautiful. The day she was born is a day that I'll never forget because I felt that I finally had someone that I could truly love and that I was sure would love me back." The next day she called Duke to let him know, but as Jordan remembers, "He could have cared less. He never came to see me when I was in the hospital." Duke ended up returning to the loft and staying with Jordan for only a few months before he left for good. With no one to help support the baby, Jordan continued to work at least part-time while she found trusted people to look after her baby. "Duke just disappeared and I never took him to court for child support because I knew that he couldn't pay. He was so strung out by that time I knew he couldn't take care of us. He had his own demons and I figured I would take care of her and things would be okay. Tracey's father never got in touch with her except for a postcard now and then in her adult years."

With a new baby to take care of, Jordan had to make some changes to her life, which included having to relocate. When Tracey was about nine months old, Hymie sold the building they were living in to new landlords. During this period, having a residence in a loft was illegal and violated building and fire codes; however, many artists found ways to disguise their spaces so that it didn't appear they were actually living in them. But now that Jordan had a baby it would be more difficult to ward off inspectors, and Hymie wasn't certain the new landlords would accommodate Jordan's situation. Although he had to ask Jordan and her baby to leave, he was concerned for both of them. Since Hymie owned another building on West Twenty-Fifth Street off Ninth Avenue, he made an apartment on the second floor in the back so that Jordan could live there with her daughter. It was similar to the loft, but in a residential neighborhood. "It was just a small place with a little kitchen, a tiny bedroom for Tracey, and a living room that I slept in. Of course I could no longer hold any music sessions because it was too small and would disturb the neighbors." Although the neighborhood was mostly safe, Jordan remembers one alarming situation:

> The apartment had a smaller building next to my kitchen window so you could open the window and climb out onto the roof. I became concerned about that when one day some guy came to the window from the roof. He knocked on the window and Tracey, who was just a little girl at the time, heard him and went to the window and opened it because he told her that he was Santa Claus and that she should let him in. So she did. I was sleeping in the other room at the time and did not hear any of this. He told her to show him where the money was because he needed it to buy her Christmas presents. So she did. I made sure that didn't happen again.

Even with all her responsibilities, Jordan always found a way to make the music she loved. Sometime in 1958, she found a singing job one evening a week (Monday) at the Page Three, a cabaret on Seventh Avenue in Greenwich Village just south of the Village Vanguard. According to Dave Frishberg from his

Written Word memoirs, "Around the time I first came to New York, during the late fifties, I got a call from a piano player named Johnny Knapp. He asked if I would be interested in replacing him with the band at the Page Three. It was a two-piece band—piano and drums. 'You have to play a continuous show,' he told me, 'the hours are 9pm to 4am, and the pay is seventy-five a week.' I told him I would be interested."[4] The Page Three appealed to alternate sexual lifestyles, and many of the customers were dressed as the opposite sex as well as a host of characters including Tiny Tim, who was just starting out his career.

Frishberg continues, "What Jimmy [Olin] and I looked forward to each night was Sheila Jordan. Sheila was magic. The customers would stop gabbing and all the entertainers would turn their attention to Sheila and the whole place would be under her spell. She was doing 'If You Could See Me Now' and 'Baltimore Oriole' and some of the other material that she subsequently put on record."[5] At the Page Three, Jordan received her on-the-job education in singing with accompanists. She worked with quite a few:

> The first accompanist was Herbie Nichols, who was a fabulous composer and a wonderful piano player. He could really play "out" and it was an incredible experience because we both really listened to each other. He was also a man of very few words. I remember one time I had just arrived at the Page Three and was getting out of the cab and he was standing there. He said to me, "You'll never become famous until you record with me." And then he gave a little chuckle. I really enjoyed working with him and learned a lot. Another pianist I really worked well with was Cecil Taylor. He came in as a substitute from time to time but I always loved the great experiences I had singing with him. Other wonderful accompanists were Johnny Knapp, Jack Reilly, and Dave Frishberg.

Eventually Jordan began singing on Tuesdays and Wednesdays along with working her office job and taking care of Tracey. "I had to have music in my life in order to survive at the time; it was really an important outlet for me."

Another accompanist who would be critical to her career was bassist Steve Swallow. "So between Steve and the different piano players on those nights I was really well covered. The drummer was usually Ziggy Willmann, who was very sensitive to singers." Swallow remembers it this way:

> The pianist John Knapp called me to work Monday night at the Page Three. I had arrived in New York only a few months before, and was still feeling my way into the city. That club became a kind of home to me. It was a gay bar, at a time when gays needed to be furtive and circumspect out in the real world. But at the Page Three they could be themselves, and offer each other loyal friendship and support, which they also extended to

> me. I was deeply grateful, and looked forward to those Mondays. Sheila was revered in that room by the regulars who constituted most of the audience week after week. There were usually a handful of other performers (I especially remember The Unique Monique), many of them not so good and treated with fond derision, and then there was Sheila. The room fell still when she sang; everything stopped. I remember one night, just another Monday, and Sheila was singing, "I'm a Fool to Want You." I was playing along, focusing on playing the right note at the right time, when suddenly tears erupted from my eyes. That had never happened to me before, and I was mightily embarrassed, did my best to cover my confusion and to keep the bass part on track. I never again took Sheila's singing lightly.

Longtime friend and vocalist Carol Fredette met Jordan through Ziggy Willmann, who took her to the Page Three one evening. Fredette fondly remembers, "The first time I heard her sing I couldn't breathe. I felt the intensity in which she sang and to me that's what it was all about. She was communicating the song, the lyrics, and also being so musical in her phrasing. I thought she was a true jazz singer and I remember her singing songs like 'I'm a Fool to Want You,' 'Sleepin' Bee,' and 'Don't Explain.' I sat in and got hired to sing there and she immediately became my big sister."

Jordan's musical connection with Swallow birthed the bass and voice concept that would be one of her shining achievements in jazz history. Swallow generously allowed Jordan to try out bass and voice arrangements while they were playing together at the Page Three. They also did some concerts at a coffeehouse in the Village called the Take Three. Sheila states, "Because I loved the way Steve played and felt so comfortable with him, I must admit that he was really the first one that I ever seriously tried to do a bass and voice duo for performance." It was also at the Page Three that Jordan met vocalist Mark Murphy, who became a lifelong friend. Jordan affectionately reminisces,

> I met Mark when he used to come into the Page Three. Everyone knew him and loved him. God was he handsome! I'll never forget when he got up on the little bandstand and sang "Willow Weep for Me." I was so impressed with his singing and I thought he really had heart and sang from his soul. There weren't many male jazz singers around at that time, at least not the way Mark sang. We became good friends after meeting up at different times. He told me that he had come down to the Page Three on the night I sang because he had heard about me through the grapevine.

Suzanne Lorge writes in an article for *All About Jazz*:

> Murphy credits the singers he was hearing when he first moved to New York with strongly influencing his musical development. "[They] spun

> around in my head and made me creative," he says. Among them was Sheila Jordan, who became a lifelong friend and collaborator.
>
> "Sheila and I met in a place called the Page Three, right next to the Village Vanguard," Murphy recalls. "I'd meet her there on Monday nights. It was usually a variety club, but on Mondays the whole scene was jazz. At 8 when the jazz band came on, the vibe changed and the people changed. Even their clothes changed. It was part of this wonderful mystery."[6]

In 1960 Jordan reunited with bass player Peter Ind and recorded the song "Yesterdays" on the album *Looking Out* on the Wave label along with Ronnie Ball on piano and Al Shackman on guitar. Meanwhile Jordan was busy juggling work, singing, and taking care of a young child as a single parent. To add to the difficulty, Jordan's daughter was biracial at a time when having mixed-race relations was not accepted and so she had to endure constant remarks, disgusted looks, and mean treatment. "So Tracey sort of went through the same thing I did," says Jordan.

> She was a very caring little girl. I remember I finally got her into a nursery school where they kept her for a few hours every day and then I'd pick her up. I'd go shopping for groceries and she'd go along with me. And I remember one day I was coming up the subway steps after picking her up and we had a bag of groceries and they fell all over the street. I was just beside myself. I thought I was going to have a breakdown right then and there. And my daughter said, "It's okay, Mommy. It's okay, I'll help you. I'm here. I'll always help you." And my heart just melted when she said that, and I thought, Yeah, she's here now. I have a family that I can really call my own. But it wasn't easy. It was never easy.

It was the early '60s, and Jordan had found employment with the Doyle Dane Bernbach (DDB) advertising agency. The agency was one of the first to team up art directors and writers and to hire people based on creativity instead of pedigree backing, which was the employment mold for other agencies during the late 1950s. In fact, many of their ads became famous for being innovative, including the popular post–World War II Volkswagen Beetle "Think Small" campaign. "Think Small" was ranked as the best advertising campaign of all time.[7] When Jordan first started at DDB, she was hired as one of the typists in the typing pool. From Jordan's account,

> I liked the company because it seemed very hip and to me it had the greatest ads going. I was promoted to secretary for Sy Collins, who I believe was the vice president in the research department. I never had shorthand training but I was a very good typist and one of my jobs was doing a progress report every month on the development of the different products we advertised along with answering phones and filing. I was very much his right-hand person and he treated me with respect. I even had my own little office.

The agency was originally on Forty-Second Street between Fifth and Sixth Avenues, but later they moved their offices to Madison Avenue. The job allowed Jordan to pay her bills so she could take care of her daughter and, as an added bonus, they provided a profit-sharing program. Jordan's voice was even used for four of their clients' commercials—for Thom McAn Shoes, Whirlpool Refrigerator/Freezer (singing to "The Party's Over"), Bulova Watches, and Softique Bath Oil (singing to the melody of "Body and Soul" with lyrics changed to fit the product). The company even had her sing at the Christmas parties each year. The job was perfect for Jordan since it had the right elements of progressive thinking, creativity, adequate pay, and respect. Jordan remembers, "One day I went to lunch with the girls in the office and one of the founders, Bill Bernbach, was there having lunch with Miles Davis. I waved to Miles and he waved back." Her boss, Collins, knew that Jordan was trying to keep her singing career active so he was very generous about letting her take vacation days during times when she had out-of-town gigs. In fact, he even gave her a temporary leave of absence when she was hired for a tour overseas. It is easy to see why Jordan held such regard for the agency and why she remained there for over twenty-five years.

Jordan was content raising her daughter and finding time to sing a few nights at the Page Three as well as several other venues. On one Monday evening a very special guest, George Russell, dropped by to hear one of his students, Jack Reilly, who was sitting in for Johnny Knapp that evening. Russell was an influential composer, theoretician, musician, and educator, best known for his development of the Lydian Chromatic Concept of Tonal Organization. From his early composition with Dizzy Gillespie of "Cubano-Be, Cubano-Bop," through the changes wrought by modal jazz as a consequence of his ideas, to his impact on the Scandinavian and European scenes, his achievements are among the most outstanding in music.[8] When Russell heard Jordan sing, he was mesmerized with her vocal sound. "George came over to me and he said, 'Where do you come from to sing like that?' And I thought, who is this guy? I told him that I come from hell and we both laughed. And he replied, 'Yeah? Well, I'd like to visit Hell.' Then he said he wanted to be in touch with me and so I gave him my telephone number. We started going out and I discovered that he was serious about finding out where I was from to sing the way I did."

It was Jordan's background growing up in the coal-mining town of Summerhill that most intrigued Russell. He encouraged Jordan to take him to her home in Pennsylvania so that he could get a look at her childhood environment, so Jordan took him home to meet her grandmother; she recalls the story this way:

> My grandmother liked to drink so we went to this beer garden up the street. So George and I were drinking and there was this old out-of-work coal miner sitting at the bar who knew me from the past. My grandmother

> started bragging about how we were from New York and how we both were famous. And so the guy at the bar asked if I still sing "You Are My Sunshine," and I told him that I didn't sing that song anymore. The guy then asked me why not and then George said to me, "well why not? Come on, let's try it, and let's play it for him." There was an old raggedy upright piano and George sat down and played the song and I started singing for this coal miner. Suddenly my grandmother pushes George off the bench and tells him, "That's not the way it goes." So I sang it with her instead. I'll never forget George saying to me that my grandmother sounded like Thelonious Monk playing that piano.

Russell was moved by the conditions of poverty he witnessed in the coal-mining towns. Jordan believes that it was because Russell was so touched by the people and how they lived that he was inspired to write the arrangement for "You Are My Sunshine." It was not more than a month later when Russell contacted Jordan about singing that arrangement for his next album.

> George called me up on the phone. He said, "I want you to come down and hear something." And so I went down and he played this incredible introduction. It was more than an introduction; it was sort of like a voice. Oh, it was so beautiful. And he stopped, and then he said, "Okay, sing." I said, "Sing what?" He said, "Sing 'You Are My Sunshine.'" I said, "Alone?" He said, "Yeah." I said, "Oh, man, I can't do that." He said, "Yeah, you can. You used to sing alone going up and down the street when you were a kid, going by the graveyard and everything. You told me that. Come on, sing it." And so I sang it. And we went in the studio and recorded it on Riverside Records. George wanted to call it "A Drinking Song," but he couldn't change the title. So that's how "You Are My Sunshine" was born in 1961.

Recorded on *Outer View*, the last album Russell made in the States until 1972, this performance is still astonishing in its power.[9] According to Jordan, "The first time 'You Are My Sunshine' was performed was at the Newport Jazz Festival in 1962. I remember that concert very clearly. It was outdoors and Max Roach and Abbey Lincoln, who were married at the time, were in the audience listening. Afterward, George Wein came over and asked me if I would do a duet with Steve Swallow—Steve was in George's band at the time—but I declined as I didn't feel confident enough to do anything at this huge festival with just bass and voice."

By this time, Jordan and Russell had developed a rather serious relationship. Russell became very involved in Jordan's life. Jordan warmly remembers, "He knew that I was working part-time, half a day in an office, five days a week and then singing in this club a couple of nights a week, which didn't really pay that much. He used to come by in his green Volkswagen on the days I was singing at night, and drive my daughter to the nursery school and sometimes pick her up too just to help me out. He did that for quite a while. He was wonderful to me."

Jordan was still married to Duke although he had abandoned her and Tracey when she was a baby. There was no doubt in Jordan's mind that he would not be returning, nor did she want him back. Russell asked Jordan to marry him and she accepted. He also offered to pay for her divorce so they could finalize their wedding plans. Unlike today, it wasn't easy to get a divorce in New York unless you could prove adultery—something Jordan could have done but was so overwhelmed with raising her daughter, working, and singing that she hadn't taken the initiative. Russell tracked Duke down and got the papers signed after agreeing to give him six dollars so he could get a fix. The two had to travel to New Mexico to legalize the divorce, and when they returned to New York Jordan had officially cut the ties from Duke Jordan forever. Since Jordan was free to marry Russell, she took the next step and had a beautiful wedding dress made for the occasion.

Russell was such a firm believer in Jordan's vocal abilities that he paid to make a demo tape of her singing to present to record labels in order to get her a recording deal. Jordan sang over an already recorded rhythm track at Nola Studios featuring her Detroit friend, guitarist Kenny Burrell. The demo got the attention of Quincy Jones, who was then the A&R person at Mercury Records, but it was Alfred Lion at Blue Note who locked up the deal. Lion was encouraged by his then future wife, Ruth, and Russell to hear Jordan sing at the Page Three. Once Lion heard Jordan, he was equally impressed with her vocal brilliance and she became the first jazz singer to record on Blue Note Records. Jordan wanted to do a bass and voice duet project, but Lion and Frances Wolff only allowed her to do a couple of songs with the bass. Instead of the typical rhythm section that uses piano, bass, and drums, it was Russell's idea to use a guitar for the trio, which at that time was rarely done. Jordan respectfully recalls, "Since I couldn't do bass and voice George said, 'Okay, we'll do guitar, bass, and drums.' I said, 'I don't know. I never sang with guitar before.' He said, 'Trust me on this.' And I said, 'Nah, maybe I'd rather do piano.' He said, 'Trust me on this, guitar, bass, and voice. Okay?' I said, 'Okay.' Because at the time nobody was using guitar. I don't remember any of the well-known jazz singers who had recorded with guitar and bass at that time, and then afterward Sarah did something and Ella did something with Joe Pass. George Russell was so ahead of his time. He was a genius. I owe him everything."

Russell suggested that they use Barry Galbraith on guitar and Steve Swallow on bass, while Lion chose Denzil Best for drums. The debut recording became one of the classic albums for which Jordan is most noted, entitled *Portrait of Sheila* and released in 1962. Swallow remembers,

> Denzil, Barry, Sheila, and George Russell, who provided arrangements for the album, were seasoned pros and I was not. Each of them took pains to set me at ease during the project. Sheila was especially sweet, occasionally steering me into a corner of the studio to reassure me I was playing just what she wanted. I was tremendously impressed by Barry Galbraith's poise. He spent most of his waking hours recording, and had his routine down, the placement of his chair and music stand, the thermos on the floor, headphones hung just so on the music stand. I watched him like a hawk, and to this day I go about securing my little area in the studio as I saw him do it.

Although Jordan would not get an opportunity to do the bass and voice duet recording she wanted until much later, she was able to record at least one song with just bass, "Dat Dere," and one with bass and drums, "Baltimore Oriole." Both songs have become some of her most requested and memorable tunes. "Dat Dere," written by Bobby Timmons with lyrics by Oscar Brown Jr., was originally written about a child with a father's point of view but Jordan cleverly altered the lyrics slightly to make it a dedication to her own daughter, Tracey. Another composition from the project was the 1946 standard "If You Could See Me Now," composed by Tadd Dameron with lyrics by Carl Sigman. Remembers Jordan,

> I was doing the Blue Note recording and I told George that I wanted to do "If You Could See Me Now," because I'd heard Bill Evans's recording of it and I loved those changes and wanted to use them for my recording. The first time I heard of Bill Evans was through George Russell. In fact, I met Bill because of George. There was a club up on Broadway and the piano was on top of the bar. Bill was playing there that night so George took me to hear him. And when the intermission came, Bill came down and sat with us. And I said, "Bill, I love your changes on 'If You Could See Me Now.' How would you feel about giving them to me?" And then George told him, "Sheila's going to do this Blue Note recording and she wants to record this tune but she only wants to record it because she heard you playing it and she loves your changes." So Bill wrote them out on a paper napkin. And I had that napkin until my old house burned down. I lost everything in that fire, but the one thing that I was most upset about losing was that napkin with Bill Evans's chord changes to "If You Could See Me Now." But I'm so thrilled that those are the Bill Evans's changes on *Portrait of Sheila*.
>
> What some people don't know is that George was very prominent in bringing Bill Evans on the scene. In fact, he wrote a composition for Bill that is incredible called "Concerto for Billy the Kid." You have no idea how many piano players I've turned on to that recording. And it's an in-

> credible solo but a lot of the introduction is what George wrote, which a lot of people think is just part of Bill's solo. George was very helpful. If he believed in you and thought you had something to say, he was out there to see that you said it. I remember one time Bill was working at Trudy Heller's in the Village, which was a club on Sixth Avenue. I went in to hear Bill and he asked me to sing with him. And I got up and I sang, of course, "If You Could See Me Now." So those are fond memories.

Portrait of Sheila was a successful project that brought Jordan recognition in the jazz community and gave her more visibility to continue her singing and to connect with other musicians for future projects. Don Heckman observes in the May 9, 1963, issue of *DownBeat*: "The most important is her new Blue Note release *A Portrait of Sheila*, certainly one of the most promising debut recordings made by a jazz singer. Her club work, too, has increased—12 weeks at Wells in Harlem last spring, two weeks at Milton's in the Bronx last July, two months at the Take 3 in Greenwich Village early this year (and again with Jimmy Giuffre at the end of March), in addition to the regular three-night-a-week job she has held at Page 3 in Greenwich Village for the last six years. Her continuing appearances in the company of musicians such as Giuffre, George Russell, and Don Ellis suggest that she holds the same favored status with the new musicians of the '60s that Sarah Vaughan and Billy Eckstine did with Charlie Parker and Dizzy Gillespie in the '40s."[10] *All Music* gave the *Portrait of Sheila* recording a five-star rating, and jazz critic Scott Yanow writes: "Sheila Jordan's debut recording was one of the very few vocal records made for Blue Note during Alfred Lion's reign. Accompanied by the subtle guitarist Barry Galbraith, bassist Steve Swallow, and drummer Denzil Best, Jordan sounds quite distinctive, cool-toned, and adventurous during her classic date. Her interpretations of Oscar Brown, Jr.'s 'Hum Drum Blues' and 11 standards (including 'Falling in Love with Love,' 'Dat Dere,' 'Baltimore Oriole,' and 'I'm a Fool to Want You') are both swinging and haunting. Possibly because of her originality, Sheila Jordan would not record again for over a dozen years, making this highly recommended set quite historic."[11]

Russell had successfully guided Jordan to her first recording date, and there were still marriage plans in the works until Russell canceled at the last minute. Though Russell "left her standing at the church door," as he puts it, for the daughter of his friend, composer John Benson Brooks, there were no hard feelings, and it was his interventions that kick-started her career.[12] "I would tease him when I saw him and tell him you know I still have that wedding dress," says Jordan.

> And we would laugh. I mean, of course I was very upset at the time but I never felt that he meant to hurt me. He was always so good to me and

> it was because of him that I made my first solo recording. And he paid for my divorce from Duke too. I'm not sure we were compatible anyway and I think George fell in love with the way I sang more than me. But we became better as friends so it all worked out for the best and I was just so grateful to know him because he truly was such a remarkable person.

Although *Portrait of Sheila* gained some well-deserved attention for Jordan, it wasn't until 1975 that she would record another solo album. In the meantime she continued to find gigs locally and was featured on other artists' recordings. In 1964 she moved to an apartment in Chelsea, where she lives to this day. Nine-year-old Tracey was growing up among some of the jazz community's finest musicians. Tracey remembers, "She always had musicians coming by the house to rehearse, and artists and painters too. I grew up with Carol and Bob Thompson. They were like my godparents. John Carter, Sonny Rollins, Ornette Coleman, Max Roach—I was really close with Max's son, Raoul. And Elvin Jones was also like my godfather. There were so many. When mom would go out on the road on tour, I would stay with Dollie and Jackie McLean. So there was a definite jazz community of kids that I grew up with."

Jordan had a few romantic relationships that tended to be abusive in one way or another. Jealously would ensue based on the attention she received from singing, paranoia about musicians she hung out with, or just simply in competition with the music in her life. Women in the spotlight have historically dealt with these attitudes from men, often resulting in physical and mental abuse, to which Jordan was no exception. A positive outcome of one of her short-lived relationships was her close friendship with Marria Banks, whom she met through Joe Banks. Jordan recalls,

> I was going with Joe for a short while and he began seeing Marria on the side. Joe and I were better friends than lovers so I gave him to Marria with my love. I always teased her and I'd say, "Some friend you are, you stole my boyfriend." I could talk to her about anything. She was always there for me and I was always there for her. She really became my best friend and when her daughter Coryelle was born, I was at the hospital with Joe to see her and the baby. Coryelle is like my niece and I consider her a part of my family.

Coryelle Kramer agrees: "I always felt like she was family. I hung out with Sheila when I was a kid. Even when I was little she fascinated me. My mom and Sheila had a very close friendship. They were always talking on the phone or they were together. I think because both of them had relationships with Afro-American men and had biracial daughters they could really understand each other. It was as if they both had a lifesaver in the middle of the ocean and together they had this bond, this power that most people couldn't understand."

It was 1968 and Jordan was featured on *Masks*, the recording by Jack Reilly on the Unichrom label, singing "Benedictus." The project was recorded live in St. Peter's Lutheran Church in New York and included Norman Marnell: tenor saxophone; Jack Reilly: piano; Jack Six: bass; and Joe Cocuzzo: drums. During that same period Jordan did some vocals on the recording of Carla Bley and Paul Haines entitled *Escalator Over the Hill* on JCOA. The project was recorded over three years between 1968 and 1971. There was quite an impressive group of musicians, including Enrico Rava, Michael Snow: trumpet; Don Cherry: trumpet, vocals; Bob Carlisle: French horn; Sharon Freeman: French horn, vocals; Jimmy Knepper: trombone; Sam Burtis: trombone, vocals; Roswell Rudd, Jack Jeffers: trombone, vocals; John Buckingham: tuba; Howard Johnson: tuba, vocals; Perry Robinson, Souren Baronian: clarinet; Jimmy Lyons: alto saxophone; Gato Barbieri, Peggy Imig: tenor saxophone; Chris Woods: baritone saxophone; Don Preston: synthesizer, vocals; Carla Bley: organ, piano, vocals; Michael Mantler: trumpet, trombone, piano, keyboards, synthesizer, vocals; John McLaughlin, Sam Brown: guitar; Leroy Jenkins: violin; Nancy Newton: viola, vocals; Calo Scott: cello; Charlie Haden, Richard Youngstein, Ron McClure: bass; Jack Bruce: bass, vocals; Paul Motian: drums; Jeanne Lee, Jane Blackstone, Jonathan Cott, Steve Gebhardt, Tyrus Gerlach, Eileen Hale, Rosalind Hupp, Timothy Marquand, Tod Papageorge, Bob Stewart, Pat Stewart, Viva, Karen Mantler, Phyllis Schneider, and Linda Ronstadt: vocals.

Jordan had met Roswell Rudd in the early '60s when she was playing at the Take Three in the Village. She was doing a bass and voice concert with Swallow, and Rudd was there at the same time performing with Steve Lacy. He liked what he heard and asked Jordan if she would be interested in doing some gigs with him. By this time the Page Three had closed down, so Jordan was looking for new places to sing. Rudd, Charlie Haden, Beaver Harris, and Jordan did some gigs at a place on Seventh Avenue called The St. James Infirmary. Rudd remembers, "We happened to be standing next to each other in a noisy club, Boomers maybe, and she just started singing very softly but very clearly in my right ear her version of Parker's 'Confirmation.' That performance absolutely bonded me to her musical personality. It was like a cantus firmus for all the future collaborations that would eventually come along." In the early '70s the two worked at St. Peter's as part of their All Nite Soul jazz concert series with the group minus Haden. Jordan admiringly recalls, "I loved singing with Roswell and we would do some trombone and voice arrangements." In 1973 Jordan sang vocals on the recording *Roswell Rudd and the Jazz Composer's Orchestra: Numatik Swing Band* on the JCOA label. The band consisted of Enrico Rava, Mike Lawrence, Charles Sullivan, Michael Krasnov: trumpet; Art Baron, Gary Brocks: trombone; Janet Donaruma, Sharon Freeman, Jeffrey Schlegel: French horn; Roswell Rudd: French horn, tuba; Bob Stewart, Howard Johnson: tuba; Mike Bresler: piccolo, flute, soprano saxophone; Martin Alter: flute, oboe, alto saxophone; Carlos Ward: flute, alto saxophone; Perry Robinson: clarinet; Dewey Redman: clarinet, tenor saxophone; Charles Davis: soprano saxophone, baritone saxophone; Hod O'Brien: piano; Sirone, Charlie Haden: bass; Beaver Harris, Lou Grassi: drums; and Sue Evans, Dan Johnson: percussion.

The following year she recorded on Rudd's release *Flexible Flyer* on the Arista/Freedom label. It was a smaller band this time with Roswell Rudd: trombone, French horn; Hod O'Brien: piano; Barry Altschul: drums; and a bass player who would soon collaborate with Jordan on a future solo bass and voice recording, Arild Andersen. Jordan was also featured on a couple of recordings with bassist Marcello Melis, one recorded in 1974 entitled *Perdas De Fogu (Burning Stones)* with alto saxophonist Mario Schiano, and the other recorded in 1978, *Free To Dance*.

Since Jordan didn't have an agent at the time (and rarely does to this day) she didn't get many singing jobs, but it worked out since she didn't want to leave her young daughter to go out on tours anyway. Fredette remembers, "Sheila couldn't go on the road like other vocalists so she couldn't tour. She would never think of leaving Tracy to do that; she was a dedicated mother." Although she did work at the Village Vanguard once or twice, the majority of her singing was reserved for special projects or recordings. After a twelve-year hiatus after her solo debut, *Portrait of Sheila*, Jordan recorded *Confirmation* at the Vanguard Studio in New York on the Japanese label East Wind (later reissued by Test of Time in 2005). Her group consisted of Norman Marnell: tenor saxophone; Beaver Harris: drums; Cameron Brown: bass; and a young Alan Pasqua on piano. The first half of the recording is dedicated to children, with a medley of songs that included "God Bless the Child," "My Favorite Things," "Inchworm," and "Because We're Kids." The remaining tracks include "Confirmation" with lyrics written by Skeeter Spight, pianist Steve Kuhn's composition "Pearlie's Swine," and a brief duet "By Myself" with Harris on brushes that segues to "Why Was I Born?" According to Jordan, "I was singing 'Inch Worm' at the Page Three before Coltrane came out with it. I used to sing it to my daughter and my best friend's daughter, Coryelle, and then later on to Jay Clayton's little son and daughter. Kids always loved that song."

Pasqua was studying with George Russell at the New England Conservatory when Jordan first met him. She remembers, "It was at Mark Harvey's All Nite Soul concert in Boston. Mark is a minister and he invited me to come up and sing, and Alan was playing piano. I was very impressed with his playing. I knew I wanted him on the recording." Pasqua had just come off the road with Tony Williams when he met Jordan again and was asked specifically by her to play on the recording. Pasqua tenderly recalls,

> I've always called her "my jazz mom," because she kind of took me under her wing and provided just a great deal of mentorship and taught me how to accompany the vocalists and, I mean, I don't even think of her so much as a vocalist. She's just another voice in the band; she's a horn as well as a singer. She's a horn player, a piano player or whatever. So she was really instrumental in my early days. I mean, after the Tony Williams records it was one of the first things I had done, and it was just an incredible experience. I just remember Beaver, especially, just how free he was and how easy it was to play with him. And how Sheila, in the studio, had the ability of going outside of herself and being able to listen to everything, and not just getting hung up on little things, maybe, that she did or that somebody did. She really had a big picture outlook, and that taught me, without even realizing it, but it kind of laid the groundwork for me in the studio of my philosophy, which is definitely, you know, it's about the spirit of the music and the big picture. It's not about an individual performance, because the spirit of the music always will transcend and supersede anything else. You can have the greatest solo in the world, but if the vibe of the whole thing doesn't match up to this great solo, then all you have is a great solo.

Jordan has commented that she would have worked with Pasqua more often but he moved to California. She did reunite with him on some performances later in her career.

Cameron Brown had worked with Jordan several years prior to the *Confirmation* recording date. Jordan had approached him about doing a bass and voice duo with her but Brown didn't feel that he was ready for the commitment it would require. Yet Jordan always felt he would be a good bass partner and her instincts proved right in later years.

When the recording was reissued, it received this review from Andrew Rowan in *All About Jazz*, published June 15, 2005:

> Sheila Jordan has the purity of heart of a child expressed through adult experience. When she dedicates this 1975 recording (originally on the Japanese East Wind label) to children of all ages, it is real.
>
> *Confirmation* has songs written by Charlie Parker and Billie Holiday (her two greatest influences) nestled alongside offerings from American popular song (Richard Rodgers, Oscar Hammerstein, Jerome Kern, Frank Loesser, Arthur Dietz, and Richard Schwartz)—as well as pianist Steve Kuhn ("Pearlie's Swine," aka "The Zoo") and something unexpected from Dr. Seuss

> ("Because We're Kids"). In lesser hands such a mélange of songs might be just a gimmick, but Jordan crafts her projects with care.
>
> She possesses the uncanny ability to simultaneously explore the changes and tell a story. Parker praised her "million-dollar ears." Listen to "God Bless the Child," a masterpiece—second only to Holiday's original 1941 recording. Realizing that this is not a gospel song, but, rather, a plaintive jazz ballad of independence informed by pain, Jordan carries the sting on soaring, held tones that descend into smoky, melismatic phrases. Would-be "American Idols" could learn something about how to bend notes with restraint by listening to Jordan.
>
> She honors Parker with "Confirmation," easily handling the light-hearted bebop lyrics written by her high school friend Skeeter Spight as she hones in on Bird's intricate melodic line and demanding harmonies. When she scats, she sounds like no one else; blowing a solo that is a marvel of concision.
>
> In the ballad medley, she introduces another masterful performance with an up-tempo "By Myself," accompanied by Beaver Harris' intrepid drumming. This high-flying opening gives way to Kern's rueful "Why Was I Born." Here the lessons learned from Holiday become even more apparent. Although she sounds nothing like Lady Day, her willingness to go to the emotional ends of a song reveals a strong connection.
>
> Every song on *Confirmation* defines the Sheila Jordan experience. To call this singer/musician merely a treasure or merely a great singer is insufficient to describe her enormous talent."[13]

George Russell was responsible for introducing Jordan to bassist Arild Andersen. Russell invited Jordan to sing at a couple of jazz festivals in Scandinavia with a group that featured Jan Garbarek on tenor and Jon Christensen on drums. Andersen was already comfortable doing bass and voice duets, so the two hit it off effortlessly, establishing a mutual admiration—so much so that Jordan recorded her first solo bass and voice recording with Andersen, *Sheila*, released on SteepleChase in August of 1977. Had they not lived so far apart, Andersen living in Norway, it's possible the duo would have continued; they both had an interest in pursuing bass and voice duets. According to Scott Yanow, "This was a breakthrough recording for Sheila Jordan. She recorded a superb album for Blue Note in 1962 and then was off records (and only working in jazz on a part-time basis) up until the mid-'70s. She cut two albums for tiny labels and then came this, the first of her vocal-bass duet recordings."[14]

That same year, Jordan would embark on a new part of her singing career as an educator and mentor. When the founder and director of City College of New York, Eddie Summerlin, invited Sheila to do an afternoon concert at the school, it initiated one of the first jazz vocal programs in the United States. Although there may have been some jazz choirs at various schools, Jordan's would be focused on being a solo jazz singer, imparting her years of experience around the instrumental masters she had learned from over the years. Although the task was daunting at first, Jordan eventually found her niche as a mentor for aspiring jazz vocalists and as an inspiration for future jazz education. (Chapter 11 covers this part of Jordan's career in greater detail.)

One of the more important and long-term musical relationships in Jordan's career was with pianist and composer Steve Kuhn. Jordan met Kuhn in the early 1960s, but it wasn't until he returned from Europe after living there from 1967 to 1971 that their musical relationship really began. Kuhn put together a quartet with saxophonist Steve Slagle, drummer Bob Moses (now known as Ra-Kalam), and bassist Harvie Swartz (now known as Harvie S). Jordan introduced Harvie to Kuhn, who hired him on the spot. Kuhn shares how he included Jordan in his group:

> And then at one point, because I'd been in touch with Sheila, she wanted to sing some of these songs with the lyrics I had written. I was kind of flattered that she really wanted to do that. So I brought her on board and the group became a quintet for a while. And then I guess for economic reasons, I decided to go back to a quartet and hold onto Sheila and let the saxophone go. That was the group I had with Sheila from the late '70s up into the early '80s, maybe three or four years, something like that. We worked a fair amount in this country with the concept being that it was really a quartet. It wasn't a singer with a trio accompaniment, even though it's perceived that way by a lot of people who see us performing and they see a singer out in front and then the trio behind. So they immediately assume that's what it is. But if they listen to the music, Sheila was really integrated into the texture of the quartet and she wanted it that way. She didn't want to be featured in any way; she just wanted to be part of the band—which, in fact, she was musically. It's just when you look at the group physically you see her standing in front. But that was the concept of the quartet. And we did a couple of recordings for ECM, which I think illustrate that point pretty well, that it was really a quartet in the true sense of the word with a dialog amongst all of us. And I was very happy that she wanted to sing some of the songs that I had written. So that was a plus for me. Then we did some other songs, too. It stayed that way until the band broke up I guess sometime in the early '80s.

The first recording Jordan participated in was called *Playground*, recorded at Columbia Recording Studios in July 1979. It featured the quartet of Jordan with Kuhn, Swartz (Harvie S), and Moses (Ra-Kalam). All of the songs on the album were original compositions by Kuhn, including lyrics that Jordan sings. One of the songs, "Poem for No. 15," was retitled from its original name, "The Saga of Harrison Crabfeathers," and was dedicated to the baseball player

Thurman Munson, who died at a very young age. The song was included in the early *Real Book* with the wrong lyrics, not written by Kuhn. The correct lyrics are included below with permission of Steve Kuhn.

Poem for #15

Now and then I think of when his teeth were so small and white
We laughed when he heard the sounds in the distant night
Later on his smile was gone
His lips spoke of silent things.
The least he could do was more than his life would bring.
Oh, what a shame
What a terrible shame to be lost and found
Below the ground beneath every child at play
His life was so short it's hard to believe today.

© Lyrics by Steve Kuhn

It was Kuhn with whom Jordan found a partnership, one that understood her desire to be part of the rhythm section, not branded as the "front singer" or "chick singer" as became the term in years later. Kuhn viewed her as an integral part of the band, learning his original songs and supporting her concept on song arrangements similar to what Billie Holiday and Betty Carter had strived to accomplish. Ted Gioia remarks in his book *The History of Jazz*, "Sheila Jordan took a similar tack, avoiding conventional readings of standards in favor of a more deeply personalized approach, best shown in her collaborations with Steve Kuhn."[15] Kuhn expresses it this way: "I know in terms of when she sings a ballad, for example, many, many times I'd be playing with her and I always get emotional. She really is able to hit that vein and that nerve in me, especially on her ballads because I can hear where it's coming from within her and it just—emotionally, it gets to me as well. Very few singers are able to do that to me and she's one of—I don't know—one of maybe two or three over the years."

Jordan reunited with bassist Swallow once again on a project on ECM, *Home*, that featured the works of the American poet Robert Creeley. Jordan joined fellow musicians David Liebman: soprano saxophone, tenor saxophone; Steve Kuhn: piano; Lyle Mays: synthesizer; Steve Swallow: bass; and Ra-Kalam (Bob Moses): drums, singing the words to the poems as arranged by Swallow. The innate ability of Creeley's verse to match jazz rhythms is no surprise, since jazz, especially bebop, with its improvisational riffs and sudden swerves from expectation, has long influenced Creeley's poetry. As he says, "To me the timing that I use, or depend upon, in poetry is very, very, very like the timing that they are using variously in music."[16] Ra-Kalam gave his thoughts on Jordan's contributions by saying,

> Swallow wrote these really gorgeous compositions that were very much in the character of the poems. Creeley's poems tend to be very minimal and every word counts. The poems have a circular quality and tend to be very short and dry but poignant. Swallow wrote the music that was exactly in that character. I liked how he set up that recording because it didn't follow the stereotypical way where the singer sings the melody and then there's a bunch of solos and then the singer takes the melody out. And in most cases on that record there was only one reading of the melody so Sheila had these really short but powerful segments and they weren't necessarily in the beginning or the end. Sometimes they were at the beginning, sometimes at the middle or the end so that kind of broke the mechanical standard approach that everybody automatically does. A lot of the pieces were only seven bars or nine bars, which is short for a jazz tune, but they didn't feel short because they had a circular nature so you couldn't easily tell where the beginning of the tune was, which made even a seven or nine bar tune seem infinite. Sheila was perfect on that and I can't think of anyone else who could have done it better.

Sadly, that same year Jordan participated in a memorial concert for her mentor Lennie Tristano, who died on November 18, 1978—oddly enough, on the same day as her fiftieth birthday. The concert was live at Town Hall in New York City on January 28, 1979, and was recorded under the title *Various Artists: Lennie Tristano Memorial Concert.* Jordan's contribution included a trio with Harold Danko: piano; Cameron Brown: bass; and Lou Grassi: drums. Jordan sang "You'd Be So Nice to Come Home To," "Yesterdays," and of course a Parker tune, "Confirmation." Although the decade ended with some significant personal losses, it was only the beginning of a chapter of enriching musical and personal experiences to come.

• 5 •

Autumn in New York

1980–1999

"I've been all over the world and there's no place like New York. There's a special vibe in Manhattan and some people have no idea about the beauty of upstate New York. It's absolutely exquisite. I love looking at the incredible sky and the stars. New York will always be my home."

—Sheila Jordan

It was during the later decades that Jordan was able to focus fully on her jazz singing career. She continued her full-time job at the Doyle Dane Bernbach advertising agency, and was still doing gigs here and there with Kuhn's group and with other musicians. Besides recording *Playground*, the group toured and performed at a variety of venues and recorded a second project in 1981 on the ECM label entitled *Last Year's Waltz*. Tyran Grillo gives a wonderful review on his blog *between sound and space*:

> *Last Year's Waltz* has everything a great live jazz album should: a present feel, gobs of atmosphere, and, oh yeah, Sheila Jordan. Right off the bat, interplay from Bob Moses and Harvie Swartz kicks us into wakefulness in "Turn to Gold." Gilded by Kuhn's indeed alchemical but always punctual pianism, this dose of smoothness is sure to please. Kuhn brings a montuno flavor to "The Drinking Song," which is deepened by Jordan's diaristic musings, both expository and speculative, and boasts enough woops from her band mates to keep our blood at a constant boil. The title track is a languid trickle that quickly crackles into a melodious and cinematic punch bowl. The key to unlocking the set's inner secrets is "The Fruit Fly," which, in both title and execution, evokes Chick Corea's blissful optimism. Downright wondrous pianism and omnipotent drumming make this the instrumental standout (the solo piano "Medley" runs a close second).

> Kuhn works his magic through "The Feeling Within," weaving a luxurious carpet for Jordan's vocal footsteps. Two standards—a decidedly upbeat rendition of "I Remember You" and the virtuosic scat-fest that is "Confirmation"—and the bittersweet yet crowd-pleasing tune "The City of Dallas" (Steve Swallow) complete this living portrait of a group in its prime. As the recording fades, members of the crowd shout, "More!"
>
> I second that.
>
> Not only does *Last Year's Waltz* show us Jordan at her best, but its explosive energy and archival importance make it by far Kuhn's finest quartet joint of the 80s.[1]

Unfortunately, the Kuhn Quartet disbanded shortly after that recording.

It was in Kuhn's band that Jordan worked with two very significant musicians who creatively supported her passion for the music that she envisioned—Harvie S (Swartz) and Ra-Kalam (Bob Moses). "I loved Sheila's singing," says Ra-Kalam,

> I definitely think of her as an innovative singer. She's one of those singers that's absolutely got her own thing and always did. I think in general that was a trait that was more happening in that generation. I think all the great singers, like Sarah Vaughn, Carmen MacRae, Abby Lincoln, or Billie Holiday—they're just instantly recognizable. Sheila's always unique. I know she's a jazz lover and in the jazz tradition but within that she was always very open to doing free stuff. She has what I would say somewhat of a native flavor to her singing. I think she has some American Indian blood in her and I certainly hear it in her voice. And that's unusual for most of the jazz singers; you won't hear that kind of quality. I can hear that in her singing and that already puts her in a different place.

Jordan continued her journey into exploring more progressive approaches to music through the musicians she surrounded herself with, and continued to explore her Cherokee roots in her improvisations. In 1982 she recorded with Ra-Kalam one of his original songs, "Happy To Be Here Today," on the album *When Elephants Dream of Music* on Gramavision. A review in *Jazzbo Notes* comments on the project: "Things get downright silly with 'Happy To Be Here Today,' sung accapella by Sheila Jordan. As a straight ballad, it doesn't really succeed, but as a piece of humor, it's pretty funny, if you imagine Sheila Jordan as a female elephant. Let's face it —if you don't appreciate humor in jazz, *When Elephants Dream of Music* won't be for you. But if you can get past the jokiness of the conceit, there is a lot to admire. The improvisations from the many musicians are uniformly muscular and inspired, the grooves are plentiful, and Moses' arrangements are unique."[2] Ra-Kalam also recorded some duos and trios with Jordan and vocalist Jeanne Lee around that same time that he still hopes to release in the near future. He continued to work on and off with Jordan throughout the 1980s in various bands and they remain good friends.

However, it was Harvie S (Swartz) who would have the greatest impact on Jordan's career, establishing the bass and voice duos that she had envisioned since her early years working with Swallow, Ind, and Andersen. According to Harvie, "We worked a lot with that band (Kuhn's quartet) and we had some amazing nights. We went beyond music and it almost became theatre without a script. Our everyday antics enhanced the show and made the music only part of the experience." Harvie and Jordan developed a complementary musical relationship and would often practice duets together when on tour. Jordan asked Harvie to join her on a concert as a bass and voice duet, which at the time was considered quite unusual. Harvie was somewhat reluctant and yet challenged at the prospect, so he agreed under the condition that they would rehearse frequently and work out specific arrangements before the concert. The concert was such a great success that they decided to continue; they became the prominent duo of Jordan and Swartz, bringing the bass and voice to a new musical level. They toured locally and in Japan, Canada, and parts of Europe, as well as recording three duo projects during the 1980s and a past live recording released in 2012. Their debut release in 1982 was *Old Time Feeling* on the Palo Alto/Muse label; it displayed to the jazz world the bass and voice concept Jordan had carried with her since her early days with Swallow. Jordan and Harvie complemented each other in astounding ways, bringing a truly unique pairing that had never been experienced. Their other classic and memorable recordings include two on the MA label, *The Very Thought of Two* (1988) and *Songs from Within* (1989), and later on a recording on HighNote, *Yesterdays*, from one of their last concerts together around 1995. (Because this is such a significant part of Jordan's musical accomplishments, a more detailed history is contained in chapter 8, "I've Grown Accustomed to the Bass.")

Jordan met composer and big-band leader George Gruntz at JazzFest Berlin sometime in the mid-'70s. Their musical relationship blossomed into the '80s and '90s, when she participated in his big band and jazz operas. Besides being the artistic director of Jazzfest Berlin, Gruntz was the musical director at Zurich's State Theater. Gruntz composed the jazz opera with American poet Amiri Baraka (LeRoi Jones) entitled *Money: A Jazz Opera*. Gruntz remembers,

> When Opera tycoon Rolf Liebermann, artistic director of the Hamburg and Paris State Operas, commissioned me to write a real jazz opera, to be performed by improvising jazz-artists only, Sheila was number one on the list of performers next to Dee Dee Bridgewater and Mark Murphy. I will never forget how deeply I was touched to hear the first time Sheila sang some of my works. At the same time she said to me "George, I'm no operatic vocalist, I

> can't do that." I told her "sure you can" and the result was her performing in three works of mine.

Jordan remembers it in a similar way: "George said that he would like me to be part of the project and I told him I couldn't do it because I didn't know how to act. So I gave him the names of a couple of other singers but he told me he didn't want anyone else to do it but me. So George was very instrumental in my doing the little bit of acting that I did." The workshop version was produced at the Off-Broadway theater La Mama Experimental Theater Club in 1982 and directed by George Ferencz, whose production was a multimedia event using music, choreography, slides, film, and black light. The story was centered on the political awakening of a nightclub singer and her saxophonist lover; Jordan played a rich woman. She remembers wearing a blonde wig, quite a switch from her own dark brunette hair.

A few years later in 1985, Gruntz asked Jordan to perform in another project, an oratorio that premiered at the Austrian "Styrian Autumn" festival. The oratorio, *The Holy Grail of Jazz & Joy*, was a ninety-minute production featuring 160 performers. Jordan comments, "I was Queen Guinevere, Howard Johnson was King Arthur, Karlheinz Miklin was Sir Lancelot, and Bobby McFerrin was Merlin. I opened up singing with George's big band before the opera started. It was performed in a cave in Austria. We had protesters because they felt the music was disturbing the birds. I remember one flew right by my face when I was singing the opening number." Gruntz included Jordan in yet another jazz opera, *Cosmopolitan Greetings*, with a libretto he coauthored with Alan Ginsburg about Bessie Smith. It was important to Gruntz that when he composed these jazz operas the singers chosen to perform the parts were actual jazz vocalists. His opinion was the following: "Nothing is more horrible than opera singers trying to sing jazz as was the case in earlier jazz operas where composers submissively served opera houses and wrote for their repertory vocalists and orchestra." The production premiered at the Hamburg State Opera in Germany around 1988 and the main characters were Mark Murphy, Dee Dee Bridgewater, and Don Cherry. Jordan shares a story about Cherry:

> During rehearsals for the opera, *Cosmopolitan Greetings*, Don would sit down at the piano and play his tune "Art Deco" during the breaks and was always on me to write lyrics for it. He said he wrote the tune for Stuff Smith and Billie Holiday. I could never find lyrics to complement Billie or Stuff. After Don died, I was walking down my road upstate and was singing the melody and for some weird and strange reason the lyrics came to me almost immediately. I wrote them for Don, who was very spiritual and very special to me. We were born on the same day and month of the year but I was about ten years older than he was. The lyrics are called, "The Art of Don."

Besides singing in the jazz operas for Gruntz, Jordan did some national and international tours with the jazz band and recorded the albums *Happening Now!* (on hat Art in 1987) and *Sins 'N Wins 'N Funs: Left-Cores and Hard Core En-Cores* (on TCOB in Switzerland in 1987–1988). Gruntz was known for putting together an eclectic group of musicians such as Ray Anderson (trombone), Kenny Wheeler (trumpet), Lee Konitz (alto sax and clarinet), Joe Henderson (tenor sax), Tom Varner (French horn), and many others. He also included different combinations of instruments such as tuba, bandoneon, and euphonium. Once again Ra-Kalam would join Jordan on some of the concerts and the recordings, and as he recalls, "To Gruntz's credit he got some really unusual and completely unique people from all over the world and somehow joined them together." It was through Jordan's association with Gruntz that she met saxophonist and composer Karlheinz Miklin. Miklin was the head of the jazz department at the Hochschule für Musik in Graz, Austria, and was so impressed with Jordan's singing that he asked her to start a workshop at the school. That program continues today and has hosted numerous vocal luminaries along with inspiring many vocal students. "George was a wonderful friend to me," comments Jordan. "He always encouraged me and it was because of his belief in me that I met Karlheinz and began teaching in Graz."

One of the many highlights of Jordan's life was to sing at a special memorial service that was held on February 22, 1982, at St. Peter's Church (located at 54th and Lexington), paying respect to jazz legend Thelonious Monk. According to Jordan, "Barry Harris was the one who asked me to sing at Monk's memorial service. They called the minister there 'the jazz minister' —John Ginsel. I sang 'Round Midnight' right next to Monk's casket. It was truly an honor." Robin D. G. Kelley recounts in his book, *Thelonious Monk: The Life and Times of an American Original*:

> Monk's own recording of "Abide With Me" was selected for the processional, as the pallbearers carried him in and opened the casket to allow the world one last glimpse of the High Priest. For the next three hours he lay there, nattily attired, awash in his own music. Old friends, new friends, and young musicians who knew Thelonious only from records, played their last respects: Paul Jeffrey, Sadik Hakim, Muhal Richard Abrams, Tommy Flanagan, Max Roach, Ray Copeland, Walter Bishop, Jr., Sheila Jordan, John Ore, Gerry Mulligan, Frankie Dunlop, Eddie Bert, Ben Riley, Larry Ridley, Ahmed Abdul-Malik, Barry Harris, Lonnie Hillyer, Marian McPartland, Adam Makowicz, Ronnie Matthews, Randy Weston, and, of course, the Rutgers Jazz Ensemble.[3]

In the April 1982 issue of *Coda Magazine*, Ted Joans mentioned that Jordan and McPartland were the only contributing women musicians; he went on to say, "It was a worthy tribute to the magnificent monarch of modern music, that classical music that we all call by its nickname, jazz, that Thelonious Sphere Monk laid on us forever and ever, he was a man . . . and we must not ever forget that man's music."[4] Jordan has many fond memories of Monk from listening to his music in the clubs to her days living in the loft. She recounts, "Monk came up to the loft one time when Duke was living there and they would talk. He used to sit down on the couch and put his head out the big window next to it. He would stare up at the sky and never say a word. But when he did speak, Monk could say in one sentence what it takes most people to say in a paragraph."

Between 1982 and 1985 Jordan recorded on several projects, reuniting her with several of her musician friends and introducing her to others. The projects were *ABC* with Aki Takase on Union Jazz, *Epilog* (*Bill Evans in Memoriam*) with Egil Kapstad on NOPA, a compilation *More Mistletoe Magic* on Palo Alto with Harvie S, and *That's the Way I Feel Now: A Tribute to Thelonious Monk* on A&M that included Marcus Belgrave: trumpet; Jervonny Collier: trombone; David Was: flute; David McMurray: alto saxophone; Michael Ward: tenor saxophone; Don Was: guitar, synthesizer; Larry Fratangelo: percussion; and besides Jordan, Sweet Pea Atkinson, Harry Bowens, Carol Hall, Donald Ray Mitchell: vocals. Don Was in later years became the head of Blue Note Records and reunited with Jordan in Detroit for the 20th Concert of Colors.

Around this same time, Jordan was introduced to the upstate New York area, specifically Middleburgh. After being invited up to a social gathering in the area with her friend, Marria Banks, she ended up becoming romantically involved with a man she met while attending the event. She began making frequent trips up to the area to see him and found the scenic beauty of the area moving, creating a longing for her to be out in nature. "I started missing the country and thought Middleburgh was wonderful. I really needed to come back to my roots again." Those roots refer to her Native American Cherokee background and growing up in the hills of Pennsylvania. So Jordan took some money from her investments and from the music gigs and decided to buy a house. She found a twelve-room house on six acres of land in a little hamlet called Huntersland outside of Middleburgh. "It was like paradise to me. The nearest neighbor was about a quarter of a mile away. I would go up there on weekends, and I had this guy that I was going with who would drive me and take me up there. He spent a lot of time at my house up there with me even though he had his own house. I decided to totally renovate the house, not remodel, but keep as it was because I liked it being old."

The relationship Jordan was in, which she prefers to keep anonymous, was fraught with problems and lasted approximately twelve years. Due to episodes of alcoholism and abuse, it was not the best experience, but it did provide the opportunity for Jordan to find the escape she needed to get back out in nature—as well as learning a new skill. "I had to learn how to drive," remembers Jordan, "and my best friend Marria decided to buy a house up there so she was nearby too. So there I was in this twelve-room house all by myself. I was working at my job in New York City during the week and going out on tour whenever possible, which eventually led to my paying off the house and property, so that I owned it outright." Marria's daughter Coryelle Kramer remembers fondly, "I remember them being just free. They would blast jazz on top of the mountains; it was really a wonderful experience for me. They made a pact that every year Sheila would do the Thanksgiving dinner and mom would do Christmas Eve. I seriously have been blessed to have Sheila in my life."

Around this time Jordan's addiction to alcohol was becoming an issue, so she attempted to give up drinking on her own, or as she puts it, to be a dry drunk. The majority of her romantic relationships had been disappointing to this point in her life. She tended to attract abusive and addictive men, which only reinforced the pattern of her own addictive behaviors, masking the real underlying problems. She was beginning to repeat the patterns of her childhood, something she swore she would never do. Jordan speaks frankly:

> Before the guy who was an alcoholic in upstate New York I went with another guy who lived half the year in California and the other half with me. He was also an alcoholic and very cruel to me. Not only was he verbally abusive, he was physically abusive. I mean, he would beat the hell out of me. He would blacken my eyes and he almost knocked my tooth out. One time I was so afraid of him I went and hid in one of my closets in my apartment. I was so terrified of him. Terrified that he was going to kill me. And I believe he might have. But, again, he was a very sick man. And you know at that time I thought, I didn't deserve any better than this. But finally I came to my senses and broke up with him after being with him for at least five years. I had to have the police come and kick him out. But of all of these guys who treated me so badly, deep down inside they had a certain caring and sweetness about them, but then the alcohol would take over and they would become violent monsters.

After getting a wake-up call from her own "higher power," Jordan left behind alcohol and began doing cocaine instead. As she put it, "I just switched seats on the Titanic." However, at that time cocaine appeared to be a reasonable diversion since it seemed to be the drug of choice for the wealthy or upper-class society. So what could possibly go wrong? With that point of view, Jordan found herself seduced with drugs until she finally pulled out and went into complete recovery for both alcohol and drug addiction. She finally took serious steps toward her recovery by dedicating herself to a well-known program that she continues to this day. At the same time, Jordan discontinued the twelve-year relationship with the man in upstate New York:

> After my last affair, I never dated anyone again and never had any desire to have a man in my life. I only had male friends and it was great. Most of the men I had previously been with were very jealous of my music except for Ken Linden, George Russell, and Frank Foster. So after the last sick relationship I started thinking more of myself and saw that I didn't have to be in abusive relationships, be they physical or mental. I didn't need to be in those relationships because I was worth more than that. I just didn't have any desire to go through all of that again. There were too many terrible relationships that I'd been in and I just didn't want to spend the rest of my life in that kind of an environment with those kinds of human beings. I was grateful to the program for helping me to realize that and so instead, I devoted all my energy to jazz music since it was my first love to begin with. I knew it would never let me down.

Jordan paid tribute to this program when she wrote "The Crossing," a song that delivers a poignant message to any person going through addiction or struggles of any kind. The message was to keep searching for an answer and a reason to become healthy again. Jordan found that answer in her music. The title actually came from the name of a piece of art she received as a gift from her past relationship. The art piece was made of wine corks with one space that she felt symbolized her years of addiction and her ultimate recovery.

The song became the title of an album released in 1984, *The Crossing*, produced by Herb Wong on the Blackhawk label (as of this writing it is out of print). The quartet on the project featured Tom Harrell (flügelhorn), Kenny Barron (piano), Harvie S (bass), and Ben Riley (drums). On this project Jordan rerecorded the song "Inchworm," which became an often-requested fan favorite. Jordan remembers that, as she was singing the song during one of her concerts, much to her surprise she noticed a tiny inchworm crawling up the microphone cord. Jordan often found these synchronistic moments would occur while she was singing or on tour. It reassured her that she was on the right path. Critic Peter Sleight of the *Sun Sentinel* wrote a review of *The Crossing* on August 3, 1986:

> Sheila Jordan, a vastly underappreciated artist, has produced something rare and wonderful—a fresh-sounding, dynamically creative vocal performance in the best be-bop tradition. Her performances on *The Crossing* are rooted in the crooning and scat of the 1940s, the milieu in which she developed amid a clan of be-bop musicians in Detroit. But her unusual phrasing, her

> warm, throaty, passionate tone and her often-abstract stylizations allow her to transcend the generally accepted vision of jazz vocalists. She is assisted by a sterling backup group. There's pianist Kenny Barron, who offers consistently creative but never overpowering accompaniment, and flugelhornist Tom Harrell, whose sensitivity meshes beautifully with Jordan's bittersweet phrasings. Drummer Ben Riley is surreptitiously supportive on drums and Harvie Swartz is brilliant on bass, particularly in sparse but compelling duos with Jordan. Jordan's song selection is flawless, moving from the playful Inchworm to the moody, eulogistic Suite for Lady and Prez, a suite memorializing Charles Mingus, Billie Holiday and Lester Young. It combines Goodbye Pork Pie Hat by Charles Mingus, Don't Explain, a Billie Holiday classic, and George Gershwin's I Got Rhythm. There are also old standards such as You'd Be So Nice To Come Home To by Cole Porter and You Must Believe in Spring by Michel Legrand. There also are new originals such as the title cut and Sheila's Blues by Jordan and Until Tomorrow by Swartz. Throughout, Jordan shows that she can swing, croon and scat with originality and, most of all, with a rare emotional intensity.[5]

A few years later, in 1986, Jordan reunited with Barron, Harvie, and Riley with the addition of Frank Wess (tenor saxophone) to record *Body and Soul* on CBS/Sony. Francis Davis reviews the recording in his book *Jazz and Its Discontents: A Francis Davis Reader*:

> Certain songs are now associated with Sheila Jordan. *Body and Soul*, a recent Japanese release (CBS/Sony 32DP 687) was practically a Sheila Jordan retrospective, with new versions of "Baltimore Oriole," "I'm a Fool to Want You," "Falling in Love with Love," and "When the World Was Young" from *Portrait of Sheila*. She has written others that deal frankly with her life (for instance, the title track on *The Crossing*). But if her singing has become more autobiographical, it has also become, paradoxically, less direct. It's no longer so intense, which is understandable; one suspects that singing no longer amounts to an emotional release for her, as it did when she had fewer opportunities to perform. For my taste, she now scats too much for someone with her gift for interpreting lyrics (although, in all fairness, it should be added that her scatting rivals Betty Carter's for harmonic aptitude and rhythmic acuity). Still, at her best, there's no one else like her. Her personal integrity has made her a role model for young women singers, including some who owe nothing to her stylistically.

Jordan had secretly prayed that eventually she could devote full time to her music but would never consider leaving her job for fear of being thrown back into a life of poverty. So it was both a shock and a blessing when at the age of fifty-eight she was laid off from her job at Doyle Dane Bernbach due to a sudden merger with another company. The company offered her a lengthy severance pay or the opportunity to become a "floater," going from office to office with a different boss every week. Jordan preferred the severance pay, and took this as a sign that she was finally meant to concentrate on her jazz singing career. With her savings, investments, money from tours and gigs, and eventually Social Security benefits, Jordan managed to create an adequate lifestyle. Jordan remembers,

> I started to cry because I was afraid and upset to leave a place that was like home to me. Then a little voice in my head said "Why are you crying? You've been praying to sing more so shut up and take the money and go sing." I have never looked back and never worked in an office again. My personal life improved in many ways because I had more freedom to be with friends, and I spent more time with wonderful musicians because I started singing more. I felt rejuvenated. I was afraid at first but my daughter Tracey was already out on her own. I figured if times got tough for me and I couldn't support myself through music, singing, and teaching part-time, I could always go back and find a typing job. Because of my financial fears, I took my social security at sixty-two years old instead of waiting until I was sixty-five, which was the minimum age at the time. So with my social security coming in every month I knew I would be able to at least pay my rent and buy food.

To her great relief during this time of financial insecurity, she found herself performing in many formats and with a variety of musicians on both the national and international front. Since Harvie and Jordan had recorded three of their most acclaimed duo projects during the '80s (*Old Time Feeling*, *The Very Thought of Two*, and *Songs from Within*), they continued to establish a musical bond and a fan base that allowed them to perform more often in concert venues. Jordan also found work doing some tours with Gruntz's Concert Jazz Band. In a *Los Angeles Times* review, A. James Liska opines:

> Switzerland's George Gruntz Concert Jazz Band made its West Coast debut here Wednesday evening at the Palace as an 18-piece aggregate with decidedly more Americans than Europeans. Promising "journeys through different landscapes," Gruntz, 55, led his brass-heavy group through an image-laden set of his own arrangements that were texturally rich and darkly moody. . . . Nowhere were contrasts more apparent though in "Happening Now," an aria from a jazz opera Gruntz is writing with poet Allen Ginsberg. The piece, sung aptly by Sheila Jordan, pitted a two-beat chase sequence against a traditional swing feel. The dreary, repetitive lyrics fitted neatly into either mode, however, as did solos by trumpeter Enrico Rava, trombonist Art Baron and tuba player Howard Johnson. Jordan was given another pair of outings that showed her in a much better light. A closing "You Are My Sunshine" was breezy and bluesy, and her lightly swinging

> rendition of "It's You or No One" was followed by alto saxophonist Lee Konitz's "It's You," a tune based on the same changes.[6]

Jordan's reputation was beginning to grow not only as a vocalist but also as a teacher by way of the program she created at City College, the programs at the Hochschule für Musik in Graz, Jazz in July, and doing workshops as she traveled (more details on teaching is provided in chapter 11, "Reel Time Mentor"). Jazz educators and professional singers sponsored a number of the workshops at colleges or in private facilities. Everyone wanted to gain the knowledge of Jordan's experiences to improve their own knowledge or share that knowledge with their own students. There was no doubt that Jordan would never go back to her secretarial days and was finally living her dream. As Kuhn says, "And it's paid off quite well because she's never had to look back since then in terms of looking for a day job. She's been able to sustain herself pretty well doing the singing and teaching, which is what she loves and which is what she should be doing."

On the personal front, Jordan's daughter Tracey had become involved in the music business working as a senior vice president for Motown. She had to relocate to Los Angeles around 1987 for the next five years. Tracey's choice to become involved in the music business was inspired by both her parents but with a different point of view. Instead of becoming a musician she was able to observe another direction for herself. Tracey says, "I think seeing what both of my parents went through, especially as hard a time as jazz musicians have in the United States where the music is indigenous, probably deterred me from becoming a musician, and that gave me a better perspective that the executives on the other end might have more longevity in their careers." Jordan and Tracey share a very close bond, so the time apart was difficult and Jordan was relieved when she returned to New York in 1992 to work for MTV.

Toward the end of the decade, Jordan was involved in several more recording projects that included *One Starry Night* with the Bill Kirchner Nonet on Jazz Heads Records (1987), *Looking Back* with Karlheinz Miklin on SOS Music (1988), and *Jazztracks* with the Goetz Tangerding Trio on Bhakti (1989, 1990). *Looking Back* featured pianist Peter Mihelic, whom Jordan had met while teaching in Graz. Jordan fondly remembers, "Peter used to play for the singers in my class and I thought he was a wonderful accompanist. He was only twenty or twenty-one when I met him. I brought him to New York City and let him stay at my apartment so he could check it out. Of course he loved it and ended up getting his citizenship papers. He's been here ever since and for the last four or five years he's been taking me to Japan as his duo partner." For the third time Jordan found herself recording an album project, *Lost and Found* on the Muse label, with the trio featuring Barron, Harvie, and Riley. Scott Yanow writes in his book *Bebop*: "Jordan, Swartz, pianist Kenny

Barron, and drummer Ben Riley form a superior quartet on *Lost and Found*. The singer digs into such songs as 'The Very Thought of You,' 'Anthropology,' and 'I Concentrate On You,' making each tune sound brand new while bringing out some hidden meanings in the lyrics."[7] Jordan shares a humorous story about Barron: "After doing several recordings with Kenny I had a couple of gigs in New York City with him. On one particular night at Sweet Basil, during intermission, he came up to me at the bar and said, 'Sheila, you're looking very current tonight.' I looked at him bewildered and said, 'I'm looking what?' Finally I figured out that he probably meant stylish and realized it was a compliment. The next night at the gig I said to him, 'You're playing very current tonight, Kenny.' We both laughed."

The decade of the 1990s got off to an inauspicious beginning for Jordan. While she was on tour in Canada with Harvie doing the bass and voice duo, there was a terrible rainstorm in Middleburgh. Disastrously, Jordan's house was hit by lightning and burned down.

> When I got back to my apartment in New York from the tour, I got a call from my best friend, Marria, who said, "Don't go anywhere. We're coming over. We want to talk to you." I didn't know what had happened. At first I thought maybe something was wrong with my daughter, because she was living in California at the time working for Motown Records. They told me my house had burned down and I was shocked. At this time I was supposed to go to London and I had a few days off. So I went up to the house because I wanted to see the damage. First of all I couldn't believe that I had lost my house, especially since I had just finished the renovation. When I saw the house, there was one wall left of the twelve-room house.
>
> This is a very strange story: I had planted a rosebush when I first bought the house about ten years earlier. The rosebush had never bloomed before and when I looked over at it there was a huge red rose that had bloomed. It was very eerie, very strange, and yet sort of beautiful like nature was in sympathy with my loss.
>
> There was nothing left but great big piles of charcoal and this one wall of the house standing. But then I saw something white lying on top of one of the charcoal piles. By this time two of my neighbors who lived down the road had come up. So I said to the one guy, "Could you go over and pick that white thing up? Be careful, though," because it was very dangerous. He told me he would get it for me, this white thing. It was just sticking out and I want to know what it was because it looked like an envelope. So he got it for me and it turned out to be a card, and the card said on the outside, "In deepest sympathy." I opened up the card but before doing so I said, "If this is signed 'God,' I'm out of here." So I opened it up and, of course, it wasn't signed God. But in a sense it was, spiritually it was a higher power letting me know at that point it would be all right, that I would be taken care of. This was a hard deal to go through, but I would survive it

as I've survived a lot of things in my life and I would continue on. And I remembered buying these cards from the Veterans where you send in a donation and then they'd send you back these all-occasion cards. All the other cards burned but this one card, it was burned just a little bit on the end. But of all cards! It was a sympathy card. So between that sympathy card and that rose, I don't know, somehow I was lifted. I thought okay, this is a terrible thing, but nobody was in the house and nobody got hurt, and thank God I have insurance. So in a sense it was like someone telling me, it will be okay, trust, it will be okay. That was kind of a strange experience for me and I never forgot that, because anytime I'd start doubting anything at all, I'd remember that experience and all the others that I've had in my life, which makes me realize that there really is a higher power.

That particular night it was a full moon and I just wanted to sit with the house, because it looked so lonely. I stayed that night at my friend Marria's house and then the next day I went back to Manhattan. But before I went back to my apartment in Manhattan I got in touch with a guy to clear everything up, knock everything down, and bury everything. And they buried the remains of my old house on my property. Then I decided to have a memorial service for the house. When I returned from my tour, my friends came up and we all held hands and we all said something about the house. We talked about all the fun we had there, because I used to have Thanksgiving dinners and cookouts and things. And then afterwards we all went and had dinner. It was like going to a funeral or a memorial service. It was really incredible.

Fortunately Jordan found herself with little time to mourn; she was busy touring, recording, and teaching. Jordan was invited to Scotland to sing at the Edinburgh Jazz Festival in Queen's Hall on November 22, 1991. Jordan recounts,

My plane was really late getting out of Heathrow airport to Edinburgh. So when I got there the guy at customs wanted to know why I had come to Edinburgh. I told him I was singing at the Edinburgh Festival and that I needed to be there now because I was going on shortly. He laughed and told me he would hurry me through. So I finally got to the hall but I hadn't even rehearsed with the pianist, Brian Kellock, and we were doing a duo performance together. I was concerned and I thought, oh my God, how's this going to work? Luckily, I travel with really good lead sheets so I'm prepared, which is something I believe that is very important for all singers. So I'm running up the back stairs of the hall, putting my shoes on and getting the music together and I see Brian. He had to start without me and do a solo piano until I got there. I knew I had to trust him. I showed him the music and told him what I wanted to do and then just told him that we would just have to do our best. And of course, that's what we did. I love to make lyrics up, so my opening number was "Everything Happens

> to Me." It was the perfect song because it's about a person who has bad luck and so I improvised, talking about my trip with the plane coming in late and of course no rehearsal with Brian. The audience loved that and it made everyone relaxed. It was perfect. Afterward I thought what a fantastic accompanist Brian was. We did a ballad at the end, "For All We Know," and his solo brought me to tears. I'll never forget that. Since that time I've worked with him off and on and he's another one of my favorite accompanists. I've never recorded with him. I'd like to one day, who knows?

One of her regular performances was, and still is, in Chicago at Dave Jemilo's club, the Green Mill. Jordan feels particularly at home there and grateful to Jemilo; it has become over the years one of her favorite out-of-town venues. "Dave is a great supporter of jazz music," says Jordan. "I just adore him and what he has done in Chicago to help keep the music alive." Jordan appeared there during the week of her birthday in November of 1992 and was reviewed by Howard Reich for the *Chicago Tribune*:

> The strange and alluring art of Sheila Jordan has a way of mesmerizing an audience, as it did over the weekend at the Green Mill Jazz Club.
>
> Jordan, who has been a regular Green Mill visitor in recent years, as always was appearing during her birthday week (she just turned 64). Once again, however, it was she who was providing the gifts. Though she's an original by any standard, the one singer Jordan suggests musically is Betty Carter, another Detroit native who clearly has been an influence on Jordan's brand of scat. Like Carter, Jordan adores distending vowels and lingering on consonants, creating sounds more akin to an irrepressible jazz horn than a human voice.
>
> But that's where the similarities end, for Jordan's improvisations seem more spontaneous than Carter's carefully planned, though still exquisite, stylings. Thus when Green Mill owner Dave Jemilo asked Jordan to tell the audience about her animals, she simply began singing her anecdotes to the tune already in progress.
>
> This is a singer who prefers working dangerously close to the edge, yet her emotionally cool tone and understated sense of swing make it all sound easy and effortless. Listen closely to the range of pitch and dynamics that Jordan traverses, however, and it becomes clear how venturesome an artist she is.
>
> The high point in Saturday night's show had to be Jordan's somewhat rarefied version of an old standard, "Haunted Heart." The slowness of her tempo was already striking, but the sense of stillness and reverie she evoked was genuinely remarkable, especially in a room overflowing with people.
>
> Yet whether Jordan was spinning arabesques of melody high in her range or whispering from down in the bottom, the crowd was quiet enough to let every nuance speak clearly. More important, Jordan imbued the song's elegiac lyrics with a lifetime of painful lessons learned.
>
> She was fortunate to be backed by some of Chicago's best jobbing musicians. Brad Williams, a versatile pianist, this time shrewdly underplayed his

> part. Like the singer he was accompanying, he kept his phrases soft, direct and insinuating. Meanwhile, Eric Hochberg drew warm lines from his bass, and drummer Greg Sergo kept the music moving with unpredictable rhythms. It was a birthday concert that surely everyone in the house will remember for a long time.[8]

When Jordan returned to New York City she was still struggling with whether she wanted to continue to have a second home in Middleburgh. Jordan recounts, "There was a minute where I felt, you know, do I want to go through this again? I'm not here, I'm on the road, I'm touring. I always had my apartment in New York City, but do I really want this house? I love Middleburgh, I love Huntersland. But do I really want to have a house up here after such a disastrous turn of events or whatever you want to call it? I mean, I had to think about it, because I thought maybe I wouldn't do this. Maybe I'll just take the insurance money and forget it." But Jordan had become attached to the area in deep ways and decided to start again. Her new house was built farther back from the road and included a memorial garden where the other house had been. Jordan also had a big red barn that she called "Charlie Parker Place." Her dream was to convert the barn into a workshop for young musicians, especially underprivileged ones. She felt that the area and the space could have made a wonderful performance center, where Jordan envisioned creating workshops and other events. Unfortunately there was never enough money to accomplish the task and as years went by Jordan realized it probably would not happen, at least in her lifetime. Lara Pellegrinelli writes in *JazzTimes*:

> What few people know is that Charlie Parker Place occupies an alternate locale hundreds of miles north: a cheerful red barn in rural Huntersland, N.Y. The barn, where a street sign identical to the one in NYC perches above chunky double doors, sits atop a tiny hill on five wooded acres. A modest house keeps it company, home of vocalist Sheila Jordan. "I was presented with that sign at the first Charlie Parker Festival, about five years ago," she remembers happily, recalling the same occasion that renamed Avenue B. "I brought Bird here to live with me." And, in a sense, he does. Photographs of Parker decorate walls and his albums line neatly organized shelves. Tiny winged figures peep from nooks and windowsills. More importantly, he is a constant presence in 72-year-old Jordan's memories and music.[9]

In some ways it's as if Jordan has two lives, her fast-paced life as a jazz impresario in New York City and small-town life as a nature lover in Middleburgh. Jordan sums it up:

> So Middleburgh is just a small place, but everybody knows everybody and it's nice. What I've accomplished in Middleburgh is being away from all this hustle and bustle in Manhattan. Sometimes that can get to you when

> you get older. I go upstate so I can relax and just live off the quietness of what's happening because there's nobody around except the wild animals and me. You hear the birds, the cows, the frogs, and it's just incredible. So I love that feeling. My little town of Middleburgh. It's also been very wonderful for my sobriety because I'm very involved with my meetings for my program there. But I'll tell you the truth, when I'm up there I miss New York City. I just have to come back and get a piece of New York, just to get the spirit of Manhattan, because I love New York City.

It's not unusual to have Jordan share her many stories of the animals that inhabit her property—stories that attest to her quirky yet beloved personality. A favorite story she likes to share is about the bebop cows:

> I found out when I first moved to upstate New York that cows love bebop. The way I found this out is I would take my morning walk, and there were several farms that had cows, and they were always out in the pasture. So I was singing my lines and practicing singing on changes, on bebop changes. I realized at one point that every time I was singing bebop on my walks the cows would come running over. And one day I stood there and I kept singing bebop and they were all there just wagging their tails. It was almost like their heads were moving in time, and I was in shock. I thought oh, here's my audience. So then I started to sing a ballad. As soon as I sang a ballad, they left. They split. The minute I sang a ballad they split. The minute I started to sing bebop they came back. So I call them the bebop cows. So there's one time when there was a knock on my front door and I went to the door and it was this old farmer. He said to me, "Excuse, ma'am, but I think my cows are up in back of your house." I said, "Oh, really? Well, you know what, I've been away for a couple of weeks, and yesterday I was over singing bebop to the cows on the farm in back. Maybe those cows told your cows, 'Hey, she's back and she's singing bebop.' So maybe that's how they decided to leave your farm and come to the back of my house." Because his farm was about seven miles down near the village. But, of course, I was going into this bebop story and he hadn't a clue what I was talking about. So I said, "Wait here, I'll get them for you." I walked up to the back and I started singing bebop. And you know those cows came right down. So those are my bebop cows.

One other story she likes to tell is about giving singing lessons to the bullfrogs and the crows:

> In the summer the bullfrogs are so loud, and they really don't have a great sound. So one night I yelled at them. "You know you guys do me a favor. Come up tomorrow afternoon in the barn and I'll give you some singing lessons." So they stopped. A couple of mornings later at about five o'clock in the morning the crows are out with that horrible sound of theirs, you

> know that cawing, caw, caw, caw. And I said, "Oh my god, listen you guys, why don't you come later today in the afternoon with the frogs and I'll give you both singing lessons." And you know what, it was like they were speaking to me, but not in words. You know what they said to me? "Do we tell you how to sing?" And I thought, no they don't. And they said "well, at least you know our sound." And that's so true, because there's a lot of birds I hear and I don't know who they are. But if a crow starts his so-called singing, I know it's a crow. So I shut up and I didn't ever say anything to them again.

During the decade of the 1990s Jordan had five recording projects of her own and eight as a guest artist. Two recordings were made with Mark Murphy, *One For Junior* (Muse), their only duo recording (once again with the rhythm section featuring Barron, Harvie, and Riley along with Bill Mays on synthesizer), and *Cosmopolitan Greetings* (Musiques Suisses), a recording of the George Gruntz/Allen Ginsburg jazz opera in which the two starred, along with singer Dee Dee Bridgewater, trumpeter Don Cherry, and saxophonist Howard Johnson. Murphy and Jordan revisited their early days at the Page Three with *One For Junior* and subsequently have performed together on many occasions in the United States, Canada, and Europe. It was Joe Fields who suggested that Jordan and Murphy should do a recording together. Jordan remembers,

> I don't remember who picked what but we just put down some tunes. Mark really wanted to do the aria from the George Gruntz jazz opera that we did together. And then the other tunes were just between us, tunes that we thought would be great to do as a duo. Then we got an order together and we went in and recorded. It was very easy. We performed the songs from the album once in a club (I think it was the Brass Rail) in Paris along with a workshop. I have a funny story from that gig that Mark never lets me forget. The promoters gave Mark and me a two-bedroom apartment to stay in while we were there. Since I had the morning workshop and Mark had the afternoon one I left the apartment before him. No one told me that you shouldn't lock one of the locks on the door because if you did, anyone on the inside could not get out. Since I didn't know about this I locked both locks when I left. When it came time for the afternoon workshop we waited and waited for Mark to appear. Finally he came in the room out of breath and furious. He said to me "You Bitch, you locked me in the apartment and I couldn't get out. I had to go out on the fire escape and scream to the superintendent that I was locked in. She was French and didn't understand me but eventually she got the message and came up and unlocked the door for me." Of course I tried to explain to him that I had no idea I had locked him out. Finally he laughed and I did too. To this day we still laugh about it. We didn't do too many gigs together because Mark was busy doing his things and I was busy doing mine. I think there was a

time when we were going to do another one, I know we thought about it, but it never worked out time-wise for either one of us. It's too bad, it would have been nice.

The album *One for Junior* was reviewed on January 16, 1994, by music critic David Royho of the *Chicago Tribune*, who wrote the following about Jordan's performance: "Sheila Jordan sounds wonderful on this release, her natural musicianship, liquid voice, and perfect intonation evident on every track. Her scat singing is so relaxed and intelligent that she may even win over some jazz lovers who usually shun singers."[10]

Jordan had always wanted to do a project with strings or a string quartet, but it was difficult to get anyone interested in producing the project. When she heard Stan Getz's recording, *Focus*, she finally had some grounds to show that her instincts about doing a project of that nature were accurate. Once again Joe Fields got behind the project, and Jordan contacted Alan Broadbent to ask if he would do the arrangements. He agreed and sent the music for her to listen: "And I started singing along with them," says Jordan, "and I dug them and so we went into the studio and recorded. Alan suggested we use the Hiraga String Quartet." In 1993 *Heart Strings* was released on the Muse label featuring Alan Broadbent: piano, arrangements; Harvie S (Swartz): bass; Marvin "Smitty" Smith: drums; Hiraga String Quartet with Amy Hiraga, Laura Frautschi: violin; Maria Lambros Kannen: viola; and Peter Wyrick: cello.

That same year Jordan recorded the track "You Don't Know What Love Is" on Lee Konitz's release, *Rhapsody II* (Paddle Wheel), which featured Harvie S and Konitz on soprano saxophone. She also recorded two tracks on the Jane Bunnett recording, *The Water Is Wide* (Evidence), which included the title track and "You Must Believe in Spring." The personnel consisted of Larry Cramer: trumpet; Jane Bunnett: soprano saxophone; Don Pullen: piano; Kieran Overs: bass; Billy Hart: drums; and Jeanne Lee on vocals. The following year Jordan recorded "Danny Boy" and "Quasimodo" with Mark Soskin: piano; Harvie S: bass; and Joe LaBarbera: drums on a project titled *Spirits—Live at Vartan Jazz* (Vartan Jazz) with various other artists.

By this time Jordan was working quite frequently and involved in projects that she found fulfilling. The bass and voice duo had been going well until after one of their concerts Harvie shocked Jordan by telling her he no longer wanted to continue the duo. After almost fourteen years of their partnership, the news came out of left field for Jordan, leaving her distraught to lose such a perfect partnership. However, with the enormous passion that Jordan had for the bass and voice duets, it wasn't long before she found a new partner in an old friend, Cameron Brown. Once again it was Jordan's tenacity that helped her find a bass partner who would be dedicated to sharing a mutual vision of the bass and voice duets that she so adored. After she joined Brown as part of an ensemble for a tour of concerts in Belgium, they quickly became musical partners. On their very first outing, as a result of the tour, they were recorded in a live performance that became the first of their recording projects. HighNote released the recording in 1997 under the clever title, *I've Grown Accustomed to the Bass*. During the same concert Jordan sang the tracks "Art Deco," "For All We Know," "Rylie's Bounce," "Remembrance," "What Reason Could I Give?/For Dad and Dannie," and "Double Arc Jake" for the OmniTone recording, *Cameron Brown: Here and Now! Vol. I.* The project featured many of Brown's own compositions and besides Brown and Jordan the band featured Dave Ballou: trumpet, flügelhorn; Dewey Redman: tenor saxophone; and Leon Parker: drums.

Jordan wrote the lyrics to both "Art Deco" and "Remembrance." Jordan called "Remembrance" "Music Is the Answer," and wrote it about the plight of the Native Americans and her unhappiness through her life. (Normally when lyrics are added to instrumental compositions it is necessary to rename the lyrics so that it's clear the original composition was not meant to have lyrics.) Remarks Jordan, "The lyrics for 'Music Is the Answer' are about finding peace and hope through music. How music can save your life if you are having a difficult time, just as it saved mine and continues to this day." Jordan had been writing lyrics throughout her jazz life, commencing with her Detroit beginnings. The songs included "Ballad for Miles," "St. Thomas," "The Crossing," "Sheila's Blues," "Workshop Blues" (mostly a free improvisation), parts of "Barbados" (along with Skeeter Spight and Leroy Mitchell), and, of course, "The Bird/Quasimodo." Jordan remembers how she came up with some of the words to "Quasimodo":

> I was writing lyrics to "Quasimodo" and of course this was well after Bird died. I got to the bridge and I couldn't think of what lyrics to put in there. So one day I was walking around singing at my job at Doyle Dane Bernbach and this beautiful Afro-American woman, who was a temp, says, "What are you singing?" And I said, "I'm singing a Charlie Parker composition." She asks, "Who?" I said again, "Charlie Parker." She said, "Who's that?" And I told her, "You're a soul sister and you don't know who Bird is? Shame on you." She was a very sweet girl. She admitted, "No, I don't." So then I told her who Bird was. I even gave her some Bird tapes to listen to. And then when I was walking home that night from work the lyrics finally came to me, "*There are those of us who really love him, oh, so many aren't even aware of his name.*" It came to me just like that. I believe I got that from Bird.

It was Don Sickler (Second Floor Music) who published her music and continues to do so, encouraging others to find these wonderful songs.

Jordan was beginning to create a buzz for herself, especially in the European jazz scene and on the East Coast. Her teaching and workshops were giving her a reputation with singers from all over the world, and she was becoming recognized as a formidable mentor. Cade Bursell put together a documentary about Jordan's life, *In the Voice of a Woman*, around 1995. Although the project never received distribution, it demonstrated the interest that people were beginning to have in the history of this jazz icon. Many of the great jazz singers had passed on, leaving only a handful left who had experienced the real jazz era of the '40s and '50s or who had sung or hung out with some of the renowned legends of that era, such as Charlie Parker, Thelonious Monk, Bill Evans, Charles Mingus, and many others. It suddenly became clear to Jordan that she had a significant message to deliver to the younger singers and instrumentalists coming on the scene by keeping the historic oral tradition of jazz intact. Jordan had a mission in her music that was beyond her own personal vocal expression. Somehow the significance of keeping the music "alive," as she often says, was more important than an ego-centered desire to perform. Her performances were laced with dedications to the musicians she knew and respected and she always had stories to tell within the context of her set lists. Whether it was her own experiences with Parker or how Miles Davis played a ballad, each performance became an intimate walk through the streets of New York and Detroit, where she had first heard these artists. As she held our hands and took us along, we listened and learned about the heart of jazz music.

Jordan spent most of her free time with her daughter Tracey and friends, especially Banks and her daughter Coryelle, whom she considered family. By this time Tracey was back in New York and the two would not only spend time together but they also loved to travel together. One of the most memorable of their trips was in 1997; Jordan remembers,

> I had gotten a call to do a festival in Israel. Israel is always very special for me. I've done about five festivals there. I especially love the Wailing Wall. So I was thrilled to go back again and do this festival. I mentioned it to Tracey and she said she would love to go with me. She suggested we go to Egypt on our way, which I found very exciting. We decided to take an extra week off to see this spectacular place. We arrived in the afternoon and had a hotel alongside the pyramids and our window looked out on them. We were in heaven. Our guide told us about visiting Moses' Mountain but we had to leave at midnight in order to reach the top. It was my first time riding a camel. When we got up to the top of Moses' Mountain, I heard someone call my name. I asked Tracey if she heard it and she said no. Then I heard it again and she said she heard too. I was so into it I thought Moses was calling me. The voice turned out to be a student who knew me from a master class I taught at the New School in New York.
>
> I will never forget that night. There were so many stars it looked like they were covering the entire sky with no breaks in between. What a sight that was. How fantastic it was to see all these amazing places. Then on our way out of Egypt to return to Israel we had to cross the border. There were

> guards who examined our passports before they would let us into Israel. I was in one line and Tracey was in another. I got through very fast but because Tracey had darker skin she was still there with the woman guard. I went back and asked the woman what the problem was. She said that the passport was not Tracey's. I said of course it is and that she was my daughter. Then the guard asked us why we wanted to visit Jordan? I was concerned that they might have thought Tracey was a terrorist and that it was a racial reaction. So without thinking I told her that we there to visit Jordan because our last name is Jordan. She looked at me as if I was insane but it was enough to let us go through. Thankfully there wasn't as much turmoil in that part of the Middle East at that time but you could tell it was in the air. I wish everyone could visit Egypt. It was the most humbling experience in my life thinking that I was just one of those grains of sand.

Jordan has always supported her fellow vocalists and especially those dedicated students who have passed her way. One of the students whom she mentored and befriended while teaching in Graz, Austria, was vocalist Theo Bleckmann:

> I encouraged him to come to the United States to go to school and I let him stay in my apartment for a week or so to make sure New York was for him. I was thrilled when he decided to stay. Later on I was doing a recording with Kuhn, and two other wonderful musicians, Dave Finck and Billy Drummond. I asked Theo to join me on the recording date because I had a few tunes that needed a male voice. One was "Oh, Henry," a song I used to sing counterpoint with Skeeter and Mitch in our old group back in Detroit. I never recorded it so I wanted it to be recorded in dedication to the group. And then he sang on "Reel Time" and my arrangement of "Every Time We Say Goodbye/For All We Know." I really wanted him on that recording and I'm glad I did because he's a wonderful singer and a beautiful talent.

The recording, *Jazz Child*, was another project produced by Joe Fields for his label, HighNote; it was released in 1998, one of many more that Jordan would do on Fields's label. Bleckmann remembers his connection with Jordan this way:

> I had long wanted to leave Germany. My struggle of having been adopted, never quite feeling at home in Germany and wanting to be closer to jazz music led me to apply for a scholarship at Berklee College of Music even before I met Sheila. However, it all came together when Sheila invited me to stay in her New York apartment for my first trip to America and as soon as I arrived in New York, I knew that I wanted to forgo my scholarship at Berklee and live in New York instead, closer to Sheila. Within months she helped arrange a scholarship in New York (at Manhattan School of Music) and in 1989 I moved to New York to begin my new life. Best of all, being

> in Manhattan allowed me to spend more time with Sheila, hear her sing and go on the road with her (she generously allowed me to sit in on almost all of her gigs and still does)—in return I drove her car, mowed her lawn once in a while and ate her food. When I first met Sheila I was completely unsure about who I was. All I had was my love and dedication for jazz music but very little sense, if any, where and if I belonged in this music at all. At some point early on I asked Sheila if my name "Theo Bleckmann" was good enough or if I should change it. She replied very dryly, "If it was good enough for Thelonious Monk [they called him "Theo" at times] it is certainly good enough for you." We both paused and then lost it laughing.

Scott Yanow reviewed *Jazz Child*:

> Sheila Jordan has yet to record a set under her own name that cannot be considered at least a near-gem. On *Jazz Child* she has a reunion with Steve Kuhn and is also assisted by bassist David Finck, drummer Billy Drummond, and (on three tunes) fellow vocalist Theo Bleckmann. Some of the material is definitely offbeat (including "The Moon Is a Harsh Mistress," Don Cherry's "Art Deco," Kuhn's "The Zoo," Gil Fuller's "Oh Henry," and trumpeter Tom Harrell's "Buffalo Wings"), but it all works. Also among the highlights are Abbey Lincoln's "Bird Alone," Jordan's title cut, and a medley of the singer's "Ballad for Miles" and "My Funny Valentine."[11]

Michael G. Nastos writes about *Jazz Child* in the *All Music Guide to Jazz*: "Her breathy, hither-come-yon, soulful voice, with an unmistakable Native American inflection and the quick witted, harmonic bebop foundation of her early days continues to earmark Jordan as one of the most important jazz singers of our time. Three cuts feature the artist with fellow vocalist Theo Bleckmann, and their voices mesh well together, especially on the kitschy, fun loving "Oh Henry." Bleckmann sounds bluesy and like a less histrionic Kurt Elling."[12] A special moment for Jordan was that she included her best friend Marria's poem "Jazz Child" in the liner notes, which became the title of the project. (See the poem at the beginning of chapter 3, "Detroit Days.")

During this time Jordan was doing small tours with various people, mostly in Europe or Japan. While performing at the Edmonton Jazz Festival in 1997 with Steve Kuhn as a duo, she met bassist Attillio Zanchi. "I loved her performance," shared Zanchi, "and I asked the director of the festival to introduce me to her. I asked her if she would be interested in coming to Italy to sing with my trio. She agreed and so we did a tour in 1998 from March 1st until the 21st. On one of the performances in Cremona there was a string quartet and Sheila was thrilled because it was the first time she sang in a live performance with the string quartet. We played everywhere in Italy and after that first tour we all wanted to work with her again so I call her every year to do concerts with us." Out of that performance came a live album called *Sheila's Back in Town* released in 1999 on the Splasc(h) label from their tours in Cremona, Koper, Busto Arsizio, Bologna, Alcamo, Forli, and Ancona. The following review is from the *All Music Guide to Jazz: The Definitive Guide to Jazz Music.*

> This disc is the fruit of an Italian tour with backing by that country's truly great E.S.P. Trio and a session with the Modern Ensemble, a string quartet. Jordan's dream has been to record with a chamber group and here it was realized during a busy tour in front of a live audience. In typical Jordan fashion, the proceedings here are elegant, lush, in the pocket, and full of surprises—like her sudden scatting in the middle of her own lyric for Don Cherry's "Art Deco." Other highlights include a stirring, heartbreaking rendition of "The Water Is Wide," with the trio being joined by the Modern Ensemble. Here, Jordan's enormous heart is exposed, raw and bleeding, full of passion for the simplest of melodies. She offers that heart in service to the song as Roberto Cipelli's piano glances through the changes and the strings slowly enter the body of the lyric. The listener can feel her mind, body, and soul being drawn into the center of the music and her voice rising to meet the well of emotion that grows with every chorus. It's a miracle that the set doesn't end right here, but then, that's Jordan. She can take and audience to a fever pitch, leaving every eye in the house full of tears and joy, overwhelmed by beauty-and still deliver more. She does so here with Gershwin and Monk (together), Brown and Timmons, and the lovely ballad "Lazy Afternoon." This album is more than a treat: it's a testament to a great singer who strives ever more to serve jazz in any way she can. This is truly a wonderful album.[13]

Toward the end of the 1990s Jordan was continuing to find popularity overseas and at home. She recorded a project in Augsburg, Germany, in 1999 with the Christian Stock Trio, *Straight Ahead*, on YVP Music, singing "Autumn in New York," "Barbados," "Sail Away," and "Song of Joy." Jordan reunited with Roswell Rudd that same year on *Broad Strokes*, an album of slow tempo tunes, singing an original Rudd track called "The Light." Harvey Pekar writes in a *JazzTimes* review, "Sheila Jordan sings beautifully during 'The Light.' She sounds amazingly youthful."[14] Jordan was in her seventies now and the reference to her youthful sound would stick with her for many more years to come. Jordan enjoyed the fruits of these years in the latter half of her life, and it appeared as though this songbird was soaring into the millennium.

• 6 •

Better Than Anything

2000–2012

> "I am very fortunate to have come as far as I have in my life. I survived and I'm still doing music and enjoying every note of it."
>
> —Sheila Jordan

Jordan's career gained momentum through the decades and as she approached the millennium, recognition and appreciation for her talents took flight with numerous awards and accolades, along with an increase in performance opportunities. As she reached the age of eighty-five in 2013, she received an overwhelming appeal to sing at concerts, festivals, and workshops, so much so that she found herself doing the unthinkable—turning gigs down. Her teaching became even more of a focal point with a demand for more workshops as well as her already established presence on the jazz faculties of Jazz in July, Jazz in Vermont, Interplay Jazz Camp, and others. It was a testament to the years Jordan had spent traveling around the world sharing her knowledge that now so many singers viewed Jordan as a mentor. Many of these singers were now teachers themselves and would set up workshops, master classes, and clinics for Jordan. Jordan's own discography had begun to flourish, and between 2000 and 2013 she had approximately twelve new recordings as a leader or guest artist.

The first album issued at the beginning of this decade was a compilation of tracks from previous Muse recordings: *Old Time Feeling* (1982), *Lost and Found* (1989), and *Heart Strings* (1993). The compilation from 32 Jazz, called *From the Heart*, helped gain some attention from new fans who were not familiar with these earlier recordings. Mathew Bahl, reviewing the recording for *All About Jazz*, writes:

> While these records deserve to be reissued in their entirety, by culling tracks from each album, 32 Jazz has created a perfect single disc showcase

for Jordan's considerable talents. Sheila Jordan is a supremely musical singer with a light, ageless, flexible voice. A true jazz musician, her performances are constant improvisations that move in unexpected and oftentimes daring directions. Yet, no matter how far out on a wire she goes musically, Jordan's commitment to the lyric remains absolute. When everything comes together, as it does throughout this CD, the results are as good as jazz gets.

Listen to the small miracles Jordan works on the opening song, "The Very Thought of You." Swinging, exuberant and infectiously playful, she so perfectly captures the mood of the lyrics ("I'm living in a kind of daydream/I'm happy as a king") that it would be easy to overlook the sheer creativity of her phrasing. The performance also demonstrates Jordan's ability to interact as an equal with the other musicians in the group.

From the Heart covers a wide variety of musical and emotional terrain. There are three voice/bass duets with Harvie Swartz including a remarkable medium tempo deconstruction of "How Deep is the Ocean?" Jordan delivers an irresistibly sexy "Comes Love" backed only by bass and drums. She sings "Japanese Dream/What'll I Do?" and "Haunted Heart" with a trio augmented by a string quartet beautifully arranged by Alan Broadbent. The tracks that find Jordan accompanied by just a traditional trio benefit greatly from the deft rhythmic attack and sheer beauty of pianist Kenny Barron's playing.

The high points of *From the Heart* are two exquisite ballads. Jordan sings Jerome Kern and Buddy DeSylva's "Look for the Silver Lining" accompanied only by Alan Broadbent on piano. Jordan drains the lyric of its greeting card sentimentality and transforms it into a statement of hope and reassurance from a woman who knows full well how difficult and unfair the world can be. Mr. Broadbent's duets with the late singer Irene Kral are legendary and his playing here amounts to a Master Class in accompaniment.

Even more extraordinary is the 18th Century Scots ballad, "The Water is Wide," on which Jordan, Barron, Swartz and drummer Ben Riley achieve an almost telepathic communion. Jordan transforms the song into a journey of deep longing and profound loss and her performance is simply staggering in the immediacy and depth of her emotions.[1]

Scott Albin did a brief review of one of the songs, "The Very Thought of You," for the online publication jazz.com:

This version of "The Very Thought of You," which she recorded at the age of 60, finds her definitely in a Betty Carter frame of mind. Beginning with only Swartz's alternately walking and prancing basslines, Jordan elongates words and alters pitches at will. As Barron and Riley chip in, she exudes a girlish charm while at the same time exhibiting an obviously mature control, toying with the rhythm and hitting effectively slurred low notes when least expected. Barron's scampering solo seems inspired by Jordan's compelling quirkiness. The singer next trades masterfully with Riley, her

> scatting as always highly musical and unaffected. She then reprises the lyrics, sometimes nearly in falsetto to contrast with her richer natural voice. This is a teasing, knowing, unassailable interpretation from start to finish.[2]

Jordan's next project was an album with a quartet including once again pianist Kuhn but with a different band this time that consisted of bassist David Finck and drummer Billy Drummond, and included special guest Tom Harrell (trumpet, flügelhorn) on four of the thirteen selections. Jordan had kept a long relationship with Joe Fields, starting with his label Muse and now HighNote. Fields understood Jordan's musical tastes and never got in the way of her instincts for choosing projects or personnel. Jordan recalls, "Joe always believed in me. He approached me a long time ago when I was at Doyle Dane Bernbach and he had the Muse label and wanted me to record with him. I never liked recording and I didn't want to record at that time. Then Joe called me again and said he really wanted me to record a project. He never gave up on me and I finally said yes. He and Barney Fields have been very good to me. I've enjoyed doing so many of my projects with them." The CD, *Little Song*, was recorded in 2002 and featured a few songs Jordan had recorded on previous sessions along with some new arrangements. Jordan had met Harrell in a club on Broadway where he was playing with guitarist Joe Puma many years before this recording. Jordan recalls, "The first time I heard Tom I thought he was incredible. He was doing duos and inviting different guests and he wanted me to do a duo with him, so I did. I also did a concert with Tom's group at a jazz festival in Greece and I did some of Tom's original tunes. I just think, for that instrument, he's the most beautiful musician alive today and he's definitely my favorite. I love him dearly and any time I have a chance to record I want him on it, because I connect with him musically."

The album showed the world the contributions of a seasoned veteran and found a place among her more revered projects. Notes jazz critic Joel Roberts in *All About Jazz*,

> There's a lot to be said for experience. That may be especially true for singers. The knowledge of how to get inside a song and really convey the meaning of a lyric isn't something most younger singers, even those with pretty voices (and faces) can do with the skill of a seasoned performer like Sheila Jordan, who celebrated her 75th birthday with a fine new release, *Little Song*, and a grand two-night stand last month at the Jazz Standard with Steve Kuhn's trio.
>
> Jordan's voice itself is limited, even fragile at times, but she knows how to make each song her own by playing with melody, phrasing and tempo. And while decades of struggle in the jazz trenches have lent a wisdom and authority to her singing, she's retained a playfulness and sassiness that's hard to resist. Listen, for example, as she purrs and flirts her way through chestnuts

> like "Hello Young Lovers," "Autumn in New York," and "When I Grow Too Old to Dream." More than just a standards singer, Jordan's also an accomplished improviser, as she proves on Charlie Parker's "Barbados" and the pair of Native American chants that open and close the set.
>
> With sympathetic backing from Kuhn's fine trio and special guest Tom Harrell on trumpet and flugelhorn, Sheila Jordan shows that jazz, like so many other things, only improves with age.[3]

Jordan didn't always get rave reviews, as many musicians and vocalists can attest to in their own careers. Not everyone is going to understand your music or do the research. In a world of recording projects being a dime a dozen, there are critics who miss the mark. Jordan recalls a review for *Little Song* that she found particularly offensive,

> I've had some wonderful reviews in my lifetime and I appreciate them all. But I got one review where this guy just had no clue. On my CD *Little Song* I do this one song, "When I Grow Too Old to Dream," that I sang for my mother, who died of alcoholism. My grandmother and my mother both were alcoholics. It's an old song and they used to sing it when they got drunk so it has some sad and deep memories for me. So this guy reviews the CD and says, "She sounded like she was drunk when she sang it. If she wasn't deliberately trying to sound drunk she is a genius." You know what that does to a recovering alcoholic? So, I guess I'm a genius, because I was not trying to sound drunk! Then I sang this song by Kenny Dorham, a wonderful trumpet player who died young. He wrote the song "Fair Weather," which is about racial equality, and having people come together. This guy said the lyrics were trite. He didn't get it and couldn't understand that after you've been on the street in a racially prejudiced city like Detroit and parts of New York, where you've been beaten up and harassed by the police because of your beliefs, you are seeking racial equality and hoping that one day we'll all walk hand in hand and it will be "fair weather." But this guy just couldn't get it.

But as *JazzTimes* critic Christopher Louden put it clearly in his review of *Little Song*:

> Certain acquired tastes are worth the effort: caviar; single-malt Scotch; Sheila Jordan. Like her friend and sometime collaborator Mark Murphy, Jordan is that anomaly peculiar to the upper echelons of American jazz—an artist too superbly innovative to attract a mainstream audience. As an improviser she knows no equal, stretching her small voice to incredible limits. It was evident four decades ago on the landmark *Portrait of Sheila* (Blue Note)—an album so boldly imaginative, so distinctly outre, that no label would touch her for another dozen years. It's just as evident throughout

> *Little Song* (HighNote), a bracing new collection of blues and standards that derives its seemingly ironic title from the nickname bestowed on Jordan by her Cherokee grandfather. Bracketed by improvised Native American chants, *Little Song* wanders freely from the awed reverence of "Autumn in New York" and velvety desire of "On a Slow Boat to China" to an agitated "Hello Young Lovers" that drips with self-deprecating humor. Along the way, Jordan injects "Something's Gotta Give" with sinful determination, ignites the smoldering edges of "The Touch of Your Lips" and peels back the delicate layers of "When I Grow Too Old to Dream" with heartbreaking tenderness. It is, though, a newer composition—bassist David Finck's cunning "The Way He Captured Me" (sort of a softer, more cerebral "You Can Have Him")—that impresses most with its evocative blend of trumped-up enthusiasm and muted envy. Throughout *Little Song*, Jordan proves conclusively that she is, at age 74, still in her prime.[4]

Most singers have a special relationship with one or more accompanists that allows them to express the music in an artistic and comfortable manner. It's important to recognize that there are infinite ways to interpret songs. A singer must have a good partnership and communication with an accompanist and often because of this brilliant relationship arrangements and musical moments occur. In jazz, as in other genres of music, there are couplings that become famous, such as Billie Holiday and Lester Young and Ella Fitzgerald and Joe Pass. Jordan is known for her pairings, especially with accompanists Steve Kuhn, Harvie S (Swartz), and Cameron Brown. To Jordan, the magic that develops when there is a bond between two musicians is the element that raises the bar of any performance. However, even two great musicians may not meet that requirement, demonstrating the importance of good chemistry when combining musical talents. There is a certain alchemic mixture that cannot be forced or produced no matter how amazing the two musicians may be, because ultimately there is more at play in this situation than just skills. Jordan puts it succinctly: "I think what is most important in accompanying is trusting and listening. If you trust each other and the accompanist listens to what you're doing, you will have a beautiful musical marriage. But not everybody plays well for singers. I mean, they may be great players, but that doesn't necessarily mean that they can play well for a singer. They may not even enjoy it or really know how to accompany a singer. I think there's an art in accompanying." That's why any time there was a chance for a duo performance, Jordan and Kuhn would jump at the opportunity. Besides their special musical relationship, Jordan reminds us that the two are very close friends: "Steve is very special to me. Aside from his wonderful music I can talk to him and he gives me good advice." The two performed in July of 2003 at the Festival International de Jazz de Montreal, ranked as the world's largest jazz festival, generally hosting over three thousand artists from thirty countries.

Jordan did some Christmas carols for the Aardvark Jazz Orchestra's recording *Bethlehem Counterpoint* on Aardmuse in 2002 and a project with Frank Mantooth, *Ladies Sing for Lovers*, on MCG Jazz in 2003, where she sang "The Ballad of the Sad Young Men." Jordan was more in demand internationally after building a reputation through her past concerts and her teaching in Graz and other workshops. It was also in 2003 that Jordan embarked on her seventy-fifth birthday tour, which included a live concert at La Ferme Asile, a venue in Sion, Switzerland. The concert was recorded by Hubert Sewer on November 8 and became the album *Believe in Jazz*, with the Serge Forté Trio, featuring Serge Forté (piano), Karl Jannuska (drums), and Gary Brunton (bass). The tour continued with various performances including a celebration in Paris that included vocalist David Linx and ended back in New York at the Jazz Standard with Kuhn's trio on her actual birthday, November 18. Canadian jazz critic and a lifelong fan of Jordan, Len Dobbins, fondly remembers the occasion:

> In 2003 I began a new friendship with Dorothee Berryman, a multi talented woman, a stage and screen actor, singer and later a jazz radio host heard across Canada, I mentioned Sheila's 75th birthday party to her and lo and behold she called to say she had Air Canada executive class plane tickets to New York and we would be attending that event. And what an event it was with people from all over the world in attendance. People like her daughter Tracey now a grown woman (who she again sang "Dat Dere" for), Frank Kimbrough, Lenore Raphael, Ian Shaw, Mark Murphy, Claire Daly, Jay Clayton, Brian Kellock, a favourite pianist, all the way from Scotland, Theo Bleckmann and Roswell Rudd, many of whom sat in with Sheila and trio of Kuhn, David Finck and Billy Drummond. Ms. Berryman was blown away by the event and on the plane home kept thanking me for including her in *my* evening.[5]

That same year began my own personal association with Jordan, leading to the concept of this book. I was moderator for a panel entitled "The Evolution of Solo Vocal Jazz Singing: Where Are We Headed?" as part of the yearly convention of the now-defunct International Association of Jazz Educators (IAJE). Vocalist Jay Clayton suggested that I invite Jordan to join the panel, which was a thrilling idea since she was definitely one of the jazz singers I admired. I contacted Jordan many months in advance and she graciously accepted, but it wasn't until that conference that I had the opportunity to meet her. The rest of the panel featured Jay Clayton, Kurt Elling, Jon Hendricks, Kitty Margolis, and Mark Murphy. It was early in the course of the conference that I actually met Jordan. Every year the IAJE Women's Caucus honored a female jazz musician deserving of wider recognition for artistic excellence and outstanding contributions to jazz with the prestigious Lil Hardin Armstrong Jazz Heritage

Award. Jordan was chosen as the 2004 recipient of the award with an event at the New York Hilton on January 23. My first glimpse of Jordan was through the doorway of the room where the presentation was held and there she sat, surrounded by singers and fans pouring their respect through their applause and laughter. Jordan and I became friends quickly and I planned to arrange some performances and workshops for her on the West Coast for the future, so we knew we would certainly meet again.

The following month Jordan was back on the road, a constant part of her life. She reunited with bassist Zanchi in Italy, where they recorded *Sheila Jordan and E.S.P. Trio: Straight Ahead*, once again on the Splasc(h) label. The personnel consisted of Paolo Fresu: trumpet and flügelhorn; Roberto Cipelli: piano; Attillio Zanchi: bass; and Gianni Cazzola: drums. Zanchi remembers, "In 2004 we finally did a CD, *Straight Ahead*, in the studio together with Sheila, the E.S.P Trio, and trumpeter Paolo Fresu, whom she liked a lot. Sheila is a bit reluctant to hear her recorded voice, even if everybody tells her how good she is. For that reason we gave her the freedom to choose what she would like to sing, and her performance was extraordinary!" Jordan wholeheartedly agrees:

> I don't really like to record. I always feel hemmed in when I'm in those booths. I hear every breath and click and it can be distracting to me. My ears are so keen they pick up every sound. I prefer live recordings. On all of the recordings I have done, after the tracks are picked and I hear the final results I never listen to it again. I am not comfortable hearing myself. If I go to a dinner at a friend's house and they are playing my CDs I ask them to please turn it off. I like to remember the deep feeling I get when I'm singing and I don't always hear that on the recordings. I become my own worst critic and start telling myself how I should have done this or that. I feel like it's over and done so let's move on to something else.

That's why the majority of Jordan's projects are recorded live, the way she prefers to record.

Jordan hadn't had many gigs on the West Coast, particularly in the Southern California area, so she was delighted when I invited her to come out to do a performance at one of the jazz venues. Unbeknown to her at the time, she would be receiving an honorary award from the Jazz Vocal Coalition (JZVOC) for all of her contributions to jazz as a performer, educator, innovator, and supporter of jazz music. As the cofounder and president of the JZVOC, I presented the award during her performance at Clancy's Jazz Club in Glendale, California, on Saturday, April 3. I still recall how convinced she was, as we drove to the club, that there would hardly be anyone in the audience. She kept saying to me, "I hope some people show up." I kept telling her that it would be packed. I don't think she had any idea what an impact she had made on jazz singers across the country. When we walked in the door she was astonished and delighted to see the room full of fans, both old and new, who were ecstatic to have the opportunity to hear her perform live. She was also thrilled to reunite with pianist Alan Pasqua, whom she refers to as her "spiritual son." They shared good memories together; he was the pianist on the *Confirmation* album in New York in 1975. Pasqua relates,

> She is really a true jazz artist, in that she improvises every moment, not just when she's soloing, but just in her interpretation of whatever she's doing. It's constant improvisation. That's just how she is. She creates all the time rather than re-creates. And to be around that at a young age, it was profound for me. She really treated me with love and she cared a great deal for me, as I did for her. And she was funny. She told me, she said, "You know, Alan, don't move to L.A., you know, you're never going to get out of there. Don't move." [Laughs] She really wanted me to stick around. It was really hard to go, too. We've had a chance to play a few times together and it's always been just great.

The evening was truly musical magic for everyone, with Pasqua's sensitive touch on the keys, joined by bassist Darek Oles and drummer Tim Pleasant. The award was presented before the second set began, a beautiful glass decorative piece with an inscription that read: "In Honor of Ms. Sheila Jordan. . . . For growing up to be a finely tuned jazz vocal artist." The award and the outpouring of love from all of the singers and instrumentalists in the room was quite touching and she was genuinely surprised that there were so many people who wanted to hear her in the Southern California area. She responded with a lovely e-mail letter to the organization expressing her feelings: "What an honor and I was so thrilled. The evening was so wonderful at Clancy's and to have this was an extra dessert. Thank you beautiful singers all of you. I especially want to thank Ellen Johnson at this time for all of her hard work in getting me out there in the first place. I am so happy to have met some of you and I hope you all hang in there together and help each other as much as you can. We singers have a long road to haul and it is not easy at times but if we stick together and help and respect one another, anything is possible. Much love to each and every one of you."

This would be one of many occasions that Jordan and I would collaborate on bringing her to the West Coast for performances and workshops. She always stayed at my home and it gave me a chance to get to know her quite personally, building a friendship over time and eventually leading to the writing of this book. However, I always had to make sure I had plenty of sleep or coffee because I was lucky if I could keep up with all of her energy!

Jordan's next CD project was, of course, a live bass and voice duet recording on her seventy-sixth birthday at the Triad in NYC on HighNote. It had been quite a while since she and Cameron Brown had done a recording, so they decided it was time. *Celebration* was another bass and voice gem that revisited some of her past duo songs and added a few new ones to the mix. Friend and vocalist Jay Clayton made a special appearance that was included on the recording. Lara Pelligrinelli captured the essence of the Jordan/Brown duo in an earlier article in *JazzTimes* where she wrote, "The chemistry shared by Jordan and Brown can be gleaned from visual cues alone. Brown's playful romps, predicted by animated facial expressions, meet with smiles and batted eyelids. . . . Jordan, in turn, sings directly into the strings, head bowed close to the instrument. 'She's right there,' Brown says, measuring about eight inches between his hands. 'Her voice and the bass almost become one thing. It feels like she gets inside the sound—that's what she wants to do.' The difference in range and timbral quality renders the effect all the more incredible."[6] Jordan has always viewed the bass and voice duo as a serious, long-term relationship that blossoms out of the dedication of both musicians. It is this concept that has made her contributions so enduring, while many artists, particularly in jazz, tend to roam from person to person. Jordan always says that she "doesn't cheat on her bass player"; it's a commitment. And although occasionally you will hear her singing with another bass player, you can be sure that it will be limited to a few songs and only because Brown was not available or part of a tour. Jordan lovingly replies, "I have made many friends through music and all of the musicians—or most of them—I am very close with. Cameron is like a brother to me. I can discuss things with him and he is very helpful and consoling—plus he is very dedicated to the bass and voice, which is a very important part of the music I do."

Jordan barely found time to breathe between invitations to perform overseas. In March, June, and November of 2005 she was back singing with the E.S.P. Trio in Italy. In the same year, Jordan made a performance in Toledo, Ohio, over Easter weekend that turned out to be a special occasion; many of her family members from the area were in attendance. Jazz writer David Dupont gave a rather animated recounting of this performance:

> Like a quirky, eccentric aunt, she arrived draped in a black gown and a glittering beret. And much to the delight of family and friends, most of them new, she sang, bringing us all up to date on her world, and the state of art of jazz singing. Sheila Jordan's appearance at Murphy's Place was something of a surprise—announced a few days before with a paragraph in a Toledo paper, sending at least this jazz lover into paroxysms of delight that bemused his co-workers.
>
> The singer, mike in her right hand with her left hand stretched out grasping the mike stand, let "Everything Happens to Me" flow. She delivered

> the words with the ease of conversation, her enthusiasm for the company expressed in ripples of melisma. She made it clear that she does not consider herself "a diva." Rather she sees herself as a messenger for this music, "a jazz messenger like Art Blakey." And yet standing there on stage she had the bearing of royalty, and we were all her subjects . . . and friends.
>
> In all her many years singing, well over 50 now, she told the audience she had never sung in Toledo, but once. Many years ago she sat in at a club; she'd gone out with her half-sister. She has family here, she announced, maybe some of them were in the house. Then a voice piped up from a front table, saying yes family was in the house. "And who are you?" Jordan asked. "I'm sister Rosie," the woman said. "When I last saw you were . . ." and Jordan measured to her leg. Quick, family reunion introductions followed. "Now you'll know what your crazy big sister does."
>
> Throughout she used songs to tell stories. "If I Had You" served as the frame for a story about Leonard Feather. During her first appearance in Los Angeles, he sat right down in front, she said, where the critics always do (and where indeed I was sitting) and taking lots of notes (I jotted surreptitiously). The next day he wrote a generally positive review, praising Jordan's swing, but saying he wished she'd stuck closer to the melody. Jordan then demonstrated for the Murphy's crowd what she imagined Feather would have liked—a decidedly square, not unpleasant, but comic reading of the tune.
>
> Jordan closed with "Sheila's Blues." Strange that she would close with this . . . it would seem that, given it tells the story of her life, she would use it as an introduction, and yet it seemed right. She told us this story now over the familiar cadences of the blues, better that we could carry it home with us. She delivered an incandescent reading of the song. The confessional style belied the craft of her performance. She played coy in the opening lines about the date of her birth, and yet in the end as she testified that it was the music that saved her, she announced that's why she's still singing for us at 76.
>
> And when she sang of being 14 and sitting in the alley behind the Sudan Club in Detroit, rapt as Charlie Parker played to her and her buddies through an open back door, I suddenly felt not just what it was to be a kid discovering this great music, not only what it was to feel the warmth of a great musician, but what it is like to suddenly be connected to the vast and powerful and enduring spirit of the music. That's exactly what happened this March night at Murphy's Place in Toledo when Sheila Jordan came to call.[7]

In April she was back on the West Coast again, performing at the Vic in Santa Monica and Dizzy's in San Diego, along with some prearranged workshops. Don Heckman comments in the *Los Angeles Times*,

> There are jazz singers and there are jazz singers. And then there's Sheila Jordan. And the very fact that one can describe her as a unique musical

> entity may be the best explanation of what is so special about her art. The New Yorker made one of her rare visits to the Southland this week, in part to teach some seminars and some individual students, in part to perform Thursday at the Vic in Santa Monica. Working with the sterling trio of pianist Alan Pasqua, bassist Darek Oles and drummer Tim Pleasant, singing two consecutive full-house sets, she was a marvel, balancing inventive musical clarity with a challenging choice of material and presenting it with wit, humor and a trace of poignant memory.[8]

As mentioned previously, Jordan had many mystical experiences surrounding her performances, including, as she likes to put it, out-of-body experiences. She describes it this way: "I have had a few out-of-body experiences, and they are incredible. It feels like you are leaving your body and floating over this form below you and the music becomes one sound. It's an incredible feeling." During the performance at Dizzy's in San Diego in April of 2005, I witnessed one of those mystical experiences. It was a warm spring day in San Diego and Chuck Perrin, who booked this unique open-space venue near the Gaslamp District, had opened the front door prior to the band starting to let in some fresh air. Jordan had just finished singing a song accompanied by local musicians Rick Helzer (piano), Gunnar Biggs (bass), and Duncan Moore (drums), and began introducing the next song. The tune was called "Bird Alone," by vocalist and composer Abbey Lincoln. In that exact moment a single sparrow flew into the room and sat on the rafters above. The bird was motionless as if listening to the music. The exact second Jordan finished the last note the bird flew toward the stage and then out the door. Everyone in the room felt the magic and Jordan put her hand over her heart and told the audience that it must have been Charlie Parker (Bird) coming to watch over her. It was something I will never forget.

Jordan had met vocalist Kurt Elling in Australia at the Wangaratta Festival around 1998 when they were adjudicating a vocal contest together. They became good friends and have shared many performances together since. Elling recalls:

> I vividly remember having her on with my "Four Brothers" show with Mark Murphy and Jon Hendricks. We did the gig outdoors at Millennium Park in Chicago and called it "Three Brothas and A Motha." Well, having her on then made me wish we'd done it that way from the beginning. Here she was walking into our arrangements with almost no rehearsal, handling them all beautifully, charming the audience, flirting with them, and juicing Jon, giving a shout out to the late Oscar Brown Jr. and helping Mark relax and play some of his best stuff. I love the brother/sister thing Sheila and Mark have. Sheila can tell Mark things no one else in the world can and he'll pay attention. The day of the performance we had chairs right on stage

> so we could all dig each other's singing, and whenever neither of them was busy Sheila and Mark sat together, holding hands. I love that memory.

The concert on July 21 during Millennium Park's "Made In Chicago" series brought together the vocal octogenarian icons for some truly memorable moments. Being at the event myself I was astounded at the electricity during the concert, the many jazz musicians present and the outpouring of affection from the audience. Elling is to be complimented for having the foresight to put together this event, which allowed a younger generation of his own fans to experience the roots from which he grew. *Chicago Tribune* arts critic Howard Reich reviewed the concert:

> From the high-flying vocalese of Jon Hendricks to the novelty effects of Mark Murphy, from the neo-hipster swagger of Kurt Elling to the make-it-up-as-you-go lyrics of Sheila Jordan, the show reminded listeners that the best singers command as much musicianship, technique and creativity as their instrumental counterparts (who tend to get a lot more respect). Listen to Elling, Murphy, Hendricks and Jordan take flight—in solo and ensemble settings—and there's no question that the jazz vocalist's art encompasses a staggering range of styles, timbres and expressive tools. . . . Jordan sounded sharper, earthier and more soulful than ever. For unfathomable reasons, she's increasingly effective every time she sets foot on a Chicago stage (which is not often enough).[9]

Due to many of these concerts and word of mouth in the United States and abroad, Jordan was becoming a more popular attraction. Even on her own home turf she attracted more fans. Vocalist and friend Tessa Souter tells a charming story:

> I threw Sheila's seventy-seventh birthday party at Sweet Rhythm in New York. It was so packed that the line snaked all up Seventh Avenue and around the corner. I took photographs very callously of the people. I say callously because it was freezing that night. I remember coming from the cake shop holding the cake in both (ungloved) hands. I stopped a young woman in the street and asked her to pull up my hood on my coat and tie the ties because I couldn't do it myself. My hands were claws by the time I arrived. But no one in the line minded at all. Everyone was smiling and excited to be seeing Sheila. I think it's her honesty that people resonate with. She is a true artist.

It's not only Jordan's honesty, but also her generosity in sharing with other singers that has proven to be a rewarding part of her life. Besides supporting Bleckmann, she has done concerts, tours, and recordings with other singers and students to support them in their jazz journey. By doing so she has been able to reach a variety of age demographics, allowing her to further fulfill her mission in spreading the message of jazz music. In 2006 Jordan was invited by German vocalist Sabine Kühlich to join her in a tour with concerts in Viersen, Köln, Würzburg, Frankfurt, and Reutlingen. Jordan says, "Sabine decided that it would be nice to do a tour called "Two Generations of Jazz." She asked me after taking lessons with me. She thought I would be interested, and I said yes. And it's been wonderful. I tour with her maybe once a year or so since we started. I really enjoy singing with another singer. I love that." The concerts with Kühlich resulted in two recordings, *Sabine Kühlich & Crisp featuring Sheila Jordan: Fly Away* (Acoustic Music) released in 2006 and *Sheila Jordan & Sabine Kühlich: Two Generations of Singers* (Digiland Records) released in 2007. *All About Jazz* critic Michael P. Gladstone reviewed *Fly Away*: "Perhaps it is no coincidence that Kühlich's style sounds very much like Sheila Jordan's on some of these tunes. On her three appearances, Jordan, who was 77 years at the time, seems to inspire both the musicians and Kühlich. On Charlie Parker's "Ornithology," the two singers spontaneously trade remembrances of when they first heard Parker's music. Jordan was a fourteen-year-old in Detroit and Kuhlich was fifteen in East Germany."[10]

In 2006, Jordan recorded on my CD project, *These Days*, singing a duet of her song, "The Crossing," and a spontaneous improvisation on a poem I had written about her called "Little Messenger."

Little Messenger
(for Sheila Jordan)

Little messenger
Singing jazz
As she passes our way
On the wings of blackbirds
That blow bebop changes
While telling Charlie's stories
Through sagacious Cherokee eyes
Not a surprise
To watch wood and flesh
Inspired by the rhythm of ancient ancestors
Calling from the heart of time
The phrases of truth
Dripping down piano keys
Just to please
The songbird
Who perches on our souls
Spreading her seeds of joy
And love
And hope

While God holds her essence
In the perpetual palm of his spirit
As a gift to humanity.

© Ellen Johnson 2004

Jordan joined me on my CD release event at the Vic in Santa Monica, which will remain a treasured memory. The room was filled with singers, instrumentalists, and jazz critics from the Los Angeles area. A brief excerpt of Don Heckman's *Los Angeles Times* review reads:

> The performance, coinciding with the release of her new CD, *These Days*, was both a celebration and a showcase for Johnson's music, with plenty of space allocated to the other artists on the album—guitarist Larry Koonse, bassist Darek Oles, drummer Roy McCurdy and percussionist and singer Ana Gazzola. And, perhaps most significant, veteran jazz singer Sheila Jordan. Parts of the CD, in fact, were stimulated by Jordan's fondness for duetting with string bassists. The program reached its climax with Jordan's arrival. She sang Oscar Brown Jr.'s whimsical lyrics for Bobby Timmons' "Dat Dere" with appropriately childlike inflection, then switched to the dark subtleties of maturity with "You Must Believe in Spring." This engaging evening concluded with a stunning duet between the two singers in Jordan's "The Crossing," a deeply personal revelation, from one who has made the journey, of what it really means to be a jazz singer.[11]

Jordan continued to tour heavily even as she approached her eighties. "I don't mind the traveling. I keep a clear head about it and tell myself this music is your life so sit back and enjoy the flight. If I have any negative feelings about traveling they leave the minute I go on stage." Bassist Finck made these observations:

> Sheila has tremendous strength, thoughtfulness, and a great dedication to her music. After turning eighty, she seems to have lost no speed or drive. You might run into her at any airport in the world running to catch a flight to get her from one engagement to the next and she's always in good spirits and maintaining her ability to see humor in things. Trust me—you cannot keep up with her. Also, Sheila has an incredible sense of humor and that is crucial. Especially in the music business where jobs, musicians, flights, hotels, and everything else are subject to change at any time.

Jordan had a heavy travel schedule, with the Taichung Jazz Festival with Serge Forté, a concert at the UMass Amherst Fine Arts Center (sharing the stage with her good friend Billy Taylor), the Art of Jazz Celebration in Toronto, the Chivas Jazz Festival in Brazil with Kuhn, the Jazz Up Close series at the

Kimmel Center in Philadelphia, Interplay Jazz Festival in Woodstock, Upstairs Jazz Bar & Grill in Montreal, Jazz in July in Massachusetts, SFJAZZ Festival, Litchfield Jazz Camp, Vitello's in Los Angeles, and more tours in Germany, Paris, and Japan.

Jordan reunited with Elling's Four Brothers Tour when she filled in for Kevin Mahogany in November of 2009 at the Royal Opera House in London. Souter, writing for the *London Jazz News*, notes:

> When Sheila Jordan fills in for Kevin Mahogany in the Four Brothers vocal group with Kurt Elling, Mark Murphy and Jon Hendricks, the band is renamed Three Brothers and a Mother. Perfect. Because Sheila Jordan is a mother, not only to her beloved actual daughter, Tracey Jordan, but to every musician, and (quite possibly) audience member who has ever been lucky enough to come under her influence.
>
> This was much in evidence yesterday afternoon at her concert in front of a full house (which included vocalist Norma Winstone) at the Royal Opera House—from the motherly way she introduced her band (making each of them take a "proper bow," encouraging them to actually scat a chorus, leaning over every now and then to hug, or receive a kiss from pianist Brian Kellock), to the way she spoke to the crowd.
>
> "Never give up on your dream!" she said. "I was 58 when I was able to give up my day job!" Actually, she was laid off, she told me recently. And as she was going down in the elevator in tears, she heard a voice within her saying, "This is what you asked for! Why are you crying!" She hasn't looked back since.
>
> Where other singers have soul, Sheila Jordan has heart. At 81, she is not a pyrotechnician, like, say, fellow octogenarian Cleo Laine. Her singing is not so much an exuberant celebration of technique as an extremely musical, direct communication from her heart to yours. Visibly exhausted between songs—more tired than I have ever seen her (she's just coming to the end of a long international tour)—she miraculously rallied for the duration of each, making you hear everything as if for the first time, really noticing, no, understanding the lyrics.
>
> It's a way of being that makes you feel as if every word she speaks and sings is a message for you and you alone. When she sings "Dat Dere," which she sings at every concert, and dedicates to her daughter Tracey, we are her children. Her rendition of "You Must Believe in Spring" is a heartfelt exhortation to all of us to (like her) keep going, even when the going is tough. At the end of the concert she came out into the audience away from the mic to thank everyone. I would guess most of the crowd couldn't hear a word she said. But everyone was touched.
>
> After the concert, a long line of people (some in tears) waited patiently to take it in turns to tell her that her message got through. "I'm going to take up painting again!" said one 50-something man, who confessed to being a

procrastinator. "When?" asked Sheila, as sternly as a mum to her teenage son. "Oh, I've got lots of things to do. Probably in three weeks," he said. "Well, make sure you do!" she said.

> In life, as in her music, she is there for you, like a good mother. Tired. Exhausted. She nevertheless rallied for us, singing better than ever, so that, unless you knew her well, you might not even have known how exhausted she was in comparison to her usual self. If she were English, where we do such things, she would have been anointed a National Treasure, or made into a Dame by now. As it is, for jazz aficionados the world over, she is an International Treasure.
>
> Sheila Jordan doesn't just sing, she blesses you with her singing and with everything she is. Yesterday's concert was as beautiful a demonstration of that as I've ever seen. Not merely a concert, but a blessing.[12]

Jordan's final two solo projects on her discography to this date include *Yesterdays*, one of the past concerts from the Jordan/Harvie bass duo days issued in 2012 on HighNote Records. This recording (described in more detail in chapter 8) was from one of the Jordan and Harvie duo final concerts and it received outstanding reviews. In February of 2008 *Winter Sunshine*, a live-recorded concert produced by Jean-Pierre Leduc and Jim West on the Justin Time label, was released. Leduc recalls,

> The first time I saw Sheila Jordan live I fell in love with her. Her charm, wit, her ease with the audience, and her utter lack of pretension were so refreshing. And then she sang. It's not just the way she engages you, but also the knowledge and wisdom she utilizes in doing so. She also contextualizes a song; turning "St. Thomas" into a Sonny Rollins homage, or stopping in the middle of "Lady Be Good" to talk about Ella, while the band comps. These were historic figures she knew; Sonny remains her great friend. It was at a little club in Montreal called Upstairs, and I was working for Justin Time Records. I immediately thought to myself, "This would make a great recording," as Sheila's between-song banter rivals that of Jack Sheldon, another hilarious yet endearing musician. We did make the record, and we called it *Winter Sunshine* (my title) as it was recorded over two cold nights in Montreal in the dead of the season. Sheila and I have been great friends ever since.

Jerry D'Souza reviewed the project for *All About Jazz* on December 19, 2008:

> Sheila Jordan has stamped her class as a jazz singer over a career that has spanned 60 years. She has an articulate sense of phrasing and rhythm and she can ad lib at the turn of a note, but it is the emotion she draws out of a lyric that makes her stand out. Jordan proves her caliber all over again with

> *Winter Sunshine* a CD she recorded live at Upstairs, a jazz club in Montreal, in February 2008.
>
> The selection of well-honed standards and originals are prime material. Jordan embodies the words of a song and brings a sense of belonging to her singing. The intimacy, her lively interaction with the audience, and an empathic band of excellent musicians makes the concert an endearing experience.
>
> Jordan's voice has an elegant arching grace that finds its beckoning right off on "Comes Love." Her agile sense of swing and scatting set the tone as she cuts into the rhythm and ad libs her way into a pulse that has the audience clapping to the beat. She has snared them from the get go and she continues to holds them in the palm of her hand until the last note has curled into the night.
>
> She pays homage to Miles Davis on "Ballad For Miles" recalling the halcyon days when Davis played at the Village Vanguard with Wynton Kelly, Jimmy Cobb, Paul Chambers, and John Coltrane. She draws Billie Holliday into the narrative and then segues into "It Never Entered My Mind" making the song as compelling as it is heartbreaking.
>
> Her medley of "All God's Chillun' Got Rhythm/Little Willie Leaps" is another winner. The blues seep into the first before the tempo opens up for the second. She bops along and scats with vivacity and infuses the story of how the lyrics came to be written. Her scatting at the end turns this into a top-notch performance. And something would be amiss if the band was not commended. Steve Amirault runs up scintillating ideas on the piano with Keiran Overs on bass and Andre White on drums adding a coruscating rhythm.
>
> Jordan continues to be at the top of her game and coming as it does at this time of the year, her *Winter Sunshine* is most welcome.[13]

That same year Jordan lost one of her dearest longtime friends, Marria Banks, to cancer. It happened quite suddenly and Jordan mourned the loss for many years. "I was holding her hand when she died," says Jordan. "The wall light over her bed flickered. It was very strange. I am so sad and just can't believe she is gone." A little more than a year after Banks's death, another old and dear friend, George Russell, passed away on July 28, 2009. Fortunately Jordan had the opportunity to pay tribute to Russell the year before and celebrate his eighty-fifth birthday in September of 2008, when she sang "You Are My Sunshine" for the last time with Russell. It was also around this time that Jordan was having health problems of her own and finding herself feeling more exhausted than she had ever experienced before. She was diagnosed with high blood pressure and Atrial Fibrillation, or AFib. But of course, Jordan found humor in the situation by saying, "I hate when I get the irregular heartbeat because I can't figure out where the hell the time is. It's so erratic and just when I think I can snap the time it does something way out." More likely the stress of traveling and the grief she suffered over such emotional losses had taken their toll. But those of us who know Jordan are always amazed at her incredible ability to bounce back and forge on in the face of adversity. Vocalist and friend Souter fondly recalls:

> I saw her performing at the 2008 London Jazz Festival and she was very worried about her heart and not doing well at all. She was exhausted! So exhausted she had to sit down between songs. If you know Sheila you know how extraordinary that is. And yet there she was giving us everything in her performance. She didn't specifically talk about her heart problems at the time but she said things like, "If I don't see you again," and "Do what you love!" and by the end of the concert people were in tears. When she sings she is like an arrow heading straight to your core and it gets right to the heart of everyone—young and old—who cares to listen. Really listen. Listen even past the songs and the singing. Past technique, past all that, to the inner meaning and emotion. She really sings the heart of a song. And the effect on your heart is like a gong hitting a bell. And this is who she is as a person, too. She is the epitome of "who you are is how you play."

Every year since her eightieth birthday and even prior to that, she has celebrated with a performance in her beloved city, New York, or on the road. It was Dizzy's on her eightieth, London Jazz Festival (eighty-first), Jazz Standard (eighty-second), and Blue Note (eighty-third, eighty-fourth, eighty-fifth) with more planned in the future. Georgia Mancio captured Jordan's eighty-first birthday celebration at the London Jazz Festival on November 18, 2009 in a review for the *London Jazz News*:

> "It's quite something to stand up and convey a song. It looks easy," mused a member of the audience at the busy Bull's Head on Wednesday night, "but it's difficult to convey overly emotive songs, and it's difficult to convey jokey songs," he concluded, having taken part in Sheila Jordan's vocal workshop that preceded this gig in celebration of her 81st birthday. On a stage decorated with pink and purple balloons and large bouquets, Sheila continued the master class, conveying all of these emotions—and more—with ease, but never complacency.
>
> Halfway through the first set, she followed the deeply moving Jimmy Webb composition, "The Moon's a Harsh Mistress," (particularly poignant in its dedication to long-term musical collaborator and friend, Jeff Clyne, who had sadly passed away on Monday) with the witty parent/child characterization of Bobby Timmons' and Oscar Brown Jr's, "Dat Dere" sung to her own daughter.
>
> These two songs and these two moments represent everything that is typical about a Sheila Jordan performance: you will laugh, you will cry,

you will understand that this is an artist in which life and music constantly intertwine and are celebrated whatever the occasion.

Tonight, she described her childhood and early musical influences by way of a humorous blues; admired the artistry of Don Cherry in her lyrics to his song "Art Deco"; reminded us of her jazz lineage by quoting Sonny Rollins (The Touch of Your Lips), honouring Ella Fitzgerald (Lady Be Good), making joyous sense of nonsense (Ooh Pa Pi Da) and evoking friend, Charlie Parker, in her ever nimble and textural scat, innate and boundless musicality and indefatigable devotion to her calling.

It had clearly been a long day and recent ill health meant that she sat down when she needed to but in a way that heightened her relaxed authority over her sensitive band, Brian Kellock (piano), Kenny Ellis (bass) and Stuart Ritchie (drums). Theirs was a co-operative venture—she clearly appreciative of their musicianship and they in turn never overshadowing hers even when storming through a trio version of Hi Fly or brilliantly, if at first tentatively, scatting to order.

Towards the end of the night her voice started to crack slightly but her smile, energy and commitment to her audience never faded and showing her mettle she dug deeper on the closing blues. She told us "No matter who disappoints you in this music or life, just do it." It seemed everyone in the audience from the inspired singers to the old friends to the novice jazz club goers was lifted by that.

At the end of a beautiful rendition of Michel Legrand's "You Must Believe in Spring" she vamped: "Believe in Spring, believe in you, believe in me, believe in jazz."[14]

Jordan's love for the bass only slightly outmatched her love for music with string arrangements. Through the last two decades Jordan has found more opportunities to present her music with a string quartet, something she hopes to do for a future recording. In June of 2006 she performed with the Ambassadors of Light Jazz Trio and the Brattleboro Music Center String Quartet at the Latchis Theater as part of the Vermont Jazz Center production. Nicolas Dauplay reviewed the event on the website bluesandjazzsounds.com:

Sheila Jordan appeared in a rare setting on Saturday, June 3rd at 8:00 when she presented a concert at the Latchis Theater in Brattleboro, accompanied not only by a customary jazz trio, but by a string quartet as well. Jordan appeared with the jazz trio called "the Ambassadors of Light," and a string quartet made up of faculty from the Brattleboro Music Center. Also featured that evening was guest soloist, Howard Brofsky on cornet.

Sheila Jordan has often sang at events benefiting the Vermont Jazz Center. For a long time she had expressed a desire to perform using some beautiful string arrangements that had been prepared for her by the internationally acclaimed composer/pianist Alan Broadbent. Although she had

> recorded them in 1993 on a project called "Heart Strings," with the Hiraga Quartet, the opportunity to present the arrangements live in public has been all too rare. Knowing that Brattleboro was a community with a rich tradition of Western Classical Music, Sheila Jordan presented her concept of fusing jazz's language and sense of swing with the timbre of a classical string quartet and was met with a warm, positive response from members of both the VJC and the BMC.
>
> Sheila Jordan performed this concert with musicians she has known and played with for over a decade. Pianist Eugene Uman, bassist Jamie MacDonald and drummer Claire Arenius have worked for many years as Jordan's accompanists at the VJC Summer Workshop.
>
> They have worked with Sheila Jordan long enough to understand the delicate balance of working with a singer who has great sense of time and who emphasizes dynamic shading during the delivery of a song. The BMC String Quartet includes violinist, Kathy Andrew, Michelle Liechti, Claudia Campazzo on viola and cellist, Zon Eastes.
>
> The show started with an introduction by Sheila Jordan, the legendary singer took to the stage and lyrically introduced the trio with the great lyrical improvisations she is known for and then sang to the crowd already by this stage she had the crowd in the palm of her hand.
>
> Sheila Jordan opened the set with "Haunted Heart" and performed the song with a delicacy that could only be provided by this sweet marriage of Sheila Jordan's own voice and strings, this interpretation was breathtakingly beautiful. Already at this point it was clear that the strings were truly a natural complement to Sheila Jordan's gentle, translucent, slightly breathy voice. The next highlight came when Sheila Jordan sang "If I Should Lose You" and you could tell she knew most of Bird's solos as she voiced her way around the tune as if channeling Bird's sax. I must also point out the great exchange between Sheila Jordan and Howard Brofsky cornet where Sheila Jordan matched Howard's cornet with such playful ease. The medley of Inchworm/The Caterpillar Song was just wonderful and makes me regret that Sheila Jordan's CD "Heart Strings" is no longer available. The balance of the evening consisted of other songs from the elusive album as well as some of Sheila Jordan's favorites such as "So Wonderful to Be Me" and "All God's Children." I thoroughly enjoyed the concert and can only thank the artist that Sheila Jordan is for still giving so much during the show.[15]

A few years later Jordan had a couple of opportunities to perform with a string quartet, first on October 5, 2008, at the Locomotive Jazz Festival with Roberto Cipelli, Attilio Zanchi, Billy Drummond, and the Heart String Quartet, and once again at Dizzy's in New York in November. Jordan reminisces, "One of my most thrilling times was on my eightieth birthday when I was able to do the string quartet at Dizzy's, with the Steve Kuhn trio, thanks to Todd Barkin. The trio at that time was Steve, David Finck, and Billy Drummond, and the wonderful string quartet, all New York musicians except on the cello it was Harold Burston, who came down to do the conducting. He had arrangements that he had made especially for me to sing. I'll never forget that. It was just unbelievable and just a magical evening." Jordan also shares one of her many animal stories from the same evening:

> I was getting ready to go to the gig at Dizzy's. All of a sudden a mouse jumps out and starts dancing all over the floor, like running around, but not afraid of me. I said, "What the fuck are you doing here?" I was furious, because he's a mouse. He scared the hell out of me. So I chased him, and he went away. He disappeared. Then I sat down at the desk getting my music all in order, and all of a sudden, who's looking me in my face but this mouse. This mouse is looking me in my face. I took the staple gun and I threw it at him, and he ran. A few minutes later I got up to get ready to go out the door, and there he was, back dancing in the middle of the floor. He was like doing a little dance. I said, "What do you want?" And it was like he spoke to me. He said, "It's my birthday, too. Isn't your birthday on Mickey Mouse's birthday?" And here was this fucking mouse dancing and letting me know it was his birthday too. How could you kill a mouse like that?

Jordan made a special reconnection to her past when she was invited by Don Was, who was the new head of Blue Note Records, to perform in the Detroit All-Star Revue during the Concert of Colors at Orchestra Hall. Gary Graff of the *Oakland Press* writes:

> But Was is also expanding the Revue's role this year. Prior to the show he'll record with the artists who are performing and add those to a selection of Detroit jazz musicians who have recorded for Blue Note (such as Donald Byrd and Joe Henderson), then combine them on an album called "Detroit Jazz City" that will come out this fall, with proceeds going to Focus: Hope. "We just wanted to do something cool and do something for the City of Detroit and help Focus: Hope out and give these Detroit jazz musicians some international exposure," explains Was, who also produced a new album for Kris Kristofferson and was part of recent rehearsals with the Rolling Stones that were filmed for a 50th anniversary documentary about the band.[16]

It was during this concert that Was discovered the amazing rapport Jordan conjures up every time she performs on stage. After singing her songs, she was asked to sing one more and she chose "Sheila's Blues" with her autobiographical lyrics, many referring to her days in Detroit. At the conclusion the audience gave her a standing ovation, applauding wildly. As she exited the stage she saw Was standing there with a big grin and he told her, "Sheila, that was great! You were amazing." To which the eighty-four-year-old Jordan replied, tongue in cheek, "Do you think I'm gonna be a star, Don?"

Between 2006 and the present time, Jordan acquired numerous prestigious awards. In 2006 she received the Manhattan Association of Cabarets & Clubs (MAC) Lifetime Achievement Award for jazz, along with Clark Terry, Betty Buckley, and Donald Smith, at the Tribeca Performing Arts Center in New York City. According to the organization, the MAC Awards began in 1986, giving awards to those artists involved in the field of cabaret, jazz, and comedy who have made a significant contribution to live entertainment. Past winners include Liza Minnelli, Keely Smith, Sylvia Syms, Joan Rivers, Stiller & Meara, Cy Coleman, The Manhattan Transfer, Kenny Barron, and Bucky Pizzarelli, among others. According to the *CUNY Newswire* on April 10, 2006, "Ms. Jordan, who lives in Manhattan, said she was so shocked when she heard the news that she fell off her chair. 'I've been doing this music for so long, I don't expect anything except the joy I get from teaching and singing. I love to carry the message of jazz,' she said." Jordan received some other smaller and local awards that she feels proud of receiving as well. She remembers,

> I got an award from Detroit from the oldest jazz club, Baker's Keyboard Lounge for their seventieth year. It was supposedly the oldest jazz club in the United States, and I went there and performed and got that award. And that was kind of nice because Baker's used to be further downtown and I remember as a kid in Detroit trying to get into that club, and I couldn't get in there. Just like I couldn't get in the Club El Sino. I was too young. So, you know, these are clubs that meant something to me as a kid. So I have a wonderful plaque from that.

The next award was in January of 2007, when Jordan was honored with the Humanitarian Award at the IAJE (International Association of Jazz Educators) convention at the Hilton ballroom in New York. The now-defunct IAJE gave the Humanitarian Award to honor their members whose love for teaching transcends the usual academic environment and was presented to individuals with twenty or more years' involvement and efforts to perpetuate jazz, and the four elements of humanism: dedication, non-prejudice, altruism, and love. The award was decided through a nomination process and then selected by the IAJE Board of Directors. I sat between Jordan and her daughter as she waited to accept the award and she was truly thrilled. The room was buzzing with singers from all over the world in anticipation of Jordan making her acceptance speech. Jordan and I both had a good chuckle prior to her introduction; the projector showed her name misspelled: Shiela Jordan. She just laughed. It was appropriate for the good-humored chanteuse, who can find enjoyment in all situations. But then her name was called and she gave the following acceptance speech:

> My daughter was sitting there and she said, "are you excited?" and I said, "No, I'm nervous as hell!" I just want to tell you what an honor this is for me so I want to thank the IAJE for even considering me. I want to give a special thanks to Ellen Johnson, who was very, very strong in seeing that I got a nomination and she's been in my corner for so long, a wonderful artist herself. Oh my God, I want to thank George Russell for putting his money together and recording me in the first place. And I want to thank my dear friends and I want to thank all the wonderful musicians that I work with and all the wonderful musicians I don't work with. And especially to Mr. Steve Kuhn, he's very special to me. I also want to thank, and you are part of this plaque and every time I look at it I will look at you all, all of the wonderful, wonderful young singers and older singers that I have worked with since 1978 when I was first at City College. So you're part of this and I thank all of you wonderful young singers for believing in me and helping me to learn how to teach. And most of all I want to thank, you know who [sings] *Charlie Parker was his name and bebop music was his fame, the Bird* [stops singing]. Thank you.

The next award came in 2008 when Jordan became the recipient of the Mary Lou Williams Women in Jazz Award. The award was presented during the thirteenth annual Women in Jazz Festival at the Kennedy Center in Washington, D.C., on May 16, captured in a review in *All About Jazz* by John Birchard:

> Next up was the singer Sheila Jordan, who was presented the 2008 Mary Lou Williams Women in Jazz Award for her contributions to the music over the years. She joins such other artists as Jane Ira Bloom, the late Patti Bown, Toshiko Akiyoshi, Marian McPartland and Melba Liston as winners of the award. Jordan described herself as "seventy-nine-and-a-half" years old, but "feeling fourteen."
>
> Jordan eased into "Lucky to Be Me" by improvising on the lyric to thank the Kennedy Center and Billy Taylor, artistic director for jazz at the Center, for honoring her. Her intonation is a little shaky these days, but she overcomes it by hitting the notes she's capable of and half-talking the rest. She was joined on stage by a stellar trio—Steve Kuhn on piano, David Finck on bass and the drummer Billy Drummond, a group certainly capable of carrying a set by themselves. Jordan was engaging and funny in her between-songs commentary, a sort of stream-of-consciousness series of ad libs that delighted the Terrace Theater audience. Following the Ivan Lins melody, "The Promise of You," Jordan had fun with Bobby Timmons' "Dat Dere." Her tribute to Miles Davis began with her own seemingly

> improvised lyric about Miles' ballad playing and segued into "It Never Entered My Mind."
>
> Jordan then introduced from the audience her former student Theo Blackman, who joined her on stage to sing "Every Time We Say Goodbye," which Jordan followed with a slow, heart-felt reading of "For All We Know." The two embraced and exchanged kisses, their obvious rapport with each other generating a warm bath of applause.
>
> Jordan closed her set with a blues that featured more apparently spontaneous lyrics including thanks to her accompanists, the Kennedy Center, her late friend Shirley Horn—a Washington native—and the audience for supporting live music. What Sheila Jordan may have lost over the years in vocal equipment, she has more than made up for in stage presence and infectious personality. It was good to be reminded of those who labor in the shadows of little recognition, but who deserve far greater appreciation. Sheila Jordan is surely one of them.[17]

Jordan is always quick to point out those who deserve recognition as well. "I was so pleased to get that award," says Jordan, "and Dr. Billy Taylor was sitting out there and he was very instrumental in my receiving that award. He's always been a strong supporter of mine throughout the years, helping me in whatever way he can. He's been wonderful to me, and a true friend. He and I go back a long time when I first met him years ago up at Minton's After Hours when Charlie Parker was still alive and all those great jazz musicians. Billy used to be up there. He was young. Hey, so was I! So I'm very grateful to him."

However, it was on January 10, 2012, that Jordan received her most prestigious award to date, the National Endowment for the Arts (NEA) Jazz Masters Award, the highest honor the United States bestows on jazz artists. Since 1982 the NEA has chosen a select number of living legends whom they feel have made exceptional contributions to the advancement of jazz. In its thirtieth year, the NEA recognized five musicians besides Jordan, including Jack DeJohnette, Von Freeman, Charlie Haden, and Jimmy Owens. The recipients receive a $25,000 grant and the opportunity to perform in a concert ceremony at Jazz at Lincoln Center in New York. Jordan remembers,

> I was just home from a tour in Toronto when the phone rang, so I put down my bag and ran to answer it. There was a long pause. The guy finally spoke and said "I would like to speak to Sheila Jordan." And I was tired and impatient because I really thought it was one of those telemarketing calls. So I was very short and I told him "Yes, this is Sheila Jordan What do you want?" He said "This is Wayne Brown from the National Endowment for the Arts and I'm calling to tell you have been selected to receive the Jazz Masters Award." I was in shock and said "Oh Wayne, I thought you were

> one of those Telemarketing guys." I laughed and so did he. I hung up and practically fell off the chair. I was in shock.

On that evening each of the 2012 NEA Jazz Masters was introduced by a short previously prepared video. Jon Hendricks, in a sailor hat and shiny indigo suit, brought out the equally irrepressible Sheila Jordan, who reminisced about life-changing experiences: hearing Charlie Parker's ReBoppers on the jukebox, studying with Lennie Tristano.[18] Then Jordan accepted her award with the following speech: "What a great thrill it is for me to be receiving this highest honor for the music I've loved most of my life. Thanks to the National Endowment for the Arts, my mentor, Charlie Parker, and the tremendous help from George Russell and Dr. Billy Taylor. I humbly accept this prestigious Jazz Masters Award." Brian Pace of the *Pace Report* writes:

> One of the most important jazz events took place at Jazz at Lincoln Center during the week of APAP last week. The 2012 National Endowment for the Arts held their 30th anniversary of the Jazz Masters Ceremony and Concert to a sold-out crowd. The event pays tribute to the architects of jazz music both living and deceased. More importantly, the NEA gives the current inductees as well as music programs and centers all over the country, grants and funding to continue the legacy of providing the community jazz programming and education to keep the music viable to public. Including this year's inductees, the NEA has celebrated the work and lives of 128 jazz musicians, awarded more than 2,400 jazz grants, and given over 32 million dollars over the last 30 years. A very important feat for the music that very seldom gets the notoriety or praise like other American black music such as hip-hop, soul, and the blues.
>
> This year's 2012 NEA Jazz Masters inductees include: Sheila Jordan, vocalist and educator; Von Freeman, tenor saxophonist and bandleader; Jack DeJohnette, drummer and pianist; Jimmy Owens, trumpeter, educator, and advocate; and Charlie Haden, bassist and bandleader.[19]

Jordan fondly recalls, "It was a wonderful day with lots of past jazz masters present. BMI sponsored a lunch for all of us and then the evening was fantastic. I sang an Ornette Coleman tune with Ron Carter playing bass and two of the other musicians who were being honored, Jack DeJohnette and Jimmy Owens. Charlie Hayden and Von Freeman would have played too but they were both ill at the time and couldn't attend." Jazz journalist Howard Mandel writes in *Jazz Beyond Jazz*: "Here are some highlights of what I saw and heard: . . . Irrepressible class of 2012 Jazz Master Sheila Jordan, 83, playfully getting an audience to sing along with her, 'Bird!' and returning to scat with '12 JM Jimmy Owens playing flugelhorn on Ornette Coleman's jaunty "When Will The Blues Leave?"—driven by '12 JM Jack DeJohnette, tethered by long-ago-named JM bassist Ron Carter, and with Ornette himself (a JM of course) listening from a front row."[20] This thrilling evening and being honored among the jazz luminaries that she so admires was one of the highlights of her career.

Meanwhile on the West Coast, the California Jazz conservatory (formerly known as the Jazzschool) vocal director Laurie Antonioli organized a special tribute concert to Jordan. The event was also a benefit concert for the Mark Murphy Vocal Scholarship given annually by the conservatory. Jordan had known Antonioli for many years, inviting her in 2002 to be one of the guest professors for the program at the KUG University in Graz, Austria. Many of the Bay Area's top jazz singers and instrumentalists were on hand to honor Jordan, performing songs in dedication to her mentorship and inspiration. Prerecorded messages were part of a video tribute from Jordan's many friends and students who could not be in attendance, including Mark Murphy, Theo Bleckmann, Kate McGarry, Alan Pasqua, Jay Clayton, Andrea Wolper, Peter Eldridge, Judi Silvano, Joe Lovano, Valerie Tichacek, Connie Crothers, Billy Drummond, Tessa Souter, and others who followed an amazing video of Sheila's life produced by videographer Jeff Foster. Vocalist Kitty Margolis remembers with affection,

> Still flying after Sheila Jordan Tribute last night. Laurie Antonioli, astute mistress of ceremonies, kicked it off with two stunning arrangements after the moving film by Jeff Foster and Ellen Johnson. Then came soulful eighty-three-year-old Ed Reed, the peerless Madeline Eastman, myself and last year's "Mark Murphy" scholarship recipient, Kyra Gordon. After Jazzschool founder Susan Muscarella and Laurie bestowed the 2013 award on Kathy Blackburn, the magnificent eighty-four-year-old Sheila gave a breathtaking performance, showing us once again what it's really all about. The house exploded with love for her. I feel truly blessed to be a part of this extraordinary family of jazz singers.

Antonioli adds, "I can only hope to be as hip, with it, energetic, and vocally intact as my lovely friend Sheila Jordan is at the age of eighty-four. Plus, we went shopping together and that woman has an eye for nice things. Just walks into a store and finds the coolest stuff—fast. A national treasure who knows how to shop. My kinda gal." Although the awards have finally come to Jordan late in life, some feel that she should receive more accolades: "I don't think she's received the due she deserves because I've seen firsthand what she has done for this music," remarks Coryelle Kramer. However, Jordan does not echo that sentiment; she says in her typical humble fashion:

> I'm not as successful as most people think I am, not in America anyway. But I don't care! I never wanted to be, you know, "a star." That's not my purpose, that's not my calling. My calling is to be a messenger of this music,

> and I'm very happy being that. I'm very thrilled with these awards I've won and the recognition that I've gotten. I used to just put all my awards in the closet and my daughter got very upset. She said, "Mom, you earned those. Put them up on the wall." I told her, "That looks like I'm bragging." She told me, "Brag."

Jordan was enjoying a period of recognition not only as a jazz singer but also as a musician who had held her own in a primarily male-dominated arena and business. "With few exceptions, before the mid-1980s, women were always second-class citizens in jazz, the most macho of all the arts."[21] On top of being marginalized as a woman, singers held their own even as they were devalued among jazz instrumentalists due to a lack of "learned" musical knowledge. Singers quite often didn't get the kind of theoretical training as instrumentalists, nor were they part of the ensemble learning process, unless, like Jordan, they made strong efforts to participate. Today, there are better opportunities for singers, but the stigma of being a woman in jazz still remains. "Long after women became accepted as writers and, to a lesser extent, as visual artists, women in music—classical, jazz, and pop—faced the nearly insuperable barrier of male chauvinism."[22] "Like elusive and untranscribable blue notes, women in jazz exist, invisible, in-between the spaces, creating voice through subversion and speaking in ways that are nearly impossible to transcribe into a discourse traditionally owned by men, and where questions of gender are nearly always overshadowed by questions of race."[23] Friend and drummer Ra-Kalam agrees: "She had tough times and I'm sure some of it had to do with her being a woman too. I know how men can be and musicians can be worse, dogging women, relating to them only sexually and not giving them respect as people or as musicians with minds. For example she was the only woman at the NEA awards." Although Jordan had to deal with her share of gender disparity, she never allowed it to get in the way of the music. Instead she refined her skills to the point where male musicians viewed her as an equal on the bandstand. Those skills included having a clear sense of time, a command of the melody, an acute ability to hear the harmonic structure, superior interpretive skills, and professionalism on and off stage. Billy Drummond adds admiringly, "It's inspiring to work with her because she's always on her 'A' game. She's welcoming to the musicians. You feel comfortable, the music is great and she sings great. I've never seen an audience that she didn't have in the palm of her hands. She's a real pro."

The other pioneers for women in jazz such as Lil Hardin Armstrong, Mary Lou Williams, Shirley Horn, Betty Carter, Anita O'Day, and so many countless others paved the way for generations of women. And although gender issues still exist, at least women like Jordan had the courage to make and share their journey. So it is appropriate that Jordan should receive the

Lil Hardin Armstrong and Mary Lou Williams awards, and that she lent her voice to projects with other female musical talents, such as Carla Bley and Jane Bunnett, and even Lennie Tristano, who according to Jordan always supported women musicians. Aside from the gender discrimination, Jordan surely endured in the jazz community; she also encountered repercussions of being female in an era when women were limited in a myriad of other ways. In retrospect it truly is astonishing that Jordan overcame the many obstacles she encountered throughout her lifetime without the kind of bitterness that can accompany these types of experiences. It would seem that for the latter part of her life, ageism would be the least of her challenges.

• 7 •

The Bird

> "There's nothing in life that will ever have the meaning for me or can give me a thrill like hearing Charlie Parker."
>
> —Sheila Jordan's lyrics to "Quasimodo" by Charlie Parker

When Jordan was fourteen years of age, Charlie Parker became her self-chosen guru, savior, and mentor. Parker, otherwise known as "Bird," was one of bebop's primary architects and was a significant influence on generations of musicians including Jordan. Sonny Rollins shared his admiration:

> Well, of course, he was my prophet. I had other idols, but Charlie Parker's music seemed to fit the time that I came up so it was great when I first saw him. There were a lot of us that were big Charlie Parker fans. I remember he was working on Fifty-Second Street and when he got off for intermission there would be four or five people, myself included, who would sort of follow him around. So the poor guy couldn't even get a few minutes rest between shows. There were a whole bunch of fans that were really loyal and he was always such a great person. He was so generous to me and nice to other people.

The music seemed to attract a generation ready for a new sound and who intuitively understood that this pied piper could show them the way. According to Kenny Burrell, "Charlie Parker was very much grounded in the past with the blues, etc., but he also had the presence of what was going on and he was pushing the envelope for the future. Now, this happens not just for jazz, this happens in all great art. He was the voice of the new movement and we all felt he was the voice of the new movement because he really moved us in terms of his music."

Parker's music instantly captured the imagination and heart of Jordan, who was struggling to find her own voice during her difficult teenage years. "I fell in love with Bird's music immediately," recounts Jordan. "I said to myself, oh my God, that's the music I've waited to hear and to sing. I'll dedicate my life to this music. And I have been a devotee ever since that day. On a wall at my upstate New York home is a framed copy I received as a gift from a wonderful friend and artist, Peter Bodge, of the 78 record I first heard, 'Now's the Time' by Charlie Parker and his Reboppers. That recording changed my life." Although at that time she had never heard any vocalists doing the music of Parker and there were no lyrics to her knowledge, she was convinced that this was the music she was born to sing. She approached the songs instinctively by singing the line, or melody. She didn't try to formulate the sound of a saxophone or any other instrument, but instead sang the melodies as she interpreted them through her own voice. "I didn't learn the songs with the intention of becoming a professional singer," Jordan comments, "I did it because I absolutely loved the music and was compelled to learn it. I did it to keep my sanity, to keep my voice alive, and because I needed to sing this music. I had to and I didn't care whether anybody ever heard me or not. It didn't matter. All that mattered was the music."

Jordan chased the Bird all the way to New York in the early 1950s, as she says, "just to be near his music." Jordan had met Parker in Detroit when he came through town along with her vocal trio friends Mitchell and Spight. Parker easily recognized his loyal fan once they connected again in New York.

> I told Bird that the reason I moved from Detroit to New York was because I needed to be near his music. He laughed (he had a fantastic laugh), and he said, "Yeah, I remember you, you're the kid with the million-dollar ears." Then he started singing the song "Parker's Refrain" with lyrics by Leroy Mitchell. "Can't you see what this could be / The way I feel for you could be music / You know that you've got my heart / Don't turn me down or tear us apart / Just take me dear and make me hear a Parker refrain like . . . (instrumental improvisation here)." We only sang it to him one time, so it was incredible that he remembered it. I told him, "I can't believe you remember that song," and he just humbly said, "Yeah."

Mitchell remembers it this way: "I wrote a tune for Bird called 'Parker's Refrain.' Bird said he liked it. He told me to write it out, so the next time he came I wrote it out and I gave it to him. And every time I talked to Bird I asked him, 'Bird, when are you going to cut it?' He says, 'Oh, one of these days I'll cut it.' But he never forgot the beginning of it."

Jordan and Parker would see each other often at jazz venues and over time their musical relationship blossomed into one of mutual trust and affection. It was after Jordan married Duke Jordan, Parker's pianist for many years, that Parker found a friend in his longtime fan. "So when I started having sessions at my loft, these two artists, Harvey Cropper and Arthur Hardie, along with one of our mutual friends, Percy Knight, brought Bird up one night. Bird had never been to my loft before, and he said to me, 'I remember you. So this is where you live.' So there he was, and he played his horn. After that we became very good friends. It wasn't a romantic thing; he was just like my big brother," Jordan clarifies.

> He's the one who turned me on to Stravinsky and Béla Bartók. He'd come to the loft with these records and say, "I have something I want to play for you. You'll dig this." So Bird would come by and would open my ears to new music or play the music I love, jazz. I had a little day bed and I'd called it "Bird's bed" because when he'd get tired he'd come up to my loft and take a rest. I think he felt it was a safe place for him, and of course I always loved having him there.

Duke and Bird had gigs called "cocktail sips," for which ladies from the black community would get together all decked out in their Sunday hats, prepare wonderful food, and dance. They would hire musicians to play, and quite often it was Charlie Parker's group. "Many times Bird would have me get up and sing a song at the gigs and it was wonderful," says Jordan. "Bird would kid me and say, 'you haven't lost those million-dollar ears.'" During that time, Duke Jordan was doing heroin and, unbeknown to Jordan, having affairs with other women while disappearing for weeks at a time. It was during these difficult times that Parker looked out for her and would come by the loft to make sure she was safe and well.

Much has been written about Charlie Parker's heroin addiction, which is not easily separated from his music. Jordan has her own view of Bird's affliction and the torment it caused in his life. She and Parker's common-law wife, Chan, each had to deal with her husband's drug addiction, and each ended her marriage due to the negative impact it had on their lives. Jordan believes that it was Bird's genius, his visionary personality, and particularly his sensitivity that probably led him into addiction. According to her, Parker had a strong need to be accepted, and despite his fame, the lifelong racial prejudice and discrimination he faced made it hard for him to find full recognition as a musician and man. Parker was often misunderstood, as was his advanced modern music. In September 1947, for example, *DownBeat* referred to Parker as a "weird wizard" and a "high priest" and described his "other-world look," perhaps alluding generally to primitivist notions of irrational black creativity and more specifically to Parker's reputation for drug abuse.[1] In the years that Jordan knew Parker, she saw clearly how it pained him to see others, who looked up to him musically, seemingly also follow him into addiction. "I didn't think about Bird as a junkie," she explains. "I never called him a junkie, never thought of him that way. He was a great man and musical genius who unfortunately had this cunning, baffling, powerful disease. I don't know that he believed he was a musical genius, and maybe it was just too much for him that everybody was trying to imitate him, everybody was putting him on this pedestal. Everybody tried to be like Bird. So I guess they figured, 'Oh well, if we shoot heroin we'll be like Bird,' which is not the way it worked at all."

It was true that many of the musicians who followed Parker considered his use of drugs a vehicle to his innovations or had such an admiration for him that in their mimicking of his life they followed the same path of using drugs.

> I had a drug habit, [relates Rollins], and Charlie Parker probably taught me because he used drugs. If Charlie Parker uses drugs then drugs must be all right, you know. So I got a habit and I was in pretty bad shape there for quite a while. Charlie Parker and my mother were the two people who got me off drugs. Maybe even Charlie Parker more so because although I wanted to do it for my mother, Charlie Parker was in my world of music. He conveyed that to me in a very profound way one day when I was doing a recording session with him. And it changed my life because it was then I realized that I had to stop, and I did stop. I went to rehab and I was so anxious to get out and tell him that I got his message but, of course, he passed away just before I got out. So Charlie Parker changed my life.

Jordan remembers,

> one time Bird came up to the loft and Duke was home, and Duke was nodding out on the couch on heroin. Bird took one look at him and yelled, "Jesus, man, didn't you learn anything from me at all?" I'll never forget that. That's all he said, because he was so disgusted at Duke. Bird got really unhappy when people tried to imitate him to the point where they took drugs. I think what Charlie Parker really wanted to do was show musicians a new way of expressing themselves musically, and he just happened to be an addict. So not only did they try to do this new music; they also tried to be like him by taking drugs. And I know firsthand that it really bothered him when he saw someone doing that. Bird even tried to teach me not to use drugs. He always said, "Don't ever do this, because it's not good and will only lead you to disaster." Of course, I didn't listen, and later on his message came back to me strong and clear.

Charlie Parker died on March 12, 1955. Though he was only thirty-four, Jordan opines that he looked as if he were in his sixties. Although the drug addiction had robbed him of his youthful appearance, his music and message remain, inspiring jazz aficionados from all walks of life. Jordan sings beautiful tributes to him through her original lyrics to Parker's song "Quasimodo" and a song she wrote especially for him called "The Bird." Her concerts always feature references to the memory of her best friend and jazz guru. "The last time I saw Bird," she says,

> he was at one of the clubs in Detroit when I was there visiting my relatives. I went to the club to see him that night, and it was amazing. Skeeter Spight, Leroy Mitchell, Willie Bolar, and I were all at the concert. When Bird saw me he leaped off the stage, took me outside in the back, and asked me what I was doing there. I said, "Oh, I thought I'd give you a surprise." He said, "Well, that's a wonderful surprise," and he gave me a big hug and a big kiss and asked me how I was feeling because at the time I was a couple of months pregnant with my daughter, Tracey. And that's the last time I saw Bird. That was in December 1954, and in March of the following year my dearest friend, Charlie Parker, was gone.
>
> I brought flowers to his grave when I did a concert at a women's festival in Kansas City. Originally he was buried somewhere else, but they moved his remains and put them next to his mother; so that's where he is now, next to his mother.

At Jordan's home in Middleburgh, New York, she has a nailed a replica on her barn of the street sign for "Charlie Parker Place." She received the sign as a gift for singing at the first Charlie Parker Festival in Tompkins Square Park, which is located between Avenues A and B on the Lower East Side. Jordan views Parker as a spiritual man who left us all with a gift from God: his extraordinary music and saxophone virtuosity.

> I remember one time when he was at my house and there was thunder and lightning. He was talking on the phone to his mother, and he said, "Do you hear that, Mom? That's God speaking." So I believe that in his heart he was a very religious man who believed in a higher power. I *know* he believed in a higher power in order to play the way he did. No one will ever know exactly what bothered Bird. You know, geniuses, a lot of times, leave very early, because sometimes the responsibility of what they know is too much to handle. I believe Charlie Parker was put here to leave his message to anyone who was ready to receive it, and then he flew away.

Jordan is often disappointed when Parker's musical contributions are shrouded due to the attention focused on his drug abuse. She wants people to understand that he was much more than his drug addiction and that there were contributing factors to his illness. Says Jordan,

> I finally saw the movie *Bird*, and I was very disturbed by it because it wasn't Bird's complete story. I felt they dealt too much with the drugs and not

> enough with his musical genius and what he contributed to the music of this country and the world. Forest Whitaker is a fantastic actor but Bird never leaned over like that or kept his head down. He always stood upright—he wasn't hiding—and if he was sad, he didn't show it aside from in his music. It just wasn't Bird and I know because I knew Bird quite well. I think anybody seeing that movie would have the wrong impression of him. The first thing they might think about would not be this great genius of jazz who invented bebop but instead they would just think of him as just a junkie. I sing this tribute to Bird called "The Bird" where I humorously refer to this and then I go into my other tribute to him called "Tribute" based on his song "Quasimodo" with the "Embraceable You" chord changes.

The Bird

The Bird, the Bird, the Bird, the Bird
Charlie Parker was his name.
The Bird, the Bird, the Bird
You heard it every day
Bird would have his way

So they made a movie about Charlie Parker
And they called it "Bird."
Thank you, Mister Clint Eastwood for making my day
By letting Charlie Parker play

But what happened to Roy Haynes
What about Tommy Potter
Miles Davis, and my ex-husband Duke Jordan?

Well, Mister Eastwood, That's okay.
I don't get alimony anyway.
No movie or book could ever really capture Bird.
Charlie Parker was his name
And bebop music was his fame.
The Bird.

Jordan brightens when she shares her many stories about Parker, revealing their special understanding and his humor and kindness to her and others. She reminds us about his deep care for her when she tells the story about when she was pregnant with her daughter, Tracey: "Bird would always send a car to take me to hear him wherever he was playing and then take me back home again. That's the kind of man he was. He might have been a junkie, but that didn't affect his feelings for people. There are a lot of guys who aren't junkies who would never even consider doing that for a pregnant woman. But Bird did." The following stories, recounted in her own words, are some of Jordan's favorite memories from her years of friendship with Charlie.

Being the Bird

"One night Bird came to one of the loft music sessions we had at my place. He had his horn, and he asked, 'Is there a piano player in the house?' And I said not yet but maybe later. He said, 'Well, I have to play now.' So he played a half-hour solo, and everyone was mesmerized. And then he just packed up his horn and left. No wonder they named him the Bird."

The Bird Meets the Bird

I had a little bird, a parakeet that I called Tori. I named him Tori because one of my artist friends, Harvey Cropper, said that Tori means bird in Japanese. I never let the bird out of his cage when anybody came over because he was a real pain in the ass and would land on your face if you were lying down. I taught him to say, "Hello, Bird, hello, sweetheart," but I would always put him in the cage when anybody came because he wouldn't talk very much when he was in his cage.

So, this one time, Charlie came up to my loft during the daytime. He knocked on my door and said, "Hey, are you home?"

I said, "Yeah, who is it?"

He said, "It's Bird."

I said, "Oh yeah, cool. Just a minute, though, I have to get the bird in the cage because otherwise he'll be jumping all over you."

Bird said, "No, that's okay. I don't really care."

So I couldn't get Tori in the cage, but I let Bird in anyway. Bird said, "Can I just rest for a few minutes?"

I said, "Of course." There was a couch that I called "Bird's bed," and I said, "You know where your bed is."

So Bird went over to his bed and lay down, and all of a sudden my bird, Tori, flew over to him. I said, "Oh shit, look, the bird's on him."

Bird was almost asleep, and my bird, Tori, said, "Hello, Bird."

Bird jumped up because it shocked him. He said to me, "What are you, a ventriloquist?" I said, "No, I didn't say that. Tori said that." He said, "Of course that was you."

I said, "No, that was Tori."

He said, "Oh yeah, sure." So he lay back down again, but this time he was a little bit more awake. My bird, Tori, landed right on the side of his shoulder, looked right up in his mouth, and said, "Hello, Bird."

Bird leaped up and said, "Goddamn, that bird *does* talk."

I said, "I told you."

He loved that, because my bird was very clear when he spoke. Tori kept jumping around and saying, "Hello, Bird, hello, sweetheart."

Bird, needless to say, didn't get a rest that day. He laughed, gave me a kiss on my cheek, and said, "I'll see you later." And he left.

Looking Out for His Sister

One time I was having a session at my loft and I went out for something. When I came back, I couldn't get in because there were so many people there. I remember saying to everyone, "Can I get into my own home, please?" I laughed because the place was so packed with people, not just inside but also on the staircase. Virginia, my painter friend who lived on the other side of the loft from me, had her place full, too.

So Bird came up, and he started telling people to get out. He said, "You can stay, you go. You stay, you go."

I said, "Bird, this is my loft. What are you doing?"

He said, "I'll tell you later. You stay, you go. You stay, you go." And he kept doing this.

I finally said, "What was that all about? Would you please tell me?"

He asked me if I'd seen this foreign movie.

I said, "What movie?"

He said, "In the movie there's an ad for a job interview for a stenographer in Italy. So all these people go to apply for this job. There's so many of them that the stairs collapse and some of them die. So I'm worried about you; I don't want this floor collapsing with so many people."

I guess he was just looking out for his little sister.

For the Birds

I went with my husband, Duke, to Philadelphia where he was doing a gig with Bird one weekend. We got there and everyone was there: Mingus on bass, Duke on piano, and a drummer that I don't recall. Bird disappeared after the first tune or so, and the owner came up and wanted to know where he was. All of the musicians said they didn't know.

So the club owner walks out of the club and sees Bird on the other side of the street, getting drugs. The owner says, "Hey, what are you doing out here? You're supposed to be up there playing. How come you aren't playing?"

Bird says, "I'm checking out the rhythm section from over here."

The owner says, "I'm paying you to play, so get in there and play!"

And Bird says, "Do you know who you're talking to? You're talking to the Bird."

And the club owner says, "I don't give a fuck if I'm talking to the eagle. I'm paying you to play, so get in there and play."

Bird told everyone the story after the gig, and he was laughing about it. He was always in a better mood after his fix.

Birdland Refuses the Bird

I was with Charlie one of the times that they refused to let him into the club that was named for him, Birdland. That evening we were just walking and enjoying each other's company, while headed in the direction of Broadway. Bird suggested that we go to Birdland, and I agreed.

So we went to Birdland, and the guy at the door (I think it was Oscar Goodstein, who was also Bird's manager at one time) said, "You can't come in here, Bird. You're not dressed properly."

I'll never forget the look on Bird's face. He turned to me and said, "Can you believe this? They name a club after me and they won't even let me in." And I said, "Yeah, I can believe it. Come on, Bird, let's go."

They refused him because he had a T-shirt on instead of a shirt and tie. I was quite upset, but I didn't show it. So Bird and I went somewhere else and got something to eat, and then he took me home and went on home, too. It was unbelievable to me that they wouldn't let Bird into his own place.

Bird's Bed

Bird came pounding on my door one morning at 5:00 a.m. He woke me up, and of course I was upset because I had to go to work.

He said, "Oh, I saw the fire truck outside and I thought there was a fire in your loft! I was worried about you and Virginia."

But I knew it was just an excuse to come up to the loft and take a rest. He had been high and up all night, and he needed a place to sleep. So I said to Bird, "If you need a place to take a rest, you know you can always stay here."

Bird on a Horse

Bird supposedly, which I hear is true, had a horse. He used to ride this horse, and kept it at a stable near Central Park, on Central Park West. I heard that one time he tried to ride his horse into a bar where a lot of the jazz musicians hung out. They threw him out and told him he couldn't bring the horse in there.

So one time Bird came by my place and said, "Let's go visit my horse." I said, "Okay."

We got in a cab and went from my loft, which was at Twenty-Sixth Street between Seventh and Eighth Avenue, to somewhere on the Upper West Side.

Bird said, "I'm going upstairs to visit my horse. You stay in the cab."

I said, "Oh, can't I go?"

He said, "No, no. I'm going up to see my horse. You just stay in the cab."

So I said, "Oh, okay." And I was kind of disappointed, because I wanted to see the horse.

He was up there for a long time. I thought, Well, should I just get out of this cab and go home, or what?

While I'm deciding what to do, he comes out and gets in the cab. He said to the cab driver, "Okay, take us to Sixth Street and Avenue A." That's where Bird lived.

So then Bird said, "So let's go to my house and see my family."

Again I said, "Okay."

When we got to Sixth Street and Avenue A and got ready to get out of the cab, Bird said, "How much is that, driver?" And it turned out to be quite a lot of money; I can't remember exactly how much.

Bird said, "Okay." He pulls out a checkbook and says to the cab driver, "What's your name?"

The driver said, "Why?"

Bird said, "Well, I'm going to write you a check."

The cab driver said, "Oh no, you're not. I don't take checks."

In those days it was unheard of to pay for a taxi with anything other than cash. So we had to go to the corner bar; I think it was on Sixth Street and Avenue B. Bird went in and they cashed his check, and then he came out and paid the cab driver.

And after spending a few minutes at Bird's house checking out the beautiful wallpaper with pictures of birds in and out of cages, which is still there today, I thought I never did get to see Bird's horse. I guess I believed we were going to see his real horse.

Jordan and the Bird shared a special bond, connected as they were to the music, as well as a deep mutual love that remains with Jordan to this day. "I felt that Bird was my brother," she reminisces.

I could lean on him. And beyond that he was, and still is, this magnificent musical guru. He is a type of spiritual or meditation inspiration that I feel I can even pray to because I know he'll help me. Sometimes when things are rough I do call on Bird, because that's how much he meant to me. His music touched me so deeply, every single note he played, that it was an unbelievable awakening to life and what music was all about. He encouraged me for all these years to do the music the way I hear it and feel it, and not to worry about what other people think. The point is, I'm singing what I believe and what I feel, and that may not always appeal to everyone.

I can still hear Bird's message to me: "Sing what you feel, even though some people might not dig it. You feel it, you mean it, and that's the important thing." Bird taught me that, and I'll never forget it.

Tribute/Quasimodo

At times I wonder where my life would be
If I never heard the music of Bird back when I just a kid.
I listened to each precious note floating out of his horn so many years ago.
What a treat it used to be for me to hear him;
The thrill of being near him.
I lived for every song that he played from his heart.
Bird brought a special world to me by leading the way.
I've learned to live my life from the dues that he paid.

He turned me on to sounds I never heard before
By putting all those magical notes into every single phrase.
Somehow I find it rather strange knowing that there are those of us
Who really love him, while so many aren't even aware of his name.
I'm so blessed that I grew up spending all of those wonderful years
Surrounded by the joy that he gave.
There's nothing in life that will ever have the meaning for me
Or can give me a thrill like hearing Charlie Parker.

Lyrics by Sheila Jordan as sung to Charlie Parker's song, "Quasimodo"

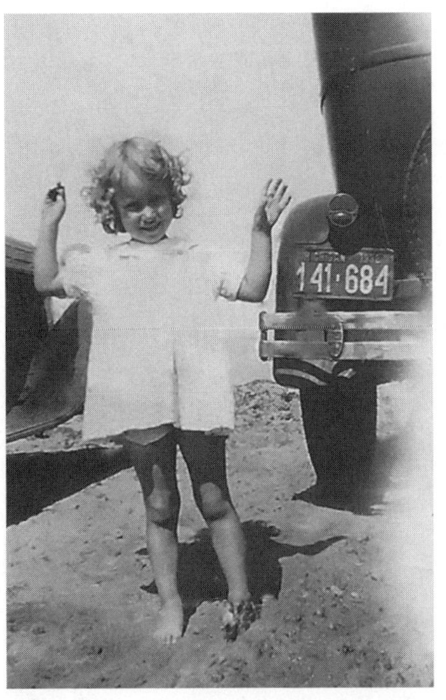

Jordan, age 3, 1931. Courtesy of Jordan Family and Friend Photos.

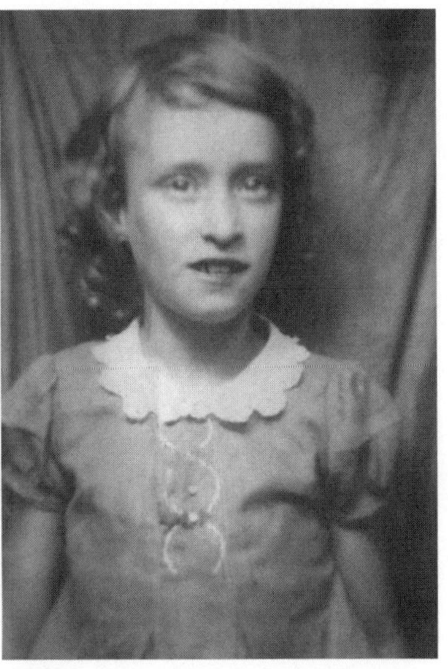

Jordan, age 4, 1932. Courtesy of Jordan Family and Friend Photos.

Jordan, Commerce High School graduation, Detroit, 1946. Courtesy of Jordan Family and Friend Photos.

Jordan's grandfather, Walter Earl Hull. Courtesy of Jordan Family and Friend Photos.

Jordan's mother, Maggie Hull, and grandmother, Irene Hull, 1920s. Courtesy of Jordan Family and Friend Photos.

Jordan's mother, Maggie, and Aunt Bobbie having fun, 1930s. Courtesy of Jordan Family and Friend Photos.

Jordan with (from left to right) Grandmother Irene, Aunt Esther, Jordan, Aunt Rowena "Bobbie," Aunt Henrietta, and Maggie. Courtesy of Jordan Family and Friend Photos.

Jordan in her early twenties, around 1948. Courtesy of Jordan Family and Friend Photos.

Jordan (middle) with Doug Watkins (left) and Barry Harris (right), 1953, at 52nd St. Club in New York City. Courtesy of Jordan Family and Friend Photos.

Tracey Jordan at one year old at her birthday party, 1956. Courtesy of Jordan Family and Friend Photos.

Jordan with Tracey, about 1958. Courtesy of Jordan Family and Friend Photos.

Jordan with Tracey at the park, about 1958. Courtesy of Jordan Family and Friend Photos.

Jordan at Jones Beach with her friend Carol Thompson, New York, 1959. Courtesy of Jordan Family and Friend Photos.

Jordan with Tracey, about 1963. Courtesy of Jordan Family and Friend Photos.

Jordan typing at Doyle Dane Bernbach, 1960s. Courtesy of Jordan Family and Friend Photos.

Debut album cover for Portrait of Sheila *on Blue Note, 1962. Courtesy of Blue Note Records.*

Jordan with Dizzy Gillespie in Oslo, Norway, early 1970s. Photographer Randi Hultin, courtesy of Jordan Family and Friend Photos.

Jordan singing at Lennie Tristano's funeral, 1978. Courtesy of Jordan Family and Friend Photos.

Jordan with poet Robert Creeley, 1983. Courtesy of Jordan Family and Friend Photos.

Jordan with (left to right) Harvie S (Swartz), Ra-Kalam (Bob Moses), and Steve Kuhn, Keystone Korner, San Francisco, 1981. Photo by Brian McMillen.

Jordan with best friend Marria Elizabeth Banks, upstate New York, 1980s. Courtesy of Jordan Family and Friend Photos.

Jordan with Shirley Horn at Fat Tuesday's, New York City, 1983. Photo by Mitchell Seidel.

Jordan with Harvie S (Swartz) at Bach Dancing & Dynamite Society, Half Moon Bay, California, March 1989. Photo by Brian McMillen.

Jordan with Harvie S (Swartz) at the Great American Music Hall, San Francisco, California, May 1985. Photo by Brian McMillen.

HighNote CD Yesterdays *(duo with Harvie S), 2012. Photo used with permission, © HighNote Records.*

Jordan with George Gruntz in Stuttgart, Germany, 1987. Photo by Hans Kumpf.

Jordan going through sheet music before performing at Bach Dancing & Dynamite Society, Half Moon Bay, California, November 1986. Photo by Brian McMillen.

Jordan with Tracey and a horse, 1980s. Courtesy of Jordan Family and Friend Photos.

Jordan sleeping next to one of the bebop cows, 1980s. Courtesy of Jordan Family and Friend Photos.

HighNote CD I've Grown Accustomed to the Bass *(duo with Cameron Brown), 1997. Photo used with permission, © HighNote Records.*

HighNote CD Celebration *(duo with Cameron Brown), 2004. Photo used with permission, © HighNote Records.*

Jordan singing with Cameron Brown. Photo by Guy Smith.

HighNote CD Jazz Child *(with Steve Kuhn Trio), 1998. Photo used with permission, © HighNote Records.*

HighNote CD Little Song *(with Steve Kuhn Trio), 2002. Photo used with permission, © HighNote Records.*

Jordan with Serge Forté Trio, Geneva, Switzerland, 2005. Photo by Juan Carlos Hernandez.

Jordan singing with Serge Forté Trio, Geneva, Switzerland, 2005. Photo by Juan Carlos Hernandez.

Jordan during her New York Times *interview in Middleburgh. Photo by Chris Ramirez.*

Jordan in front of the barn at Charlie Parker Place, in Middleburgh. Photo by Chris Ramirez.

Jordan at her home in Middleburgh, by the piano. Photo by Chris Ramirez.

Jordan with (left to right) Ellen Johnson and Jay Clayton, adjudicating the Ella Fitzgerald Vocal Competition for JVOC, 2006. Photo by Jeff Foster.

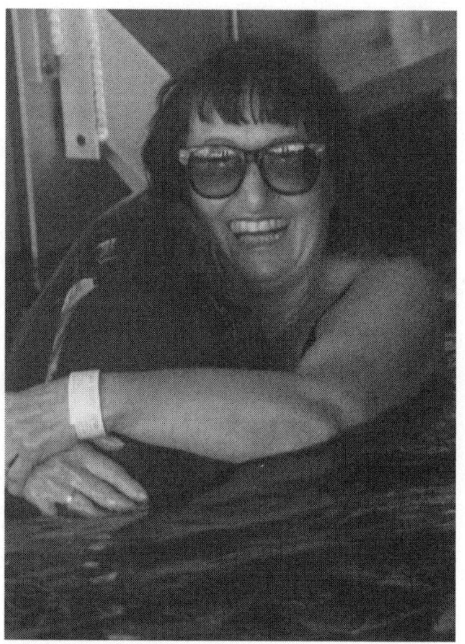

Jordan hugging a dolphin. Courtesy of Jordan Family and Friend Photos.

Jordan with Ellen Johnson in Long Beach, California, 2006. Photo by Jeff Foster.

From left to right, Billy Drummond, Cameron Brown, Jordan, and Steve Kuhn at the Charlie Parker Jazz Festival, New York City, 2013. Photo by Tessa Souter.

Jordan and Hendricks at "Meet the Artist" interview with A. B. Spellman at the Lensic Performing Arts Center, Santa Fe, New Mexico, July 28, 2012. Photo by Jim Gale.

Jordan with Cameron Brown at the New Mexico Jazz Festival, 2012. Photo by Jim Gale.

2012 NEA Jazz Masters Jack DeJohnette, Sheila Jordan, and Jimmy Owens. (Not pictured: Von Freeman and Charlie Haden.) Photo by Michael G. Stewart.

2012 NEA Jazz Master Awards Concert with Sheila Jordan, Jack DeJohnette, Jimmy Owens, and 1998 NEA Jazz Master Ron Carter, performing 1984 NEA Jazz Master Ornette Coleman's composition "When Will the Blues Leave" at Rose Theater, Frederick P. Rose Hall, Lincoln Center, January 10, 2012. Photo by Michael G. Stewart.

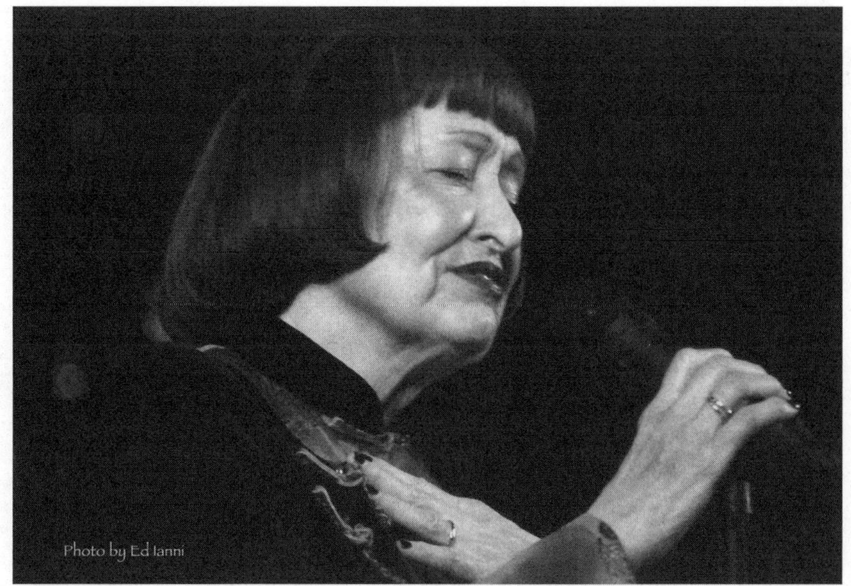

Jordan performing for her 80th birthday at Dizzy's in New York City, 2009. Photo by Ed Ianni.

Jordan reflecting during her New York Times *interview in Middleburgh. Photo by Chris Ramirez.*

Jordan singing with the UMass Orchestra, directed by Jeff Holmes, 2011. Photo by Bill Sitler.

Jordan performing at the Jazz in July UMass faculty concert around 2010. Photo by Edward Cohen.

Jordan performing at the Jazz in July UMass faculty concert around 2009. Photo by Edward Cohen.

• 8 •

I've Grown Accustomed to the Bass

"My favorite way to sing is with the bass. In fact I think I may have been a bass player in a former life."

—Sheila Jordan

Jordan has always said that her real love affair was with the double (or often called, upright) bass. Her natural fascination with using space was a perfect match for the bass and voice duo format. Without the clutter of chords she was able to find the freedom and subtleties that her instrument required to be fully expressive. She adored the quality and sound of the bass and had a deep yearning to investigate the ways it could be used to interpret songs with a solo voice. Long before singers entertained the idea of crafting a musical relationship with this key instrument of the jazz rhythm section, Jordan was already setting the creative parameters on what was possible in such a unique duo format. Throughout her career she has been recognized as the primary innovator of the bass and voice duo.

Jordan spent time trying out tunes with many bass players, particularly in the Tristano sessions. She learned quickly that there had to be a special kind of trust and a keen listening skill in order to master the bass and voice duo. Peter Ind, a bass player from London living in New York at the time, was one of the first musicians whom Jordan experimented with, singing standards such as "Yesterdays" and "There Will Never Be Another You." However, the first time Jordan performed a bass and voice duet in public was in 1954 in Toledo, Ohio. She was pregnant with her daughter Tracey at the time and was visiting her family. She heard that Mingus was in town playing with Lee Konitz, so she went to hang out and listen. The trio consisted of saxophone, bass, and drums, which was an unusual combination in those days since there was no chordal instrument included such as a piano or guitar. According to Jordan,

"Mingus asked me to come up and sing something with him and I told him no because there wasn't a piano. He said, 'well you're not worried about that when you're at Lennie's singing with the bass so why don't you come up and sing a song with me?' At that time I was studying with Lennie and Mingus would occasionally come to the sessions. I did the tune 'Yesterdays' because that was one of the first tunes I did at Lennie's with Peter." And so history was made that night for the woman who would later become one of the most accomplished bass and voice duet visionaries in jazz.

In 1956 she made appearances with bassist Steve Swallow, pianist Johnny Knapp, and drummer Ziggy Willmann at the Page Three in New York City. While performing at the club, she used the opportunity to experiment with ideas for bass and voice arrangements. "Steve was the first bass player I ever tried ideas with in public. I felt so comfortable with him and the way he played. I just loved his playing." The Tristano sessions and her own explorations on gigs inspired her to record a bass and voice track with Steve Swallow on her 1962 Blue Note LP, *Portrait of Sheila*. Jordan originally wanted *Portrait of Sheila* to be entirely bass and voice, but Alfred Lion, who was the head of Blue Note, turned down the idea. Both he and Francis Wolff told her she could only do a couple of tunes with the bass. Jordan firmly believes today that the concept was far ahead of its time. Jordan would have used a pianist on her recording, but George Russell suggested that she record with guitar. The one track she chose to do with just bass was the celebrated Bobby Timmons composition "Dat Dere," with lyrics by Oscar Brown Jr. Although the song is a clever conversation between a father and his young son, Jordan thought it would be more appropriate for her to do as a conversation between a mother and daughter. In her version the lyrics to the song are slightly altered and dedicated to her daughter, Tracey.

In the late 1960s Russell invited Jordan to sing at two jazz festivals in Scandinavia. One was with Jan Garbarek's group; that was where she met bassist Arild Andersen. They instantly created a musical bond and seemed to have effortless communication doing bass and voice duets. Because of their mutual admiration for this type of duo format, the two decided to create an album together. Andersen had already had some experience working with bass and voice duets when he toured in 1969 with the Norwegian vocalist Karin Krog. In August 1977 they recorded an album in Oslo, Norway, for SteepleChase Records entitled *Sheila*; it was Jordan's first recording featuring only bass and voice duos. The songs on the recording included "Song of Joy," "Hold Out Your Hand," "Lush Life," "The Saga of Harrison Crabfeathers," "What Are You Doing the Rest of Your Life," "On Green Dolphin Street," "It Never Entered My Mind," "Don't Explain," "Better Than Anything," "The Lady," and "Please Don't Talk About Me When I'm Gone." According to Andersen, "We recorded at the same studio the German record company ECM was using. The recording went very easy as I remember, with only one or two takes. 'Green Dolphin Street' was added because the producer wanted more music on the record. Since we had not rehearsed that song we just made up a version right there."

It was clear that Jordan had a natural disposition for working with the bass and that she had a specific vision in mind in regard to her choice of bass players and arrangements. Jordan, well known for her vocal nuances and raw delivery, clearly allowed her dynamic vocal range to emerge, culminating in a spectrum of impressionistic colors while Andersen provided the space she required with solid support. There were moments on the recording where they didn't quite lock in on the interpretations, but considering that they were both delving into uncharted territory, the sessions revealed a particular sense of courage and abandonment that they shared. And certainly they did not allow themselves to be distracted by previous performances or expectations. This first bass and voice recording was a kind of launching pad for Jordan; it wasn't until later in her career that she found her muses in both Harvie S and Cameron Brown. "Later I kept contact with Sheila and I visited New York several times around 1972 through 1974," relates Andersen. "I always stayed at Sheila's and we played some gigs now and then around New York. It was a very important and creative period for me. Sheila, being a Scorpio, as I am, felt like my big sister. We always had very good communication on and off stage. She is a remarkable person."

One night during the late 1970s Jordan went to listen to Lee Konitz at the Half Note in New York City and heard a young bassist, Harvie Swartz (now known as Harvie S). Konitz invited Jordan up to sing a couple of songs with the band. "I was thrilled with the idea," said Harvie. "Sheila somehow even got Lee to sing along with her and it became the 'Liverwurst Song' and it was quite a funny and wonderful experience." Jordan was so impressed with the bassist that she asked him if he would be interested in working with her on some of her upcoming trio performances. Harvie was already familiar with Jordan since he had first heard her on the Russell recording *Outer View* when he was in high school. He told her he would be honored, and that was the beginning of their musical friendship. They did gigs at the Tin Palace, Sonny's, Gulliver's, and others with a variety of piano players such as Hod O'Brien, Jack Reilly, Johnny Knapp, and of course Steve Kuhn. Harvie recalls, "While we were on the road the drums and piano were at the club but my bass was always with me because I love to play. Sheila would encourage me to bring the bass over and run some tunes. That really was fun and stretched my ears because I had never done anything like that before." Eventually Jordan asked Harvie to do a concert with her of bass and voice duets for a radio station benefit in Philadelphia. Originally Harvie thought it wouldn't work since he believed that "you can't do a concert with bass and voice for two hours and expect the audience to sit through it." But he agreed on the stipulation that they would rehearse twice a week for the two months prior to the performance. Harvie also made an oath to himself that he would never use sheet music on the concerts, and he never did.

Since they both lived in New York City, Jordan went over to Harvie's loft after her day job twice a week to rehearse, according to their agreement. Jordan would choose the songs, keys, and tempos, and together they would work out ideas for the arrangements. "Harvie is such a creative and beautiful musician. He was significant in helping me get the bass and voice off the ground with such wonderful arrangements and ideas." Harvie tells it this way: "I was the entire band and the arranger. Sheila always picked the tunes and we did them at the tempos she wanted and of course the keys that suited her best. I had to play in A♭ minor, B major, D♭ major, F♯ minor, and other keys that were very challenging for an acoustic bass with no frets and no piano to buddy up to. I had to practice the music a lot and work on my time because there were no drums to rely on. I was on my own." Jordan also contributed to the duo by preparing stories with the bass and by creating interesting medleys and combinations of songs such as "Miles's Medley," which included "Blue Skies," "All Blues," Miles's solo on "Freddie the Freeloader," and Miles's solo on "Now's The Time." The stories would come out of her experiences through the years with her musical heroes: Charlie Parker, Miles Davis, Thelonious Monk, Sonny Rollins, and others. "Through the years I started putting together different medleys dealing with certain musical subjects like the Fred Astaire and Ginger Rogers dance medley, the swing and bebop medley of Fats Waller and Charlie Parker, and a children's medley that consisted of all tunes dealing with kids. I wanted to tell musical stories about these subjects."

When the concert in Philadelphia finally came about, Jordan and Harvie were quite shocked when they received multiple standing ovations along with four encores. After that performance, it was clear to both of them that their bass and voice duo had a future. However, they also felt that their creation was more appropriate on concert stages than clubs. At first they mainly performed in the New York area, where they did a few performances with Kenny Barron and Ben Riley at Visiones, selling out all four nights, and later the Third Street Music Settlement, concerts that Cobi Narita organized at the Jazz Gallery, Saint Peter's Church, and St John the Divine. Eventually they got booked at concerts throughout the United States and internationally in Germany, Finland, England, Scotland, and France, along with many tours in Japan. The audiences always seemed to love them and once again they received standing ovations and encores. "I was always amazed that an audience would listen so attentively to a bass and voice concert and still want more even after two hours," said Harvie. "I think the magic we created came from somewhere else because we just allowed our emotions to flow into the music, come what may."

The two began receiving positive reviews wherever they performed. A 1981 *Variety* review claims, "Bebopesque vocalist Sheila Jordan and bassist Harvie Swartz are a fine pair whose talents complement each other as smoothly as their gray outfits did visually Tuesday night at the Vine St. Bar & Grill. The spontaneous chemistry at work between Jordan and Swartz was stunning."[1] On the West Coast, Andrew Gilbert of the *Santa Cruz Sentinel* writes:

> Few singers have the confidence or ability to survive with identity intact the test Jordan so frequently subjects herself to. Just a voice, a bass and a microphone—it's like watching tight rope acrobats performing without a net, or an escape artist being lowered in chains underwater. It was almost eerie how much Jordan and Swartz's musical personalities complemented each other and the degree to which they anticipated each other's moves. She sang a line and he played it back to her, embellishing on it. At one point, Jordan sang a series of improvised wordless phrases so fragilely beautiful it seemed an untimely cough from the audience would shatter the moment.[2]

However, Jordan's love affair with the bass, like most relationships, wasn't always easy. Most people who had not heard the duo had a difficult time imagining how a bass and voice could hold the attention of a concert or festival, even with the success of their previous concerts. Venue owners and promoters didn't want to take a chance on bass and voice duets because it was such an unusual combination at that time and they had a difficult time imagining how a concert could be accomplished without drums and piano. However, whenever Jordan was booked for a bass and voice performance, everyone was pleasantly surprised and satisfied. "Most people felt that the idea was too 'out' and that it couldn't be done. But when Peggy Lee came out with the recording 'Fever,' I started thinking that maybe I wasn't so crazy after all," comments Jordan.

> I remember one time Harvie and I were doing a bass and voice duo at the Ottawa Jazz festival in Canada. When the first tune was finished a guy said, "Where's the piano? Where's the drums?" because he couldn't imagine anybody just singing with a bass. So I told him, in my head, man, they're all in my head. Then he stayed around and at the end of our gig he apologized. He said, "Man, what you two did was fantastic." In the beginning there were a lot of venue owners who didn't know what to think, not that they disapproved, but they didn't know if they wanted to take a chance

> on the bass and voice. But when they did they were always happy with the outcome.

Jordan and Harvie's first duo recording was *Old Time Feeling* on Muse Records, produced by Herb Wong and recorded in October of 1982 at Eurosound in New York City. The songs on the album included "I Miss That Old Time Feeling," "Sleeping Bee," "How Deep Is the Ocean," "The Thrill Is Gone," "Tribute," "It Don't Mean a Thing (If It Ain't Got That Swing)," "Lazy Afternoon," "Whose Little Angry Man Are You?," "Let's Face the Music and Dance," "Some Other Time," and "Barbados." Because the two had been making music together since the late 1970s, they were able to bring a well-crafted set of standards to the session. From the very first track you can instantly hear their remarkable rapport along with the counterpoint of the two instruments weaving together in rock solid time. Changing meter or key was never an obstacle for the two and it always sounded effortless. Harvie masterfully used pedal tones, textures, and repeated patterns to complement Jordan's vocal articulations and interpretations.

Harvie's impressive technique and Jordan's "million-dollar ears" formed an equitable musical partnership and a consummate artistry. Harvie bends notes, bows with purpose, and comfortably sits in silence in appropriate moments as demonstrated on the Jerome Moross and John Latouche ballad "Lazy Afternoon." The two suspend time so effectively one almost experiences the heat of the day and hears, as the lyrics say, "the grass as it grows." When Jordan improvises, she quite often references her Cherokee roots with a wordless vocal, and for "Lazy Afternoon" she includes an eerie vibrato, sounding like a wild animal lamenting in the landscape. Harvie complements by using harmonics so creatively that they almost sound like an African kalimba at times. The finale of this song is a soulful few measures of "You Are My Sunshine," a stunning reference to the deep emotion that Jordan captures within this song. It's obvious from the beginning to the end of this bass and voice adventure that Jordan and Harvie have incredible musical chemistry. Each song is a well-thought-out portrait of expression cleverly and beautiful executed. *Old Time Feeling* inspired countless jazz singers to discover the inventive accompaniment possibilities of the bass and voice duo.

Jordan acutely understood the qualities that made the bass and voice duo desirable. "I like to work out ideas, feelings, and moods," relates Jordan. "I need a bass player who can go in all directions, along with swinging and walking a beautiful bass line, because I love that, especially on bebop tunes or swing tunes. I also like to do things where we both solo at the same time, and that comes from knowing the tune, knowing the chord changes, knowing what was written there originally, and having that melody in my head. It's more than just the bass player accompanying me; it's a musical conversation. You listen to what I have to say; I listen to what you have to say." Harvie tells a wonderful anecdote that confirms Jordan's incredible knowledge of the tunes she performs. "One night we were doing a gig at Seventh Avenue South and Sheila wanted to do 'Confirmation.' I started making up an intro and thought it was pretty good, but Sheila just kept her head down and wouldn't come in. I kept playing and playing, but she wouldn't sing. She finally looked over and whispered 'key of C.' It was then that I realized I was playing in the original key, which was F major, and she sang it in C major. She has great ears. Very few singers would have noticed that, at least not until they started singing."

The Crossing was the next release that included just a few tracks of bass and voice with Jordan and Harvie. The three tracks of bass and duo included "Little Willie Leaps," "The Crossing," and "Suite for Lady and Prez (a medley of "Goodbye Pork Pie Hat," "Don't Explain," and "I Got Rhythm"). The 1984 Black Hawk recording (out of print at the time of this writing) was not primarily a bass and voice project; it also featured pianist Kenny Barron, drummer Ben Riley, and flügelhornist Tom Harrell. The title track was written by Jordan and repeated in other recordings throughout her career, due to the personal significance it has to her alcohol and drug recovery. It begins with a droning bass introduction, tasty harmonics, and a powerful wordless vocal before moving into Jordan's original lyrics (complete lyrics in chapter 9). For the first time, Jordan records "Little Willie Leaps," a Parker composition taking her back to her days in Detroit with the clever lyrics written by the vocalists from her old group, Skeeter Spight and Leroy Mitchell. On the solo section Jordan improvises spontaneous lyrics recalling the past vocal group. Her soaring phrasing, on par with any horn player, reminds us of her strong roots in the bebop tradition. The "Suite for Lady and Prez" is significant to Jordan because of her deep admiration for Billie Holiday and Lester Young and their seamless connection both musically and emotionally, similar to the relationship Jordan and Harvie managed to share in their interactions. According to Harvie,

> The "Suite for Billy and Prez" was put together at rehearsals and we performed it quite a bit and were always tweaking it. The recorded version that came out on Sheila's CD *The Crossing* has an interesting story. We recorded it at the studio and it took quite a long time to get it right. I felt the big problem was that we were separated in booths. We finally got a good take and it was the last thing to be recorded on the session. I went to get my car and came back to get my bass. Everyone looked so crestfallen. I asked, what's wrong? They told me that the assistant engineer accidentally erased the take. I told them I would be back in ten minutes after I parked my car again. I came back and Sheila and I did the whole suite, perfect in one take and that's the take on the recording.

On February 4, 1988 Jordan and Harvie recorded a live concert at Vario Hall in Tokyo, Japan, which was released as *The Very Thought of Two* on MA. At this point the duo had been working together for close to ten years and their ensemble technique was at a high level of musicianship. On this recording the duo perform "The Very Thought of You," "Lost In the Stars," "Honeysuckle Rose/Ain't Misbehavin'," "You Are My Sunshine," "Dat Dere," "The Bird/Quasimodo," "Spirits Arise/Mourning Song/The Water Is Wide," "Let's Face the Music and Dance," and "You Must Believe In Spring." During this recording Jordan revisits two pieces she had first recorded in 1962 on *Portrait of Sheila*, "Dat Dere" and "You Are My Sunshine." "Dat Dere" quickly became one of the most requested of her signature bass and voice songs. "You Are My Sunshine," the track on the George Russell recording *Outer View*, was quite often the first exposure most people had to hearing Jordan. On the Tokyo concert, Jordan adapts the tune to fit with the duo by singing it simply but with a bluesy feel and a gutsy vocal quality. Jordan doesn't disguise the pain that this song elicits as its memory takes her back to her impoverished childhood roots.

The duo had a penchant for medleys and segues with clever arrangements that flowed from one song and key to another while never missing a beat. On "Honeysuckle Rose/Ain't Misbehavin'," the two are at their best with their signature playful repartee. As Harvie always seems to know exactly what, how, and when to say something, his instrumental interpretations are on par with Jordan's vocal storytelling. A full rhythm section is never missed because the two know how to use space and fill space with subtle conversation. A good example is the medley combining two originals, "Spirits Arise," composed by Harvie, and "Mourning Song," Jordan's composition. Harvie cleverly adopts a drum-like pulse reminiscent of indigenous tribal dancing in a sacred ritual. Jordan's voice enters like a shaman calling the spirits. Once the frenzy has stopped the poignant and understated version of "The Water Is Wide" brings the listener to a peaceful finale. The tale has been told to satisfaction for the listener.

Harvie's imagination is in rare form with his "tap dancing" solo on the wood of the bass, a device he incorporates to capture the essence of the dancing of Fred Astaire on "Let's Face the Music and Dance." The two reveal not only their collaborative abilities but also their outrageous sense of humor as they promenade through the song, just like Ginger Rogers and Astaire, never missing a step. And of course when Jordan laments her life story on" Sheila's Blues" we hear a different side of the wispy-voiced chanteuse, a powerful belting blues. Those who are only familiar with the gentle side of Jordan's voice should listen to the way she can knock a song out of the park with her vocal strength. As always, Harvie seems to know when it's appropriate to take center stage or to just support Jordan. Something other accompanists could take note of on these recordings. The final track of this set is the stunning ballad "You Must Believe in Spring." Jordan has often been quoted saying that her purpose in singing jazz is to be a "messenger of the music." It's clear that her choice to end with this song was purposeful in its intent to inspire the audience as she sings, instead of "believe in spring," "believe in jazz." (A side note: MA Recordings decided to add bonus tracks to this recording and to *Songs from Within*. Unfortunately, these tracks are by different artists from the MA roster and their presence on the Jordan discs seems to take away from the mood so well established by Jordan and Harvie. In other words, what were they thinking?)

The third recording of Jordan and Harvie, *Songs from Within*, was released in March of 1989 on MA Recordings and recorded in Tokyo with producer Todd Garfinkle. Jordan clearly remembers the session because it was in a very cold studio with rattling pipes. Jordan was wearing a winter coat and Harvie could barely move his fingers, but the two managed to persevere and made their special magic once again. The songs on this recording include "Dedication," "If You Could See Me Now," "Waltz For Debby," "Good Morning Heartache," "St. Thomas," "You Don't Know What Love Is," "My Shining Hour," "We'll Be Together Again," "Alone Together," "In a Sentimental Mood," "I Got Rhythm/Anthropology," and "Birmingham Jail." Besides interpreting a variety of standards on this album, there is one original song, "Dedication," as well as Jordan's lyrics to the classic Sonny Rollins composition, "St. Thomas": "I dance and I sing when I hear Sonny Rollins, / I dance and I sing when I hear Sonny Rollins, / play this song, / all night long, / play St. Thomas, Sonny Rollins."

The opening number, "Dedication," showcases Harvie's bass as he continuously searches for ways to squeeze every bit of eloquence out of his instrument. Bill Oddie wrote the lyrics for this version of "Waltz For Debby," and Jordan recounts, "I heard these before I heard Gene Lees's lyrics. I stayed with these lyrics because I could identify with them because they reminded me of the beauty of nature around my home in upstate New York." Kevin Whitehead, jazz critic for National Public Radio's *Fresh Air*, reviewed *Songs from Within* in the September 1993 issue of *Pulse!*: "Singer Sheila Jordan, 65, is a master of understatement. Accompanied by her longtime pal, bassist Harvie Swartz, she can take the music down to a whisper, and let silences linger, to increase the intensity of their musical intimacy. *Songs from Within* exemplifies their strengths: Jordan's remarkable combination of high-wire chops and girlish enthusiasm; Swartz's ability to shadow her like a detective, imply an orchestra (or classical cellist) or melt out of her way."[3] Music critic Robert Palmer raved in the *New York Times*, "Her ballad performances are simply beyond the emotional and expressive capabilities of most other vocalists." Jordan demonstrates the proof of this statement in her renditions of "Good Morning Heartache" (dedicated to Billie Holiday), "You Don't Know What Love Is," "We'll Be Together Again," and "In a Sentimental Mood." Both Jordan and Harvie had an acute sense of how to pace and program songs for a recording or performance, taking the listener from one emotional arch to the next.

The last project to date was a live concert recorded around 1995, *Yesterdays*, produced and edited by Harvie for HighNote Records. The project was released in 2012 and was quite possibly the final performance between the dynamic musical bass and voice duo. According to Jordan, "There were so many wonderful people during that time who helped book concerts for us. One of them was Brenda Bayne, a singer and events coordinator at the Thomas Center. She used to book a jazz series and invited us to perform there. I was thrilled because she was keen on keeping jazz alive in her area. It was always people like that, who really understood what we were trying to accomplish with the duo, who helped us find our best gigs." Since Jordan prefers being recorded in a live concert situation, as opposed to a studio recording, she thought this was a first-class representation of the duo, as did Harvie in the following statement: "I feel the only full CD that captured the real duo is the recording *Yesterdays*. Before that we had made three duo recordings that were done under very bad conditions and we were not able to even scratch the surface of what we could unleash. On *Yesterdays* you can hear us creating, laughing, smiling, crying, and being ourselves in the music. I'm grateful to High Note Records for putting it out."

It's clear that by this time Jordan and Harvie had reached a pinnacle of excellence, becoming a single unit of perfected sound, a complement of dual expression, and the perfect musical marriage. One can hear the growth of their relationship as newlyweds from their first duo album to a seasoned couple now comfortable with each other's idiosyncrasies in this final recording. They are so familiar with each other that every phrase is completely effortless, with a musical freedom that can only be achieved through a deep trust. Many of the songs had been recorded before, such as "The Very Thought of You," "You Don't Know What Love Is," "Fred Astaire Medley," "It Don't Mean A Thing (If It Ain't Got That Swing)," "Fats Waller Medley," "Mood Indigo," "Waltz For Debby," and "Lazy Afternoon." It makes no difference because every time Jordan and Harvie perform a song, they bring something fresh into each moment. "The Astaire Medley on *Yesterdays* was made up 'on the spot' and Sheila just led me on a crazy, fun journey," says Harvie. "I had one very scary moment when Sheila went into the song 'I Could Have Danced All Night.' I didn't know the tune that well and had never played it in that key either. When it came to the bridge I prayed hard that I was going to go into the right key. Luckily I did or it wouldn't have been a very good moment. Sheila has a real gift of putting together tunes that tell a story."

The genius of this duo was their ability to continually take risks while preserving the craftwork of every arrangement. This recording is a testament to the brilliance of Jordan and Harvie's journey into the unknown landscape of voice and bass duets, ultimately ending in a body of work that will no doubt be considered among the great treasures of jazz. According to Kirk Silsbee, who provided the liner notes for this recording, "The previously unreleased recording at hand captures the duo at a concert near the conclusion of their partnership. It's full of musical adventure and playful spontaneity: like her humorous recounting of a questionable review in the middle of 'The Very Thought of You,' and the flight into steeplechase time on 'Honeysuckle Rose.' Harvie points out: 'You can tell we were having fun. And the audience was fantastic; they stayed on our every note.' He's clear on the recording's worth: 'I feel vindicated by this album. We only recorded three other CDs but the magic is on this one. This recording is us; it's what we did best.'"[4]

Silsbee's liner notes were supported by many of the reviews the project received from the critics. Paul de Barros of the *Seattle Times* notes in a January 31, 2012, review, "Jordan's high, light, mischievously supple voice and Harvie S's toffee-rich, dexterous bass achieve an orchestral completeness that never for a minute makes you feel anything is missing. Spontaneity and a sense of play are paramount. On 'The Very Thought of You,' Jordan improvises a recitative rebuttal, mid-song, of a review that complained she didn't sing the melody last time she was in town. But that's Jordan's thing: She inhabits the architecture of a tune, then celebrates it by messing with it."[5] And Lloyd Sachs writes in *Jazzespress* on January 26, 2012, "I don't know why it's taken so long for *Yesterdays* to see the light of day, but if you wanted to put a Jordan performance in a time capsule, you could hardly do better than this one. As always, she takes standards you've heard a million times, and makes you hear them for the first time with her fearless approach. Springing off Harvie S's big, plummy tones, she makes every note count, heightening the meaning of the songs with finely tuned scat, stream of consciousness-style phrases and Native American-style chants."[6]

The duo worked on and off for about fourteen years, developing their original style and delighting audiences with their stellar performances and repartee. Sadly, sometime around 1995 and immediately after one of their performances, Harvie told Jordan he no longer wanted to continue the duo. As Jordan described the break up, "It was a musical divorce. It was quite shocking but I guess at that time Harvie wanted to do his own music and pursue his career with his band." One can't help but wonder, after being thrilled by the virtuosity of these two great musicians, what another twenty years would have produced.

Jordan was adamant that she wouldn't give up on the idea of the bass and voice, an idea she had been passionate about since her days singing with

Swallow in the 1950s. Shortly after Harvie left the duo, Jordan found a new partner in Cameron Brown. Oddly enough, Jordan had wanted to start a duo with Brown when she heard him back in the '60s, but Brown felt he wasn't ready. They did perform one little bass and voice gig for the opening of an art show by Jacki Clipsham, but the duo never took off because, as Brown tells it, he became involved with a group with Archie Shepp, George Adams, and Don Pullen. They did work together from time to time in other groups, and in fact Brown was the bass player on Jordan's second album, *Confirmation*, as early as 1975. But as fate would have it, the two reunited almost thirty years later. "Cameron was thrilled to work with me on the bass and voice project and willing to rehearse," said Jordan. "Besides being a great duo partner he is a very caring and considerate person. He constantly supports everything I do and that is so important to me."

In 1997, Jordan joined Brown as part of an ensemble for a tour of concerts in Belgium sponsored by Jazz'halo, a pioneering arts organization. Brown wanted to do his original compositions and wanted to include the voice as part of the instrumentation. The band consisted of Dave Ballou (trumpet), Leon Parker (drums), and Jordan with a couple of cameos by tenor saxophonist Dewey Redman. The organization's goal, besides the concerts, was to have the band create two live recording projects out of three ninety-minute sets from three different concert sites. The project was completed under the titles *Cameron Brown and the Hear & Now: Here and How!* and *Cameron Brown and the Hear & Now: Here and How! Volume II*, both recorded by David Baker and released on OmniTone on October 21, 2003. The majority of the songs are with the trio, but there are a couple of very special bass and voice moments with Brown and Jordan, one of which is "Mourning Song," with some exceptional bass work by Brown. This is an outstanding recording that needs much more attention for its originality and creativity. Frank Tafuri wrote in the liner notes: "*Here and How!* brings Cameron full circle by harkening back not only to his roots in the music, but also to the very roots of modern jazz. 'To work with somebody like Sheila who literally goes back to Bird, that we're trying, in some living way, to preserve the feeling of this music, it just has a tremendous meaning for me,' says Cameron."

Brown and Jordan rehearsed for the Belgium concert for about a year, and during the course of their rehearsals they decided to create a long-term bass and voice duo partnership. So along with the pending concert material, the two found time to work on some of the bass and voice material for potential performances. For the recording in Belgium, Brown recalls, "Jordan looked at me at one point and said, 'Listen, I'm not going to scat this whole record. We've got to write some lyrics to some of these songs.' So I wound up writing lyrics to a bunch of songs and of course some songs didn't have lyrics." As fate would have it, one of the scheduled performers had to drop out on the last day of the festival and an open slot was offered to Brown. Brown seized the opportunity to premiere the bass and voice duo with Jordan and that became their first public performance. Since Baker was already recording Brown's sets, he offered to record the duo; the result became their first recording.

Their debut album was cleverly titled *I've Grown Accustomed to the Bass* and released on HighNote in 2000. That recording became a documentation of exactly what happened on their first duo outing. More importantly, it gave Jordan another shot at presenting the music with the instrument she so adored. Ken Dryden writes on the Jazz'halo website:

> The concert at De Werf Brugge from 11.11.1997 marked the first time that vocalist Sheila Jordan and bassist Cameron Brown had performed live as a duo. Nerves aside, they had their Belgian audience captivated from the opening of the set. Jordan improvises much like a horn with her interesting choices of notes as she sings the lyrics to standards like "The Very Thought of You," while Brown is also a superb musician, comping perfectly for her and launching on inventive solo flights of his own. Jordan scats an introduction to the playful "Better Than Anything" (a good song that is often subjected to lackluster interpretations), adding a few interesting twists of her own as they take it into new musical territory. "Dat Dere" sounds even better in a vocal/bass setting; Jordan's humorous interpretation proves to be infectious. One unusual part of this performance is her series of medleys that are connected without interruption, blending her originals with standards and favorite jazz compositions into a stunning tour de force. The duo wraps the session with "I've Grown Accustomed to the Bass," with Jordan wryly altering the lyrics to "I've Grown Accustomed to Her Face" to craft a fitting tribute to her duo partner."[7]

Since it was their first outing, Jordan relied on songs that she had done in the past in other bass and voice duets. She was focused at this point on the connection that Brown and she were building, so she wanted to keep the song choice familiar and meaningful. The songs included "The Very Thought of You" (recorded in 1993 with Harvie Swartz), "Better Than Anything" (recorded in 1977 with Arild Andersen), "Dat Dere" (recorded in 1962 with Steve Swallow), "Mourning Song," "The Bird/Tribute (Quasimodo)/Embraceable You," "Goodbye Pork Pie Hat," "Good Morning Heartache," "I Got Rhythm/Listen To Monk (Rhythm-a-ning)," "Sheila's Blues," and "I've Grown Accustomed to the Bass." On "Dat Dere" Jordan introduces the song as she always does, dedicating it to her daughter and on this recording she includes: "to all of your children and your grandchildren and the children that you're going to have." Brown intuitively knew just how to support Jordan's vocal antics, adding his whimsical flair with slides and grunts on the bass accompaniment.

Even in her programming of material, Jordan tells a compelling story and understands exactly how to take us on a journey into her jazz world. Brown's solid foundation on this recording continuously provides the frame for Jordan to paint her sonorous pictures and sing her heartfelt messages. Jordan loves to dedicate her songs to those musicians who have touched her heart, and her last dedication is to Thelonious Monk, using Gershwin's "I Got Rhythm" as she soars into "Rhythm-a-ning" (with the lyrics "Listen To This Cat" by Jon Hendricks). This is where the duo proves that this honeymoon recording is destined for a long-term relationship. The two are playful and relaxed, listening and responding to each other's phrases in a collective conversation. Jordan's charming ability to use her improvisations, both sung and unsung, to tell stories is highlighted on this recording. And no one does it better than Jordan. She loves to communicate lyrics in the moment with the audience, a skill most singers have yet to master. What some critics believe Jordan lacks in vocal strength (she has often been accused of having a scant vocal quality in comparison to other singers), she certainly makes up for in interpretation, invention, and subtle nuance. Jordan can hold an audience in the palm of her hand indefinitely, and the result is simply magical. The last song on the recording is a tender yet humorous comment to Jordan's affection for the bass, "I've Grown Accustomed to the Bass," a nod to the Lerner and Lowe composition, "I've Grown Accustomed to Your Face." Jordan's changed lyrics go, *I've grown accustomed to the bass / It almost makes my day begin / I've grown accustomed to the sound / I love it pound for pound / The highs the lows, The strings the bow / Are second nature to me now. / Like breathing out and breathing in, / I was serenely independent and content before we met. / Surely I could always be that way and yet, / I've grown accustomed to the tone, / Accustomed to the drone, / Accustomed to the bass.*

Once again Jordan received rave reviews for her bass and voice experience. In September of 2000, Mathew Bahl wrote in *All About Jazz*,

> Sheila Jordan is one of the most creative, intelligent and original singers that jazz has ever produced. Like Carmen McRae, she has the ability to deconstruct a song harmonically without sacrificing the coherence of a lyric. When she dispenses with words, Jordan's scat singing is fluid, inventive and often quite playful. Her latest recording happily finds Sheila Jordan back in the musical format of which she is the acknowledged master—the bass/voice duo. Her partner on this outing, recorded live in concert in Belgium on November 11, 1997, is the talented bassist Cameron Brown. Singing with only an acoustic bass is a guaranteed way to expose vocal deficiencies. However, the CD, recorded one week prior to her 69th birthday, finds

> Jordan's voice in remarkable shape and her sense of musical adventure firmly in place.[8]

Sometime around 1997 Jordan met bassist Attillio Zanchi while performing with a trio at a festival in Edmonton, Canada. The following year she went on tour in Italy with the E.S.P. Trio, which featured not only Zanchi but Roberto Cipelli (piano), Gianni Cazzola (drums), Gloria Merani (violin), Alessandro Franconi (viola), and Filippo Burchietti (cello). The tour was recorded on albums entitled *Sheila Jordan & E.S.P. Trio, Live in B.Arsizio*, released in 1998 on Pro Music, and *Sheila Jordan & E.S.P. Trio: Sheila's Back in Town*, released in 1999 on Splasc(h). On the recording *Sheila's Back in Town*, Zanchi and Jordan do a bass and voice duo on "Morning Song" and "Dat Dere." The string section was active during "Morning Song," so it wasn't strictly a duo, but it's important to mention; the instruments provide a bold and mysterious texture to the familiar bass and voice piece recorded on Jordan's past sessions. Zanchi's seamless segue to "Dat Dere" and his rapport with Jordan is stellar; he always manages to keep up with the swinging phrases and unique nuances. The two clearly had a chemistry and sense of humor that would have been interesting to see develop over time. However, the fact that Zanchi lived in Milan, Italy, would have made it difficult to practice, and by this time Jordan was committed to her new duo partnership with Brown.

In 1999 Jordan and Zanchi did a duo bass concert opening for Wayne Shorter and Herbie Hancock at the Arts Centre's Martha Cohen Theatre, as part of the Calgary Jazz Festival. James Muretich from the *Calgary Herald* writes, "And the opening duo of legendary vocalist Sheila Jordan and bassist Attillio Zanchi also demonstrated the timeless dynamics that exist even within the sparsest arrangements. The ageless Jordan, who began singing in the 1940's, scatted and improvised while Zanchi's bass provided every note and nuance needed. Combined with warm, human touch between songs, just as with Hancock and Shorter, it was a night of jazz that left one wondering where the time went, if it ever existed at all."[9] It was during this concert that Zanchi recalls an incident showing Jordan's keen wit and professionalism. "I was a little nervous because this was an important gig. I put a microphone near the bridge of my bass to have a better acoustic sound. When Sheila started singing my microphone fell down to the ground (making a loud sound) and I was very embarrassed. But Sheila kept singing and stayed in the moment adding to her scat, 'I knew this was going to happen' and all of the people laughed." Jordan frequently uses unexpected situations to add to the spontaneity of her performances; often those are the most memorable moments.

Although Jordan and Brown continued to perform regularly at concerts locally and internationally, it took seven years after their debut release to record another project of bass and voice duets. This time the live recording was at the black-box cabaret on Manhattan's Upper West Side, The Triad, for Jordan's seventy-sixth birthday party, with two dates on November 17 and 18, 2004. The much-awaited recording, *Celebration*, was released in 2005 on HighNote. The recording kept the feel of being at the live event by including much of the performance banter from Jordan—for example, her opening remarks bemoaning the fact that she had left the shoes she planned on wearing for the performance at home making for a clever segue into the first tune, "Hum Drum Blues." It's obvious that the relationship between Jordan and Brown had grown deeply through the years. The comfort they share with each other can be heard through Jordan's voice sailing across Brown's expressive strings. Even the new repertoire speaks to the development of their own style together: a swinging version of "It's You or No One," a delightful duet with guest vocalist and Jordan's good friend Jay Clayton on "Birks Works," and a haunting elegy "Brother Where Are You?" with music and lyrics by Oscar Brown Jr. Jordan has consistently acknowledged her profound love for the music of Miles Davis, performing tribute medleys of his music in concert and on past recordings. This is the first recorded venture with bass and voice entitled "Blues Medley for Miles," and begins with "Blue Skies" in a 6/8 feel with a bass riff that segues neatly into "All Blues" with Oscar Brown Jr. lyrics. The final tune in the medley is "Freddie the Freeloader" with vocalese lyrics on the Miles solo by Jon Hendricks. By this time Jordan had become a fan of Brazilian composer Ivan Lins, so she included a touching bossa nova version of "The Promise of You," including on the vamp her distinctive Native American chant. In the Astaire/Rogers Medley Jordan adds two new songs to the earlier arrangement of this same medley, "I Won't Dance" and "Pick Yourself Up." Later on, the duo gives a nod to pianist Mal Waldren and vocalist Abbey Lincoln in the very soulful civil rights song of struggle, "Straight Ahead," and Jordan revisits the Fats Waller Medley newly titled "Fats Meets Bird Medley" with the addition of the Parker classic, "Scrapple from the Apple." On "Birks Works," both Sheila and special guest vocalist Jay Clayton dazzle with their scat improvisations, the two complementing with their hallmark techniques, bebop and free style. Other tracks include "Mood Indigo," "Sheila's Blues," and an encore of Jordan's own composition, "The Crossing." Unfortunately as of this date there are no other bass and voice duo recordings with Brown, but perhaps we can look forward to another on the horizon.

Until then, these two recordings remain an explicit example in every aspect of the art of the bass and voice duo. Jordan and Brown continue to perform concerts as well as club dates, most recently at the Detroit Jazz Festival, at the Green Mill in Chicago, and quite often in New York City—especially at Jordan's favorite place to do bass and voice performances, Cornelia Street Café. Jordan and Cameron extend their activities together by giving clinics specifically in the bass and voice duo, privately and for schools and universities around the globe. The two have even been invited to do private performances at people's homes called house concerts, which has become a popular way to hear more intimate or obscure music. A jazz enthusiast, Libby Graham, shared a review of a house concert she attended in February 2012:

> I had the utmost pleasure of attending an absolutely stellar concert, as part of Nich Anderson's popular JazzVox house concert series, in Auburn on February 10th featuring NEA Jazz Master Sheila Jordan. To see this indomitable vocal jazz veteran cozy up with her long-time bassist Cameron Brown was a sight that won't soon be replicated. After all, they originated the "base and face" concept in jazz and totally mesmerized us with their nuanced, heartfelt delivery on such classics as "I've Grown Accustomed To Your Face" and "It's You Or No One." Also of note were her fabulous "Freedom for Humanity" interpretation of Martin Luther King's teachings and a medley of infectious blues standards to close out this extraordinary evening.[10]

Besides her full recordings of duets with Brown, Jordan has recorded one or two versions on a variety of projects with other bassists. There is one bass and voice duet, "Dat Dere," in the live recording *Winter Sunshine* (Justin Time) from a performance in Montreal in 2008. The bassist was Kieran Overs; the rest of the trio featured Steve Amirault (piano) and André White (drums). It's obvious that Jordan knows her way around the bass and feels comfortable no matter who is behind the wood. However, Jordan is adamant that she prefers to work exclusively with Cameron Brown, stating, "I am musically married to Cameron. I might do one tune or improvise on a bebop tune during a performance with a bass player in the trio but that's about it." Jordan cherishes the memory of bass players she has shared wonderful duo experiences in trios or live performances with, such as Steve LaSpina, Jon Burr, David Finck, Mike Richmond, and Jodie Foster, among many others. She encourages other singers to carry on the tradition, often by providing workshops about the bass and voice duo and supporting those vocalists who continue to bring this art form forward. Her friend and colleague Clayton has done concerts with bassist Jay Anderson and Jon Burr, and Jordan acknowledges a few other singers who have been working on bass and voice duets, such as Katie Bull and bassist Joe Fonda; Teri Roiger and bassist John Menegan; Lynn Stein and bassist John Burr; and myself (Ellen Johnson) and bassist Darek Oles, where Jordan was a guest artist on her original composition "The Crossing" on *These Days* (Vocal Visions Records) and at my CD release event in Los Angeles in 2007. Most recently Clayton and Jordan created the group Bebop to Freebop. The two vocalists split time on stage, Jordan doing her bass and voice duo with Brown, and Clayton doing a duo with guitarist Jack Wilkins. Eventually all four trade off into different musical configurations, intertwining bebop and free improvisation. The group has primarily performed internationally in France, Norway, Switzerland, and Canada, doing venues as well as the Burlington Jazz Festival, Rochester Jazz Festival, the Vision Festival, and the Women's Jazz Festival at Kennedy Center in Washington, D.C.

Although Jordan has inspired many singers who share her love of bass and voice duets, she feels strongly that the art of singing with the bass requires complete dedication. "I don't do the bass and voice to be different," she says.

> I have a deep feeling for the bass and I feel totally involved when I'm singing with Cameron. It's such a very special way to present music. I try to encourage young bass players and singers who want to present the music this way to rehearse and get their own thing happening. Rehearsal and trust are the two main ingredients and last but not least—don't give up! It's respect, too. Respect is very important, especially when it's two people creating music in an unfamiliar situation like a bass and voice. You have to trust one another and you have to listen to one another, and you just pray for those out-of-body experiences that happen every once in a great while to let you know, yeah, this is the right way to go.
>
> Accompanying is listening. Sometimes musicians don't listen to one another. So they're not going to take chances. They're not going to be listening so closely that they will go where you go or you might not be listening so closely that you will go where they go. So, for me it's about trusting, listening, and trying to become one. And maybe not all the time, but most of the time. I don't like to turn around and say, "Don't walk, or don't do swing or do this or do that," I don't like to do that. I like it to be free, and we are communicating so well together that we both know. In other words, Cameron knows. I don't have to turn around and tell him in front of an audience. He'll know from the way I'm singing, because he's listening, he's trusting, and he's communicating.

In fact, Jordan is convinced that her dedication to singing with the bass comes from a deep spiritual drive inspiring her efforts. She acknowledges this drive through a past dream:

> I had a crazy dream once and I'll never forget it. I was by the oceanfront walking along the shore when I saw four basses lying there. Who would leave these beautiful instruments lying so close to the water's edge? I was in shock and saw that the tide was coming in. Luckily, there was a house in back of the shore. I carried the basses one by one and stood them up against the side of the house where they would be safe. As I started to continue my waterfront journey, four guys came walking up to where I was. I recognized them immediately. It was Ray Brown, Charles Mingus, Ron

> Carter, and Charlie Hayden. They took their basses, gave me a nod, and walked away without a single word.

Back when Jordan first imagined singing with just the bass, she visualized these four bass players as her musical partners. She has shared this dream on numerous occasions with friends and other musicians, eventually having a poem written about it by Lara Pellegrinelli entitled "Sheila's Dream," which Clayton recites and dedicates to Jordan during her performances. "When Sheila showed me the poem," says Clayton, "I knew it would be something I could make a piece with and most of all a chance to show my respect for the passionate person Sheila is and to highlight her love for the bass."

Sheila's Dream

Treading across soft sand
she came upon their dusky silhouettes
Smooth, shapely, shimmering in the moonlight
Like whales, an eerie sight on land
Their rumbling voices silent
Four basses, how came they to these shores?
Bridges strung with pounds of pressure
so large and yet so fragile
Treading across soft sand,
She saved them from the coming tides.

© Lara Pellegrinelli[11]

Clearly Jordan's rescue of these basses demonstrates a subconscious responsibility she has chosen to accept. There is simply no one who has devoted the time and effort to bringing the bass and voice duet to the level that Jordan has for the past sixty years. Her courage and contributions to the bass and voice duo will forever be revered and admired by musicians and remain the foundation for future artists.

• 9 •

White in a Black World

> "I wouldn't be singing the kind of music I'm singing today if it hadn't been for African American people and learning from them and their beliefs."
>
> —Sheila Jordan

In the summer of 1943, when Jordan was fourteen, altercations between blacks and whites broke out in Detroit, causing a race riot that lasted for three days. Thirty-four people were killed, twenty-five of whom were African Americans. According to Detroit vocalist Leroy Mitchell, "It was worse than the Twelfth Street riot of 1967." Despite Detroit's racial and economic climate, its black community managed to create a supportive social, cultural, and intellectual environment for pianist Tommy Flanagan, drummer Elvin Jones, tenor saxophonist Yusef Lateef, vibraphonist Milt "Bags" Jackson, guitarist Kenny Burrell, pianist Barry Harris, saxophonist Frank Foster, vocalists Betty "Bebop" Carter, Skeeter Spight, Leroy Mitchell, and the white members of this cohort: baritone saxophonist Park "Pepper" Adams, drummer Art Mardigan, and vocalist Sheila Jordan.[1]

Yet a racist environment prevailed during Jordan's youth, and this set the stage for what would be a constant struggle for her, dealing with discrimination. Although she was white, Jordan's passion for African American music, specifically jazz and bebop, exposed her to the ugly realities of what her African American friends and partners had to endure. Having grown up in poverty where other children made fun of her, Jordan could easily relate to these prejudicial experiences. For many reasons, she identified deeply with black culture, and at one point in her life even expressed a desire to be black instead of white. Jordan remembers how her mother and aunt used to get upset about the hatred toward "colored" people at that time. Oddly enough, these family members never shared the hatred that was so prevalent in Detroit. However, the majority of whites *did*, making any type of biracial relationship almost impossible. This made it hard for a color-blind jazz prodigy to have the freedom to socialize without getting into frequent altercations. "Even the principal of my high school brought me into the office one day," says Jordan. "She said, 'you dress so nice; why do you want to hang out with colored girls?' and from that point on that made me question people of authority."

The bebop "culture" created an atmosphere where musical collaborations helped to bridge the racial polarization that existed in Detroit. A variety of interracial friendships, romantic ties, and a continuous dialogue that questioned the social inequities of the time grew out of the inspiration and excitement of the musical environment. The highly creative and complex musical language of jazz crossed racial barriers, which in turn violated white supremacy rules. Certainly the bebop musicians and fans were an integral part of an ever-growing change of climate that gained strength throughout the '60s and '70s. "Oh yeah, we had a lot of trouble," recounts Leroy Mitchell.

> I remember we were singing in a big club on East Grand Boulevard that was mainly for whites. We came out to scat our tune and half of the people got up and walked out. They couldn't handle two black guys with a white girl. Another time we were in a taxi and the police pulled us over and blocked the taxi. Then they came over to us and said to Sheila, "What are you doing in a car with these niggers?" Sheila stopped them dead and said, "You mean I can't ride with my own brothers?" And they looked at her and looked at us with perplexed expressions. [Mitchell laughs.] They just told us to go ahead. But that's what I mean—we always had a lot of trouble.

In order to pursue her music, Jordan was faced with a constant barrage of frightening, frustrating, and hostile situations—based on the color of her skin as she kept company with the black people she so adored. Jordan observes that today the majority of young people are not faced with the sort of experiences that she endured during the mid-1940s. She was ahead of her time as an advocate for a movement that was just beginning to be born, one that would bring together people of all races and nationalities. When the civil rights movement became more visible in the 1960s, Jordan had already experienced firsthand the injustices being perpetrated upon the black community, and had demonstrated her own courage in confronting them. Resistance to racial prejudice became a centerpiece of her life, from Detroit to New York and beyond. The music, style, and philosophy of bebop musicians critiqued the ideological justifications used to naturalize an economic system that perpetuated racial and social inequities.[2] In the same manner, the interracial friendships, professional collaborations, and romantic relationships in the bebop scene publicly flouted the dominant values by violating white racial taboos.[3] Jordan remembers,

It was very hard growing up with racial prejudice. I have many stories where people were almost killed, myself included. My white friend Jenny King and I went to hear Barry Harris one time. Barry's gig was in a bar in Hamtramick, which was an all-white and Polish section of Detroit. Skeeter Spight and Leroy Mitchell were at the gig, too. Barry asked us to come up and sing with him. So after we sang we continued to hang out with the musicians, which was great. Then we left to go catch the Woodward Avenue streetcar. But first we waited outside the club for Barry, because he and the other black musicians were going to go take the streetcar with us. So here are these two white girls with all these black musicians, and all of sudden Barry yells, "Run! Run!" These white Polish guys from the bar were chasing us, screaming "We're going to kill you!" We ran as fast as we could, and fortunately the Woodward Avenue streetcar came and we all jumped on. Thank God the streetcar came. Barry continues to remind me even today about the time I almost got him killed. We laugh about it now but it wasn't funny at all back then.

During the late '40s and early '50s, black Americans were becoming more racially and politically aware and in Detroit the local NAACP chapter became the largest in the nation. Complaints about police harassment of blacks were frequent, and the police, like the white rioters, saw it as their task to draw the line on what were acceptable interactions between blacks and whites.[4] "For interracial couples in Detroit at that time it was very hard," relates Jordan's former boyfriend, musician Frank Foster. "I had to always be on my guard. The police frowned on interracial relationships. The police were, as far as I can recall, quite racist. I'd been stopped on the street on more than one occasion. They wouldn't think anything of stopping somebody just because they saw a black and white together. And if you happened to be doing drugs that made it worse." Jordan experienced these biracial atrocities firsthand on numerous occasions when she hung out at black clubs and with friends. A stunning example of this type of harassment is the following story:

One time I was going out on a picnic with my then boyfriend, Frank, who was Afro-American, my friend Jenny, who was white like me, and the Afro-American guy she was going out with, Gunther. So the four of us drove in Gunther's car to a place in Detroit called Belle Isle where you could have a picnic, swim, and all kinds of activities like that. A lot of people stopped going there because they said that all the so-called colored people were overtaking it. So on our way to Belle Isle we got stopped by some plainclothesmen.

They said, "Where are you going?" We told them we were going on a picnic. They said, "Come with us." Of course, at that time we didn't know we could ask them what they were holding us for, so we went with them. They separated the two guys from us and took us into another area and gave us the third degree. "What are you doing with these niggers? What's your parents' telephone number? We're going to call them up."

I told them I didn't live with my mother and that I lived on my own. I told them they could have my mother's number but she wasn't going to care one way or the other. So this one detective said to me, "You know what? I have a nine-year-old daughter at home. If I thought I was going to find her like I found you two tonight, I would take this gun and go home and blow her brains out." I couldn't believe he said that to me, it was so shocking. I told him, "I'm not going to be here too much longer anyway, I'm moving to New York." He said, "Oh, where it's so cosmopolitan." I thought to myself that this detective is very dangerous, so I'm not going to say anything else. I'm going to be very cool, because I think he could try to hold us on something. But eventually they let us go.

Right after that, Frank went into the Army and I moved to New York so I could be closer to Charlie Parker and his music. I also decided I didn't want to live in Detroit anymore because I couldn't take the racial prejudice. As much as I loved my musician friends Tommy, Barry, Skeeter, Mitch, and Kenny, I just needed to get out of Detroit. I wanted to go where I thought I could be free to relate to the people and musicians I cared about.

So Jordan left for New York, not only to be near Charlie Parker's music but in the hope that she would escape the prejudice she witnessed daily in a city so full of discrimination and ignorance. Surely the sophistication of New York would bring her relief from the brutal world that ostracized the black culture and the music she so admired. However, the Big Apple was to prove a disappointment in that it was no more a refuge from racial thugs than Detroit had been. Jordan did not realize that the confrontations she had been subject to on a regular basis in Detroit were part of a trend of violence erupting in many urban areas in order to sustain segregation between blacks and whites. In addition, her trust in police officers had been tarnished from her Detroit experiences. However, some police officers appear to have been sincerely concerned about preventing racist violence.[5] Jordan recalls,

I used to have jam sessions at my loft in New York City. One time while a session was going on in my loft, I went to get something to eat with my two black artist friends, Percy Knight and Arthur Hardie. On the way back from the restaurant four white guys saw us together and came out of this bar on the corner and chased us down the street. They jumped us in front of my loft. Three of the guys held my two friends while the fourth guy threw me down on the street, beat the hell out of me and knocked my tooth out.

Then a guy dressed up in a suit walked across the street toward us with a gun. So I thought, after all those years dealing with hostility in Detroit,

I'm going to die in New York instead, which was supposed to be so cosmopolitan. For some reason I wasn't afraid, and I just waited for the shot. I figured, at least I'm going to be killed for doing something that I really believe in and that I know is right.

But it turned out the guy with the gun was an undercover detective. He said to the four white guys, "Why are you assaulting this young woman? Are you related? Do you know her?" Then he asked me, "Do you know them?" And I told him that I didn't know any of them. So he put the white guys up against the wall and frisked them. My two black artist friends were free to go. The detective asked me if I wanted to press charges, but cautioned me that they had already seen where I lived. I asked for his advice, since he had literally saved my life. He said, "If I were you I wouldn't press charges. Unfortunately, the way the world is today they're liable to come back and really do you in. But you do what you want. Whatever you want to do, I'm with you." So I didn't press charges. Even today I wonder if I made the right decision.

A pioneer for interracial relationships at a volatile time during the 1950s in New York and other parts of the country, Jordan audaciously married an African American musician, Duke Jordan. Although musical collaboration among whites and blacks was becoming commonplace on Fifty-Second Street, interracial sexual relationships still had the power to shock.[6] It wasn't until 1967 that the Supreme Court deemed anti-miscegenation laws unconstitutional, to the horror of many people who still believed the mingling of the races to be sinful and wrong. For decades, Jordan was faced with racism regarding the most vital areas of her life: her marriage, her friendships, and her professional music collaborations. "I found it difficult to find places for Duke and me to live because of the discrimination toward biracial couples. When we first decided to live together we were lucky to find a rooming house that was run by a lovely Jewish woman who accepted us, and next door was another interracial couple, so that was cool."

Other friends and musicians experienced exclusion, not only from society but from their own families. Jordan's friend from Detroit, Jenny Devries King, worried about telling her family. She relates, "I remember what my mother said when she came to see my husband and me and we hadn't even told her where we lived because of the racial thing. She was such a wonderful woman and I didn't want to hurt her. She said, 'How could you marry a black man? What about his parents? And I thought you'd come back here to live but now you can't live here because you're married to a black man.'" Sonny Rollins talked about it this way:

I was interracially married and of course we lived our life. We went through being ostracized. We're all human beings so we're going to commingle.

> I was married to my wife for over forty years and we had a wonderful relationship. And knowing people like Jordan and seeing her go through this early on just let me know that these things are possible in life. So it was never a big deal for me to be in an interracial marriage. It was normal. Those times that she came up in, those difficult times to have a black person having a white friend and a white person having a black friend—Jordan exemplified that so much in her life. I think she's a courageous woman.

Along with the disparagement from both Caucasians and African Americans for her marital status, there was yet another challenge for Jordan. In 1954 she became the proud mother of a biracial daughter, Tracey. Her maternal joy was often overshadowed by anger over the treatment of her innocent daughter, who from a young age had to cope with a myriad of ugly situations.

> After my daughter, Tracey, was born, I started taking her to the beach every Sunday. She loved to play in the water. I remember one time in particular we were on the subway going to Reis Park. Tracey was about nine months old at the time. There happened to be a white woman sitting across from us. She looked at Tracey and said, "Oh look at the cute little colored baby. Where did you get her from?" The lady had two small children sitting with her, so I asked her, "Are those your children?" She said yes. And my answer to her was, "I got my baby the same way you got yours." Then she looked puzzled. I don't know where my remark came from. It's almost like my higher power said to me, here, give this comment to her and let her digest it.
>
> Another time, we were at the beach when a group of white teenagers saw us. They came over to where my daughter was playing and formed a little circle around us. They began taunting us over and over: "Look at the little nigger baby. Look at the little nigger baby." It was horrible, really horrible. It was so devastating to watch my beautiful little girl being tormented by these ignorant teenagers. It was so cruel. We had to leave, because I didn't want her to hear any more of the mean things they were saying.

Fortunately, as Jordan's daughter became older the racial stigma was changing, especially with the help of young people and visionary leaders like Martin Luther King Jr., John and Robert Kennedy, and other forward-thinking politicians. Jordan's daughter, Tracey, recalls, "Growing up in that era there was a lot more tolerance. It was still very black and white but I think the walls were starting to meld together into just one community. I was a kid, so I probably didn't notice it since the group of friends my mother was with, the other artists, jazz musicians, actors, and whatever, treated it like the norm. Multiracial was kind of just normal to me anyway. I'm sure my mother saw it because she was older and from a different vantage than I did." Although times had improved, there were still difficult situations for the next generation, as Coryelle Kramer remembers:

> I used to get teased a lot when I was a kid and would tell Sheila about it as she was like my aunt. I would tell her that I just got accosted, beat up, and kicked, spit on and other things, all because I was biracial. She would be absolutely livid and she'd tell me that I have to let people know that they can't do that, that I was a human being who deserved to be treated with respect. And more importantly that I didn't have to take it and she gave me the strength to tell people this and to believe in myself. Sheila always had amazing people who came to her place of all races and cultures. She didn't care what you looked like on the outside; she cared about what you were on the inside. Because of her example, I have a wide variety and cross mix of friends too.

To this day, Jordan remains an advocate for racial equality and the African American community through her constant message of tolerance, unity, and love. "Today, I am overjoyed when I walk down the streets of most cities and witness the peaceful interaction of interracial couples and families. Not only that, but the fact that we elected a biracial president really blows my mind! I realize that my efforts and those of others in the past were not in vain."

• *10* •

The Crossing

"Take your troubles to The Crossing. It's where joy outweighs the pain."

—Sheila Jordan

Jordan's introduction to alcoholism came early in her life from observing her mother's binges to having to bring her drunken grandfather home from the beer gardens. As a young child she was always uncomfortable around her family when they were drinking and as a result developed a hatred of alcohol. She could never understand how one minute the grownups acted loving and caring and the next day they would be hungover and in a foul mood. Jordan remembers, "As a kid I was always embarrassed about their drinking. One time at school there was a boy who told me that my mother was nothing but a falling-down drunk, which was a mean thing to say. I couldn't have been more than ten years old and those words stayed with me forever. I thought to myself that I would never be a falling-down drunk. I hated alcohol and I told myself that I would never do that." But those words would come back to haunt her later in her life, and regrettably Jordan would lose her mother to the advanced stages of alcoholism.

Jordan started drinking at about fourteen years old, when she moved to Detroit. It was her desire to be accepted by the groups in high school, so she would join them when they drank at parties. Her drinking lasted for a couple of years until she met vocalists Skeeter Spight and Leroy Mitchell, who informed her that if she wanted to sing with them she had to stop drinking. That was the motivation she needed to make her quit, and she did. Says Jordan, "It wasn't like I was drunk every day. It was mainly at parties with friends from school where I would drink even though I was not yet of age. So I'd always find booze somewhere. After I stopped I never started drinking again until after I was living in New York." Until that time Jordan's worst habit was smoking cigarettes, which was not uncommon for most people during those days. Although she didn't take drugs, she did notice the effects from watching others, especially Parker and her ex-husband Duke Jordan. Both musicians were using heroin, which was prevalent on the jazz scene. "When I was around Bird," said Jordan, "he never influenced me in any way to use drugs. If anything, I think he was proud of the fact that I didn't take anything. At that time I wasn't even tempted by drugs or alcohol."

Jordan's drinking began after she started singing at the Page Three in the Village in the early '60s. Part of the criteria for working in the room was to mix with the customers and allow them to buy drinks to further the revenue of the club.

> So I told the owner, Jackie Howe, that I really didn't want to drink alcohol because of my childhood experiences. I told her the whole story. She told me to just spit back. I didn't know what that was and she told me to take a drink and instead of swallowing it you have a chaser of water or whatever and then you spit it back into the water. You pretend like you're drinking. I would order this drink, Cherry Herring, because it was sweet and red. So I remember one night there was a couple in the club who loved my singing. They bought me a Cherry Herring and I spit it back into the water chaser and they caught me. I was embarrassed, so I told them it was an accident and then drank the Cherry Herring. That immediately set off the phenomenon of craving for alcohol. So that's what got me started again.

Alcohol consumption for musicians or performing artists was often related to professional socializing, performance demands, and ways to deal with inhibitions, so it wasn't unusual that Jordan would succumb to these pressures. Vocalist Carol Fredette confirms, "In a lot of clubs, especially at the Page Three, you were expected to mix with the people. You'd sit down and it was about drinking, it was about making money for the clubs."

However, Jordan didn't allow herself to get completely immersed in drinking because she realized that she needed to keep it under control in order to maintain the responsibilities of raising her child. Although alcohol eventually took over her life, it did not happen until after her daughter was much older. It was important to her for her daughter not to have the same experience that she had endured as a child. According to Jordan, "Everybody thought they were going to be able to play better if they got high, especially with heroin. They thought it was going to help them play or sing better. Of course that wasn't true and Bird tried to tell them. He tried to tell Duke too and fortunately I never got involved with heroin, it was mostly booze and later cocaine."

One can't imagine the challenges that musicians faced during this time, including discrimination, financial insecurity, maintaining a musical reputation, and the constant demand for creativity. Society tends to focus on the addiction as opposed to the causes of these types of afflictions, which can be a result of early childhood instability, abuse, and genetic predisposition. According to a study on psychopathology and its relation to creativity among jazz musicians in the bebop era by Geoffrey I. Wills, PhD, "Seven subjects (17.5%) experienced an unhappy or unstable early life: for instance, Dizzy Gillespie and Charles Mingus remembered being beaten by their father, and Charlie Parker's father deserted the family when Parker was 10 years old." And in regard to heroin-related disorders:

> Twenty-one subjects (52.5% of the sample) were addicted to heroin at some time during their lives. It must be noted that heroin use was widespread among modern jazz musicians in the period after the Second World War and there were a number of reasons for this. After the war there was a dramatic increase in the availability of heroin because supply routes from the Far East and Turkey were re-opened by the Mafia. Heroin travelled via Marseilles directly to New York and was made easily accessible (Shapiro, 1988). It "flooded urban black neighbourhoods to plague the lives of average working-class African-Americans" (DeVeaux, 1997). Modern jazz was a revolutionary music that was rejected by the general public, and heroin, like the music, was defiantly anti-establishment (Hentoff, 1978). It thus tended to be adopted by disaffected musicians.[1]

Jordan remembers a particularly embarrassing occasion when Tracey brought home her boyfriend to meet her. Jordan recounts,

> She brought him up to the apartment and I had been drinking. I used to drink on the weekends since I worked in the office during the week. So I stood up to meet this guy my daughter wanted me to meet and I fell down from drinking and passed out. And I'll never forget the look on her face. But did that stop me? No, I just kept right on drinking. I look back on it now and think that I did the same thing my mother did. That's something I've had to work on and make amends for to my daughter because it must have been as terrible for her as it was for me. Unfortunately my daughter had to see that, so I'm not proud of that. I have made my amends to Tracey because she saw me intoxicated and not in a good space. I would tell her that I was sorry and she'd tell me, "You did the best you could." Tracey is such a beautiful person and I am so grateful for her understanding.

Tracey concurs: "We've been through a lot together. She's my best friend, and I love her dearly, dearly. I wouldn't trade anything for our friendship." But in Jordan's heavy-drinking days she was convinced she had things in check:

> I mean talk about denial, I would pass out right in front of my apartment building and whoever was with me would take me up to my place. And

> still I wouldn't face the fact that I was an alcoholic. I wasn't an everyday drinker, but all I needed was someone to drink with like my friends or the men I was involved with, who were also alcoholics. It's just that if I took the first drink I couldn't stop in most cases. Once in a while I'd try a little controlled drinking like telling myself I'll only have two drinks. But it was never okay because I was always thinking about when I could have the next drink.

One can only speculate about the causes of addiction, yet it was clear in Jordan's case that besides a history of family alcoholism she had been physically abused, bullied, harassed, and abandoned with a daughter in an environment of racism, not to mention her highly sensitive and artistic character. These are the types of conditions that would easily lend themselves to addictive behavior. Besides that, her daughter states further, "I know that she went through a traumatic era in history where it was really tough for women, especially being a Caucasian jazz singer in basically a genre of music that's pretty much identified with African Americans. But you can't really sing the blues unless you've lived through them, and I think that's colorless."

Jordan's awakening came one day when she was on a drinking binge with a boyfriend. She remembers passing out and waking up to a voice: "I woke and heard a very clear and strong message. 'You know what I gave you is a gift, and if you don't start taking care of that gift I'm going to take it away from you and give it to someone else.'" It was an eye-opening experience, forcing Jordan to finally realize that she was an alcoholic. She decided not to drink and stopped on her own, which she calls a "dry drunk." It would be eight years before she sought the program that helped her maintain a sober lifestyle to this day. In the meantime, she starting snorting cocaine, or as Jordan puts it, "I switched seats on the Titanic. I thought since rich people do it that it was okay." Jordan had convinced herself that cocaine was a pleasant drug that would not be addictive but she soon found out the truth. Her second "spiritual awakening" came with the same voice saying "Did you hear me? You hear what I said? I told you that if you don't take care of the gift I've given you and you don't respect it I'm going to take it away and give it to somebody else." This was the moment Jordan decided to seek help for her addictions by becoming a friend of Bill W. Every year on March 9 she celebrates her recovery of more than twenty years. Because of her perseverance in obtaining sobriety, Jordan attained a greater understanding of the issues that brought her to what she calls "this cunning, baffling and powerful disease." According to Jordan, "A lot of my use of alcohol and drugs had to do with my insecurity within myself, low self-esteem, and not being supported as a child. It took me years to discover that I was okay, I wasn't a bad person. I was given a gift and I have learned to respect it, take care of it, and share it with the world."

Jordan values the lessons and opportunities she has been given and knows that because addiction is an illness she must always stay away from alcohol and drugs. "That's what I teach young people if they wonder how I got sober and straightened out my life. I tell them there is help and you can find a solution to this disease. You have choices, and as long as you approach it one day at a time, you can find a way out." During Jordan's recovery period, she was inspired to write the song "The Crossing" as a way of encouraging others who are struggling with addiction. "I was walking on the mountain near my home in upstate New York and this song came to me. I was filled with such gratitude from being given this gift of sobriety, probably one of the greatest gifts in my life besides my daughter and my music. The Crossing can be anybody's crossing, whatever demons are in your life, you'll find an answer if you look for it and believe that you can find one."

The Crossing

There are moments in your lifetime
When the whole world seems insane.
If you search beyond the madness
There is peace of mind to gain.
Where there is not time or season
And there is no fear or strain.

Take your troubles to the crossing
It's where joy outweighs the pain.
Oh the crossing, oh the crossing,
It's been known by many names.
Some have found it through religion
Putting faith in God each day.

When your world seems lost and shattered
And your dreams have gone astray,
Never seek out self-destruction
There's a crossing that can help you find your way.
Oh the crossing, oh the crossing,
What a blessing it can be.

When you're feeling down and lonely
There's an answer there's a key.
And for those of you who wonder
What the crossing means to me,
It's the love I feel when I'm singing for you
Oh the spirit of the music sets me free.

• 11 •

Reel Time Mentor

"If I had a school, it would be a school from the heart and soul, and it would be a jazz school. It would be dedicated to Charlie Parker."

—Sheila Jordan

In the autumn of 1977, Eddie Summerlin, founder and director of the Jazz Department at City College of New York, invited Jordan to do an afternoon concert. That invitation initiated her maiden voyage as a jazz educator and master teacher. Jordan recalls the afternoon: "I sang some songs and talked to the students. I was a little nervous. I wasn't nervous when I was singing, just when I was talking about the music. And then I thought, I'm just going to talk about the way I feel about my experiences with the music. So that's what I did." After Jordan finished, Janet Steele, one of the classical voice teachers at the college, asked her if she would be willing to do a workshop with the singers. She wasn't sure she was up to the task since she didn't have a degree in music and lacked experience as an educator. Still she agreed to do the workshop and decided that she would talk about her own experiences learning to sing jazz. With the encouragement of Summerlin, John Lewis (pianist and director of the Modern Jazz Quartet), and the classical vocal teachers, Jordan soon discovered that her style of teaching was exactly what the program needed. It was refreshing to have Jordan giving real-life instruction to the students and passing down the mentorship she had received from so many of the jazz icons in her life. Over time, City College asked her to teach more often, and according to Jordan, in 1978 she created one of the first jazz vocal programs in the country.

It was the start of a new chapter in her career, as a jazz educator and mentor to aspiring jazz vocalists. Often it is through teaching others that we learn to teach, and so it was for Jordan. To this day, she is still surprised when she realizes the tremendous impact she has had and still has on so many singers of all genres. Even as an octogenarian she continues to travel all over the world, helping singers and instrumentalists to understand what jazz really means from someone who grew up learning to speak the language from the founders of its creation. She spreads the message of jazz through her own performances, and by sharing her experiences through workshops, clinics, colleges, and other private venues. Jordan humbly states, "I tell the students how I learned jazz and the particular things I've learned about the music. So when I'm doing a workshop or one-on-one teaching, I put my heart into it, the same as I do when I'm singing. I get the same feeling when I'm teaching as I do when I'm performing the music. I get wonderful e-mails and telephone calls all the time, from singers who tell me how much they've learned from what I shared with them. And that's how I know I'm doing the right thing."

From the very beginning Jordan applied her professional experiences to her teaching by emphasizing the songs from the Great American Songbook and insisting that singers learn the melody of compositions from the original sheet music, and not just from the recordings of other singers. In Jordan's opinion, melody notes are the stepping-stones to improvisation: "I was very insistent that the singers learn the tunes the proper way, at least from my point of view—from the source—the original lead sheet of the music with the melody line and correct chord changes. Just learning from a recording isn't enough, since the recorded vocal versions aren't going to stick to the melody. You're not ever going to know the actual melody and lyrics unless you get to the source and learn that first, because then you can go anywhere you want to with the tune."

When Jordan began teaching, jazz education was a new and developing field. Unlike today, teachers with degrees in jazz education were almost nonexistent; most teaching was based on the oral tradition, with teachers passing on their knowledge to students through demonstration or verbal explanation. Up until at least the mid-1980s, the majority of jazz vocal teachers were professional musicians who had worked in the "trenches" of the jazz clubs. The academic world created an opportunity for jazz artists to elevate jazz singing to a higher status, as well as gain some much-needed income along the way. However, the teaching was limited to a class here or there, a vocal jazz ensemble, or some private lessons, so there was not enough of a jazz curriculum to build a solid program. When Jordan created a program at City College it was one of the first in the nation that emphasized "solo" jazz singing and improvisation in real performance situations. Jordan based her program on the knowledge she had received from the jazz geniuses who had nurtured her during her formative years: Lennie Tristano, George Russell, Charlie Parker,

Charles Mingus, and countless others. Her mentors had supplied her with the necessary ingredients to become the unique and impressive interpreter of jazz and improvisation that she remains today.

In her approach to teaching jazz, Jordan credits Parker and focuses on the bebop tunes that she felt—and still feels today—are so necessary for singers to incorporate into their repertoire. Jordan explains,

> I always felt the singers should at least learn a bebop tune, so they could feel what was going on in the music. After that, I would teach them a little guideline (choosing a simple melodic line based on the chord changes or scales to the tune) so they could improvise on it. Then I would show them how they could create a solo without filling every space. It's important that all musicians know how to leave space, like Miles did. Then there's a little exercise I do that teaches the singers how they can build a solo. If they want to continue this later on in their life they can, and if they don't and they just want to do it for fun, that's great, too.

When Jordan left City College to go on tours, she always recommended teachers whom she respected, such as Jay Clayton, to fill in for her. As a result, she and Clayton often give workshops together or teach at other programs as a team. Jordan continued with the program at City College for twenty-seven years, and the culmination of her efforts was the creation of one of the premier places to study vocal jazz. Her accompanists for the program were pianists Reggie Moore and Ray Gallon. Gallon admiringly remembers,

> I first met Sheila in the late '70s when, as a student at CCNY, I enrolled as an apprentice accompanist for her weekly Jazz Vocal Workshop class. Within a few years, I became the full-time accompanist for that class and, soon after that, Sheila started calling me for gigs. Her loving support and constant encouragement helped me to feel confident enough to pursue a career as a jazz pianist. I can certainly tell you that accompanying Sheila's vocal workshops has spoiled me. She is such a natural teacher. Always open and willing to share all of her knowledge and experience, Sheila teaches with a lot of love, though it is often tough love. She always insists that her students learn the correct, original melody and lyrics of each of their songs (learning songs from recorded interpretations is not the way to learn songs) and Sheila's remarkable encyclopedic knowledge of the American Songbook allows her to instantaneously correct any and all mistakes. Another priority for Sheila is that students learn how to communicate with their accompanists and how to do all things necessary in leading a band. She consistently offers her students wonderful arranging ideas that are both creative and practical and sees to it that the students are well aware of a wide variety of possibilities for intros, endings, interludes, vamps, tags, rubato, and more.

Gallon continued as the accompanist for Jordan's classes until she left City College in 2004. Today the rapidly growing jazz program offers a bachelor of fine arts, with a curriculum under the direction of Suzanne Pittson that focuses on the development of vocabulary and language for improvisation. But the heart of the program will always be the practical performance applications first bestowed on its students by a "jazz child" from Detroit with a bebop message. "I feel that I really started that jazz program at City College and I'm thrilled that it turned out to be very successful and continues to this day." Gallon adds,

> In the thirty-plus years I have been fortunate to work with Sheila, both on the bandstand and in the classroom, she has taught me so much: a deep appreciation of working with singers; the art of accompaniment; how to teach with love and humor while remaining firm and not tolerating any BS; how to arrange songs in an interesting, creative way; how to organize set lists; making every note count; playing every note as if it is your last; hidden gems of the American Songbook; the importance of finding just the right tempo and mood for every song; always swinging; the beauty of bebop and the blues; and the amazing stories of her friendships with so many of my musical heroes. Above all, she always teaches, by example, the importance of artistic honesty and integrity.

The art of scat singing, or improvising using wordless or horn-related syllables or sounds, has been the defining feature of many great jazz singers. Amazing vocal improvisers such as Ella Fitzgerald, Jon Hendricks, Betty Carter, Sarah Vaughn, Anita O'Day, Mel Tormé, and Mark Murphy, among many others, set the bar and continued the evolution. The majority of these singers learned to scat sing in the big bands and small jazz combos by listening to the great horn players who surrounded them. Because the majority of Jordan's musical models were jazz players rather than singers, it was only natural that she learned scat singing the same way. Her years of immersion in Parker's solos began early, and her ability to sing them and even write lyrics to some of them deepened her understanding of soloing on chord changes. In fact, her mastery of bebop changes and phrasing contributes in no small part to her reputation as one of the world's finest improvisational singers. At her concerts and club dates, it's not unusual to see the players on the bandstand stretching out and admiring her creativity and skill in developing a high-quality solo. It's apparent to anyone watching the interaction of Jordan and the band that she is embraced as a respected member of the ensemble instead of just another singer to accompany. In addition, the fact that she can interject substantial musical and rhythmic ideas creates the kind of depth and spontaneity that jazz artists revere.

However, when working with students, Jordan always insists that being a jazz singer does not require having to scat or even feeling obligated to prove that one can. From Gallon's observations, "Sheila encourages scatting but always points out that it is not a requirement ('Billie Holiday was the greatest jazz singer of all time and she never scat!'); but, when scatting, she always emphasizes the importance of connecting with the changes and listening to the accompanists. Sheila also stresses how important it is for young jazz singers to listen to the great instrumentalists and not just other jazz singers." At every workshop, Jordan brings up scat singing in her own clever yet poignant way, to emphasize the importance of recognizing whether or not scat singing is the right choice for a singer:

> I call it a "scat virus," because I find that in today's jazz singer's world, many singers feel that if they don't scat sing, they're not jazz singers. I find that very disturbing, because there are too many great singers who either didn't scat or chose to only infrequently. A prime example is Billie Holiday, who wasn't known as a scat singer. I'm not saying she couldn't, because I used to have a tape that someone gave me of her scat singing one time at a party. The people at the party were yelling, "Scat, Billie, scat!" and so she did—and she sounded great! Unfortunately, the tape was destroyed when my first house in upstate New York burned down. But my point is, she didn't scat or record scat singing, even though she could. Even Sarah Vaughan didn't scat that much, nor did Carmen McRae. Now, the main scat singers, in my opinion, are Ella Fitzgerald, Anita O'Day, Betty Carter, Jay Clayton, Mark Murphy, Jon Hendricks, Bobby McFerrin, and Kurt Elling. But today the "scat virus" can be dangerous because, although many singers aren't comfortable scat singing, don't enjoy doing it, and don't have a passion to scat sing, they feel that if they don't do it, they won't be considered a real jazz singer. My personal feeling is that there's a scat virus going around, and they don't have an antibiotic. So I always talk about my antibiotic—bebop—and about how I learned to scat by listening to bebop: Charlie Parker, Dizzy Gillespie, Miles Davis, Bud Powell, and all those great players. That was my music. I got turned on to jazz music when I was fourteen and I heard Bird play for the first time on a jukebox. So it was Bird who turned me on to jazz music and scat singing. I sang with Bird through his records, and it left no room for "shoobie-doobies." Today a lot of the young singers use very corny syllables because they're uptight about what to use. I think that if they would practice singing more bebop lines it would eliminate a lot of the corny syllables, and eventually they'd find their own syllables, as I've done throughout the years. Even I wasn't ready to jump right into scat singing. I scat sang as a teenager, but when I did my first recording on Blue Note [*Portrait of Sheila*], I didn't scat at all. I was just singing the tune straight from my heart. I just didn't feel like scat singing at the time. It wasn't until much later that I started recording any of my scat

> singing, but that doesn't mean I couldn't do it. I just wasn't pressured into it the way some of these young kids and professional singers coming up are today. And if it comes from being pressured, in my opinion, it doesn't sound real. It doesn't sound honest. Sometimes singers sound so much better when they just sing a song and sing it from the depths of their soul. So I personally think that the antibiotic for scat singing is bebop.

In our technological society, we often lose touch with the oral teaching tradition between master craftsman and student. But this philosophy, along with Jordan's musical and life experiences, shapes what she offers in her workshops, classes, and private coaching. Her basic approach is revealed and emphasized in what she calls *the four main ingredients*: what happens with your foot (accurate time), what beats in your chest (emotional expression), and what's attached to your head or your ears (deep listening), and then how it is expressed (articulation and pronunciation). Since the interest in jazz singing is now worldwide, Jordan does include a fifth, more practical, ingredient intended for international students. She recommends that singers who don't speak the English language learn to do so, in order to preserve the intent of the composer's and lyricist's message and deliver their music with both accuracy and understanding. Last but not least is dedication to the music. This dedication is part of the message Jordan brings to the world—the lesson that just learning the music is not enough, that you have to be as devoted to it as you are to the family members and friends whom you love throughout their highs and lows, and their trials and triumphs. "Really loving the music is what counts," Jordan insists. "Loving it so much that you dedicate your life to it, whether you become a star, which in most cases you won't, or just sing for the joy of doing the music and keeping it alive. That's what dedication to the music means to me."

In terms of teaching style, Jordan believes in giving love and encouragement to all of her students, from beginners to professionals. This quality has especially endeared her to her students. "What I want to do as a teacher is be a friend," she says.

> I don't want to put myself up a few notches from you and be on a power trip. I refuse to teach that way, and if I have to be on a power trip to teach, then I don't want to teach. I just want to show you how I learned jazz, how it came into my life, and how important it is for me. Hopefully some of that desire will rub off on my students. That's all that I want to do. I just want to keep this music alive by inspiring others to love it as much as I do.
>
> I had a student at City College I'll never forget. She was very shy, and I think embarrassed because she had a lot of facial hair. Boy, could she sing! I'll never forget how I managed to bring her voice out and how good it made me feel. So I was looking forward to having her perform at our

> concert. The day before the concert, she came up to me and said, "I'm not going to do the concert." I said, "Why not?" She said, "Well, I'm just not comfortable doing it." Well, I encouraged her to go on in spite of her fears, and I told her, "You'll be very comfortable because you sing beautifully." So she did sing in the concert. Years later I saw her again, and I noticed she'd had the facial hair removed. She said, "I want to thank you for giving me the courage to sing that day, because I don't think I'd be where I am today." I always remembered that, and it made me realize what an influence we can have on our students in so many other ways besides teaching them to sing. I was so happy that I'd made a difference in her life.

In the early 1980s Jordan became a featured educator with the annual Jazz in July program at the University of Massachusetts in Amherst. She was hired for the program by two of its three cofounders: Dr. Frederick C. Tillis, a well-known saxophonist and published poet, and Dr. Billy Taylor, the renowned pianist and educator (the third cofounder was legendary drummer Max Roach). Dr. Tillis remembers, "It started—I think, and I'm not absolutely certain, but I would say—probably around 1973 maybe, or something like that, '74. I came to the university in '70. In 1972 Max Roach and Archie Shepp came, and about two years after that somebody else in 1974. So as these big stars and famous people came to the University of Massachusetts, I decided, well, why not get a program that would highlight them. And that's how we came up with the Jazz in July, because it was right after the 4th of July." Although the program started out with instrumentalists, at some point a vocalist was brought into the program to teach singers. Dr. Tillis remembers that she was a good vocalist, but as he put it, "she was a little hard on the vocalists, not as gentle and nice in handling the variety of vocalists we had." One evening he attended a concert at UMass where Jordan was performing and thought that she might fit in well with the program due to her personality and skill. Dr. Tillis recalls, "And she really was a little hesitant about doing it because she said, 'I don't want to take anybody else's job.'" Jordan eventually took the position and remembers,

> The teacher at the time was a little rough on the kids, and so they got their spirits broken very easily. I found out early on in teaching that you don't break a student's spirit. It does nothing for you as a teacher, and it absolutely does nothing for the student. Unfortunately, some teachers are on power trips, and because they may not be working professionally they don't understand the pressures of being out in the jazz scene struggling to keep the music alive. They're insulated in a teaching environment, and it can cause them to either lose perspective or be musically frustrated. At least that's what I've observed. I try to be a different type of example for the students. I sing from my heart, and I teach from my heart, too. If I can't

> do that, then I don't want to do music or teach others. If you can't do it from your heart and your soul, why bother? That's why I've never been classified as a diva. I prefer to be the messenger of this music. So I went up to Jazz in July, and I was quite surprised that they'd want me, but obviously it worked, because I'm still there.

Jordan continues teaching every year at Jazz in July, and Dr. Tillis sums it up: "I know that she's contributed a great deal to the teaching of jazz. It so happens that she loves the music and she loves it so much that she gives of herself. There's nobody who sings some of the kinds of music that she does. So this puts her in a different category from other singers. Let's put it this way, she sings jazz in such a way that it's personalized. Nobody sings like she does."

One of her former students and now an established jazz artist in her own right, Tierney Sutton, tells of her summer experience with Jordan:

> I first met Sheila Jordan in the summer of 1986 at U Mass Amherst at "Jazz in July." Sheila was with the vocalists the first week of the program, but because she had a commitment, another vocalist was with us for the second week. During the week with Sheila, I watched even the most timid and inexperienced vocalists blossom. There was warmth and honesty, a kindness and life experience that Sheila offered, that I never forgot. The vocalist who was with us for the second week of the program was an excellent and skilled singer, but her spirit was not in the same league as Sheila's. I never forgot the contrast and have always held Sheila's example as the paradigm for great and generous teaching.

In 1985 the Austrian "Styrian Autumn" festival premiered George Gruntz's oratorio *The Holy Grail of Jazz and Joy*, featuring Sheila Jordan, Bobby McFerrin, Howard Johnson, and saxophonist and composer Karlheinz Miklin. As a result of that performance, Jordan became friends with Miklin, who was the head of the jazz department at the Hochschule für Musik (KUG University) in Graz, Austria. With his encouragement, Jordan set up a vocal jazz program there and taught from March until June 1988 and from October until January in 1988–1989, 1994–1995, 1996–1997, and 1999–2000. Jordan remembers her teaching experiences in Graz: "There was a workshop before mine but as Charlie [Karlheinz] told me at the time, they wanted someone who could teach the singers more straight-ahead music. The previous teacher was teaching them more free music. I think Charlie and I both felt these young singers needed to know how to sing 'in' before they sang 'out.' I agreed to teach in Graz and sent subs to my City College gig." However, due to the length of the program in Graz, it became difficult for Jordan to commit to the schedule so she rotated with other singers. "I recommended and opened the door for a lot of other singers to teach in Graz. My first replacement was Mark Murphy. The kids loved him. Then I got Jay

Clayton to fill in for me and they loved her also." Laurie Antonioli, vocal director of the California Jazz Conservatory, remembers,

> Nancy King was invited to come out, and couldn't do it. Nancy talked to Sheila and they came up with the idea of inviting me to come in Nancy's place. When I arrived at Graz I was brought into the "rotation," which was to be passed around to the other vocal artists. Once I was there, the school decided they wanted a full time vocal professor and invited me to stay on. Thus, the era of rotating professors that Sheila started had come to an end. Now Dena DeRose is there in a full-time, tenured position and probably will remain until she retires. But back in the day, when Sheila was involved, the three main people who taught in Graz were Sheila, Mark Murphy, and Jay Clayton. Some of the other teachers included Andy Bey, Michelle Hendricks, Lauren Newton, and Tom Lellis. Sheila was deeply loved in Graz and famous for starting that vocal program. It was the first of its kind in Europe and I'd go as far as to say that Sheila changed the face of vocal jazz education in Europe. Since she started that program, others cropped up in Germany, Switzerland, and Italy.
>
> Always a favorite workshop presenter, Sheila traveled throughout Europe doing workshops and educational residencies. But it was in Graz where she developed a stationary program that lives on today at a major institution, where young singers from all over Europe can come study the music. I have Sheila to thank as the one who got my career in academia off the ground.

When Jordan first took the position in Graz, she found that she was homesick since she didn't speak the language or have many friends. Jordan recalls, "Of course, this lonesome feeling didn't last long because I had wonderful students I became very close friends with Theo Bleckmann, Melanie Bong, Peter Mihelic, and Fritz Pauer. The musicians were wonderful and the school was fantastic. On top of all of this, I made a really nice salary; it was enough to pay my mortgage on my house upstate." Antonioli remembers Pauer fondly:

> Fritz was a pianist who not only worked with Sheila for several decades—in fact, even when Sheila wasn't in Graz teaching she'd go to Europe and work with Fritz as her pianist—but it turned out that Fritz, who passed in 2012, had worked with many, many American jazz musicians, most notably Art Farmer, and was my saving grace while living and working at the university. The jazz world is small and the connection with Fritz was one of the most monumental experiences I had being in Graz. Fritz loved playing for Sheila. As it turned out, Fritz and I became songwriting partners and subsequently wrote over forty songs together—his music, my lyrics—until he passed, a relationship that continued even after I came back to the states.

Besides Jazz in July, Jordan continues to teach for one week each August at Brattleboro's Vermont Jazz Center, under the direction of pianist and composer Eugene Uman. "Eugene is a wonderful piano player and educator," Jordan comments, "and I have enjoyed doing that workshop since I started." Hungarian guitar player Attila Zoller started the summer program, and although he and Jordan were friends it wasn't until Uman took over that a vocal component was created. According to Uman, "I had noticed that there were a lot of vocalists in the Southeast and Vermont area and that their needs weren't being met. I wanted to change things and bring in some singers. So the first summer that we included vocalists we invited Sheila up to do a three-day program, three out of the six days, just as a pilot to see if it would work, and that was in 1997." Uman had met Jordan sometime in the mid-1980s and stayed in touch with her until one day he was asked to be the replacement pianist at City College for Gallon, who was on the road. Because he already knew that Jordan had experience starting programs and because of her status as a major jazz artist, Uman felt she would be the perfect choice. Uman recalls,

> And I didn't even know how to set it up. So I asked Sheila what to do and she said, "Just make sure that I have a bass player and you come in and play piano with me a little bit when you're not doing stuff." And so it ended up being a bass player named Tyler Gibbons who joined us and I accompanied on piano. And as you can imagine, it worked out really well. The next year, in 1998, we did it the whole way through with vocals and to this day we have to turn away vocal students because there's such a demand, because they enjoy the program so much. Sheila is a wonderful advocate for the Vermont Jazz Center. She gets students to come from all over the world. Whenever she does a concert and finds people who are singers, she invites them to her programs here in the United States.

Once the program started getting popular, Jordan invited her friend, vocalist Jay Clayton, to collaborate with the program, which continues to expand. Uman sums up Jordan's contributions to jazz and jazz education:

> First and foremost, there's her connection to the lineage, but then you've got to connect that to her generosity and her desire to communicate that with others. And then, that flows directly into the other most important part about Sheila, which is that she is a great jazz educator, and it's not just because she's a great musician, but it's because she has been able to break down what it is that she learned through the old-school methods that is then practical and applicable toward learning the music even in this day and age. I think one of the most important things about Sheila is the fact that she is a great singer who has come up through the old-school convention of learning tunes by ear through being able to sing back solos by Miles

> Davis and Charlie Parker. And because she actually knew Miles Davis and Charlie Parker and the cadre of great musicians who hung out with them and is part of their group, Sheila is a really important touchstone for all of us who love the music. She is, without a doubt, one of the most important historically connected individuals on the planet.

Among Jordan's other regular commitments is the Interplay Jazz Workshop in Woodstock, Vermont, during the month of June, under the direction of pianist and saxophone player Fred Haas and his wife Sabrina Brown. Founded in 1996, the workshop provides a holistic experience with a professional music faculty that focuses on key aspects of jazz improvisation, integrated with daily yoga and meditation. According to Jordan, "It's a great place for the students to learn the music and at the same time feel nurtured and safe to express their creativity." Over the years, Jordan has taught at hundreds of other workshops and clinics in the United States and abroad, including the Litchfield Jazz Camp in Connecticut; Fionna Duncan Workshop in Edinburgh, Scotland; the Jazzschool (now California Jazz Conservatory) in the San Francisco Bay Area; Jazz Camp West in California; Corfu Jazz Camp in Greece; the Banff International Workshop in Jazz and Creative Music in Canada; and the Sardinia Workshop in Italy. "All the workshops that I do, I enjoy very much, and if I didn't, I wouldn't do them. It's not about the money; it's about the attitude and spiritual feeling going on."

When Jordan began teaching thirty-five years ago, jazz education was in its infancy. New jazz instrumental programs continue to emerge in colleges, universities, high schools, and even K–12 programs. Unfortunately, vocal jazz programs, specifically those that train solo jazz vocalists, have not kept pace with instrumental jazz programs. Aside from private studies with professionals or workshops such as those Jordan offers, aspiring solo jazz singers have had a limited number of schools to offer them training. As a result, only a handful of solid programs for singers exists, and there have been few opportunities for jazz vocal educators to develop curricula for the future. Worse still, some of the iconic vocal singers have died without being able to pass down pertinent information to the next generations of singers. This is why Jordan continues to be a significant mentor for jazz singers. As one of the few remaining icons of the early jazz era, Jordan views her role today as that of a messenger of the music in all areas of her career. Today she recognizes other mentors and a new group of talented vocalists and educators who are passing along the torch:

> Mark Murphy, who has been teaching about as long as I have. Definitely Jay Clayton, and she and I teach together, too. I think of Theo Bleckmann, Kate McGarry, Peter Eldridge, Laurie Antonioli, David Linx, Tierney Sutton, Madeline Eastman, and Ellen Johnson. They are all wonderful teachers

> and singers who treat their students like friends, like they're people they really want to help, and they're not on a power trip. And, of course, I know Jon Hendricks teaches from his heart, and to me he is the genius of "vocalese." Also schools like the Jazzschool [now California Jazz Conservatory], Art of Jazz in Toronto, Jazz Camp West, Manhattan School of Music, and Queens College. So these are some of the teachers and schools. Actually, the students today are very fortunate because they can learn technique, take piano classes, and become highly skilled musicians. That only helps your singing. When I was coming up, there were no such schools, so that part is really an advantage. Not to mention all of the wonderful summer camps and workshops for people who work regular jobs to make a living, like I did, and don't have the chance to study in a school program. In the summer, you have all of these camps you can go to and learn the music. And it's a nice vacation, too.

According to an article in *All About Jazz* by Suzanne Lorge,

> Over the years Murphy and Jordan also have offered some of the best teaching available to up-and-coming jazz singers, devoting a significant part of their careers to imparting the knowledge they learned in the edgy jazz clubs of their youth.
>
> Still, vocal jazz is a tough thing to teach from an academic setting, a situation that gives Murphy pause.
>
> "They're trying to put [how to sing jazz] into books now and the books are marvelous, but you can't get the feeling from that," Murphy explains. "To be a jazz singer it takes a lot of study. You've got to know the chord changes and the words" first off, he asserts, but when it comes to improvisation, the litmus test for serious jazz singers, you can only learn by doing.
>
> The way I learned was I'd just get up there and at first the more complex parts of the improv weren't there. But you try them again and it flows a little more. You have to fall in love with it and that's what gives you the courage and the inspiration to go on further and further and further. And then, all of a sudden, things start to happen.[1]

With commercial music dominating the music scene today, how can young singers find places to practice and develop their art and craft? Jordan's advice on this matter is simple: Devote less time to getting a CD out and more to finding places to sing. "Singers can go into a lot of places that have an open mic night, or they can sit in with instrumentalists," she points out. "Or look for a school—sometimes music schools have a regular singers' jam session night. You have to be singing jazz constantly, wherever you can. It's the best way to become good at the music. My feeling has always been that if you want to do this music you will find a place to do it. I don't care who you are or what you play, you will find a place to do this music and that, again, is part of the dedication."

• 12 •

Where You At?

> "I feel blessed that I grew up spending all of those wonderful years surrounded by the joy that he gave. There's nothing in life that will ever have the meaning for me or can give me a thrill like hearing Charlie Parker."
>
> —Sheila Jordan

There was no vacation from jazz for Jordan as she entered the year 2013. Although she had promised to pace herself, she was tempted by even more offers to perform due to her NEA Jazz Master recognition. It was an exhilarating time, filled with commitments to past work and opportunities for new projects. "Well, you know, I'm in my eighties now," says Jordan,

> and it's shocking to me that I've lived this long. A lot of it has to do with my attitude, and the fact that I had this music in my life. It's almost like it keeps me alive. In fact, I know it keeps me alive. I know I wouldn't be around if I didn't have music. I've been ill a few times. In 2010 I had pneumonia for the very first time in my life. I've had irregular heartbeat, AFib, which is under control now.
>
> I've had some scares like that, but to tell you the truth, the only time I ever canceled a concert because of illness was when I had to go in the hospital with pneumonia. I'll never forget it. I went to my doctor, and I told him I was feeling a little dizzy. I wasn't feeling very steady, and I wanted to make sure everything was okay, as I told the doctor, because I had to go to Toronto on a week's tour the next day. He said, "You're not going anywhere." I said, "Why not?" He said, "Because you're going in the hospital." I said, "Why?" He said, "Because you have pneumonia, my dear." So it was very upsetting to me that I had to cancel, because I know how hard a friend of mine, Yvette, had worked to get this tour together.

But they were all very understanding. I thought they'd probably never have me back again or they'll never trust me again, but they did.

And I'm very fortunate to know wonderful musicians all over the world who love to do music with me. There are two piano players in Germany and I have a wonderful trio in Italy, Attilio Zanchi and Roberto Cipelli, and sometimes Paulo Fresu, the wonderful trumpet player, flügelhorn player. I work with them because they bring me overseas to do concerts with them, which is thrilling. They call *me*. And I feel that we really do communicate well. When I go to England, I usually work with Nick Weldon and his trio and they play wonderful for me. Then when I go to Scotland, I work with the great Brian Kellock and his trio. I'm lucky because I've got trios who are arranging tours for me just about all over the world.

So I'm always busy even at this age. True, I get a little tired sometimes from the travel, but the minute I get on stage and see all those beautiful faces and those wonderful people out there, it's like I'm twelve years old again. It's a beautiful feeling. So I feel very blessed. I owe a lot of this to my sobriety. That gave me the courage to go on and do what I felt I had to do in my life. But I never in my life, expected that I would get this far in the music and that no matter what age, I would be able one day to travel the world and spread this music around.

Early in the year, on Valentine's Day, Jordan and her daughter attended a special wedding celebration for her friend and past student Theo Bleckmann. Jordan describes the event:

One of the highlights of 2013 was attending Theo's wedding to Preston Bailey. As I have said thousands of times, Theo is like a son to me. He couldn't have met a more wonderful, kind, and generous partner in Preston. I was honored that Preston accepted Tracey and myself as family. After all, he has been making these fantastic Thanksgiving dinners for us for the past couple of years. You can imagine what kind of a dinner he gives since he's a famous and incredible events planner. When the wedding plans were being made, Theo called me to find out what day I would be around. He wanted to make sure I would be able to attend. Thank God Tracey and I could see this beautiful wedding take place. Joan Rivers joined them together and all of their closest friends were in attendance. I used to think about gay people and the terrible times they went through years ago when I first started working at the Page Three. They were constantly being called names, harassed, and even physically abused, very similar to the hatred of the Afro-Americans. I used to wonder if the day would ever come when people could love whomever they wanted to and live and walk freely in life without the fear of abuse. It's always been my belief that if two people love each other, regardless of their sex or race, why shouldn't they be able to live a normal life minus all the hatred? So this wedding was a very special event for me. I saw it as a stepping-stone to progress for my gay friends and people in general.

Shortly after that, Jordan toured Italy from March 3 through 10 with the E.S.P. Trio and then went on to perform in Japan with pianist Mihelic from April 10 through 18. Jordan always kept a positive outlook on her travels, no matter how difficult the situation. Jordan's posts on Facebook for April 11 and 14 read,

> I'm stuck in Anchorage, Alaska. Our plane was on the way to Tokyo and the electricity in the main cabins and bathrooms went out. No electricity except for overhead lights. We have to stay overnight here and then get a new plane to Tokyo tomorrow. Thank God it happened before we started flying over the Pacific Ocean. Better safe than sorry. What's on my mind are the trials and tribulations we all go thru to keep jazz music alive.
>
> Being stuck in Anchorage, Alaska was one thing but how about earthquakes? Yesterday there was one in Western Japan. I'm in Tokyo, which is east I believe but I was sitting in my chair and it started moving around with me in it. It was like a scary movie. Just an aftershock. It was weird but the music is always well worth it. And how was your day?

Jordan returned from that trip and turned around to go back on the road again. On April 26 she was in Massachusetts singing with a full string orchestra and big band at UMass under the direction of Jeffrey Holmes. As Jordan recalls, "Jeffrey wrote such beautiful arrangements for the strings and the big band. It was a wonderful evening full of love and joy." The longtime friendship between Jordan and Jay Clayton began sometime in the late '70s when she was singing at the Tin Palace in the East Village. The two already had a mutual respect for each other's work. Clayton remembers,

> I knew about her but I had never met her. I was already playing my own gigs with Cameron Brown. So one night our gig stopped early and I said, "Please, Cameron, can we go to the Tin Palace? I want to meet Sheila." And that's when I met her in person. She had already heard about me and so then she came to hear me at the Top of the Gate. That meant so much to me. At that time, she'd been teaching at City College and I would go there and watch her workshops. She wanted to take a couple years off from her City College teaching and she asked me if I would be interested in teaching for her. So I did it for two years. So then we got to know each other better and she even used to babysit my kids when they were little. Then I moved away to Seattle but I used to come visit her. I can remember being up in the country with her and we would take walks and she'd tell me, "You've got to move back." So I did. And we became very close, closer than I ever thought we would, honestly. I mean, she's Sheila Jordan.

> I always tell her that. She's just this really enjoyable, amazing, wonderful, interesting person that you'd love no matter what. And then on another hand, you look at her and you go, oh yeah, and she's also Sheila Jordan.

Clayton became a great support to Jordan after her dear friend Marria Banks passed away. Jordan affectionately remembers, "I had a wonderful friend, Marria, who was like my sister and we were very close. I could talk to her about things that bothered me that I never told anyone else. We drank together and we got sober together. We even bought houses in the country very close to each other. Her daughter Coryelle is like my niece. I was closer to her than most of my own family. Jay has taken Marria's place since her passing. Jay was always a good friend to me and we tell each other things that we would never tell anyone else." The two became constant companions, often hanging out to hear music or spending time socializing at Jordan's apartment or her upstate home. So it was no surprise when Clayton came up with an idea for a group with Jordan called Bebop to Freebop. Clayton was as well known for her free vocal improvisation as Jordan for her bebop. During the concerts, the two vocalists divide the evening with duets featuring Jordan, Brown, and Clayton with guitarist Jack Wilkins. Eventually they all share the stage in a combination of duets, trios, and a quartet. In late spring of 2013, the group did a two-and-a-half-week tour in Europe, ending with a concert for the Women in Jazz Festival at the Kennedy Center on May 16. Francine Schwartz of *DC Metro Theater Arts* shared the following in a live performance review on May 17, 2013:

> Sheila Jordan brought the crowd to its feet with her renditions of "We Thought About You," "So In Love," "Little Willie Leaps," and "Ballad For Miles," which included "My Funny Valentine" and "Lament." Jordan has an infectious, droll style, and has developed into a superb scat singer and improviser, often compared to Blossom Dearie. Like Blossom Dearie, she has received well-deserved recognition for her unique talent late in life. She has also produced many critically successful recordings, and has appeared with many prominent jazz musicians during a 40-year career in and out of the music industry, as well as being a notable jazz educator. Jack Wilkins, a well-known accompanist on the guitar, collaborated and provided standout accompaniment. Cameron Brown on double bass added rhythmic depth to these showpieces of Bop. Jay Clayton regularly performs as a singing duo with Ms. Jordon all over the world. Both Clayton and Jordan specialize in wordless improvisation, a facet of free jazz, which uses the wordless voice as a powerful instrument rather than the usual emphasis on lyrics and narrative. Through the use of innovative mixing, Clayton speaks and sings over a percussive background of her own voice on tape, which showed off the bluesy talents of Wilkins as well as the two scat singers.[1]

Jordan has been a longtime friend to Mark Murphy, sharing a special bond as well, so it was not unexpected that she was invited to sing at a tribute to him at Joes's Pub in New York City. "Mark Murphy: Celebrating the Life and Career of the Master Jazz Vocalist" was a collaboration between the Jazz Foundation of American and Lunched Management & Booking, with the proceeds going toward helping musicians in need. It was also a celebration of the release of Murphy's EP, *A Beautiful Friendship: Remembering Shirley Horn*, on Gearbox Records. The evening included Jay Clayton, Amy London, Janis Siegel, Tessa Souter, Theo Bleckmann, Francesco Pini, Roz Corral, Milton Suggs, and other artists. Jordan says fondly,

> I love Mark like a family member. The last time I heard Mark sing was at Joe's Pub when a group of singers got together to honor him. We all did a song and everyone sang from the heart. Mark sang last and I wheeled him on stage. He improvised long solos and his voice was the same old Mark. I sang "Sheila's Blues" and improvised about Mark and what he means to me. It was a lovely evening. I have been through many times with Mark both good and bad. When his partner died, I was there for him to lean on. He has been to my house upstate and use to come to my dinners on Thanksgiving and he always bragged about my turkey. He still asks me to make him a turkey!

The celebration of Murphy's recording remembering pianist and vocalist Shirley Horn was particularly special for Jordan. Jazz critic and Grammy Award–winning jazz journalist Joel Siegel introduced Jordan to Horn, and the two immediately became close and dear friends. Jordan affectionately recalls,

> She came to the club in Washington, D.C., where I was working one night, called the One Step Down, and brought me a beautiful bunch of red roses. Shirley would invite me to sing at her gigs and for me, the way she played ballads was out of this hemisphere. Nothing like it and nothing since. I loved Shirley and boy, she sure could cook. One time when I was in D.C. working, she invited me for dinner. Wow, what a meal. She also made a little jacket for me too. Unfortunately, I didn't get to see her as much as I wanted to because of our touring schedules and living in different cities. The only gig we ever did together was at Fat Tuesday's. It was Shirley Horn with her trio, Helen Merrill with her group, and me and Harvie. Helen opened the set, then me and Harvie, and then Shirley. I joined her at the end of her set to do some blues.

In 2004 Jordan performed at the Kennedy Center in tribute to her friend. Mike Joyce of the *Washington Post* writes, "The vocalists were a diverse and impressive lot: Newcomer Lizz Wright, seasoned baritone Kevin Mahogany and the great jazz veteran Sheila Jordan, whose custom-tailored arrangement of "The Very Thought of You" simultaneously revealed her bop roots, eternally youthful spirit and great affection for Horn."[2] Jordan remembers the concert:

> Shirley was very upset when she found out that I wasn't included with the rest of the singers who were there to honor her. She insisted that I be part of the celebration. I was so happy to be part of this wonderful tribute. She already had her amputation and was in a wheelchair at that time. She sang at the end of the concert; the tune was "Here's to Life" and she wanted to accompany herself. A few people backstage were concerned about it but I said "Hey, Shirley will be fine, trust her, I do." And of course she was so moving and at the end she pointed to the audience and told them, "Here's to you." That was my last time seeing her and hearing her. I miss her big time.

Summer brought a fitting occasion and Jordan was included as one of the jazz luminaries for the Charlie Parker Jazz Festival. The twenty-first annual event was on August 25, and Jordan shared the stage with fellow Tristano alumnus and legendary saxophonist Lee Konitz and his quartet featuring Christian Scott (trumpet) and Aaron Diehl (piano). The event covered three days and began with the Jimmy Heath Big Band performing a new arrangement of Heath's orchestration of the works of Charlie Parker, originally commissioned by the Charlie Parker Jazz Festival in 2004 and reworked for a big band, entitled "Bird Is The Word." Also performing at the event were Kenny Garrett, vocalist Cecile McLorin Salvant, drummer Kim Thompson, alto saxophonist Jaleel Shaw, and multi-instrumentalist Warren Wolf. Jordan enjoyed the idea of celebrating her guru, Parker, and sang with a trio consisting of Kuhn, Brown, and Drummond.

Jordan has fond memories of the festival: "I did the very first Charlie Parker Festival, which was always either on or near his birthday in August. At the end of the concert, they gave me a replica of the street they named after him at that concert, "Charlie Parker Place," and I put it on my barn upstate. That was the most wonderful gift I have ever been given besides my daughter."

The autumn found Jordan traveling from the East Coast to the West Coast and the Midwest, along with her other tours. She was invited back to perform in September at the Detroit Jazz Festival, this time with Alan Broadbent and an eighteen-piece string orchestra. Mark Stryker of the *Detroit Free Press* gave Jordan the compliment of having the "best ballad" at the festival. He comments, "Detroit-born singer Sheila Jordan still brings it on a ballad. She used her now slippery pitch to storyteller advantage and turned "Haunted Heart" into autobiographical confession with a perspicacious string orchestra arrangement by pianist Alan Broadbent behind her."[3] Andrea Canter writes in *Jazz Police*: "Pianist Broadbent has a well-earned reputation for arranging and accompanying the likes of Irene Kral, Natalie Cole and Detroit heroine Sheila Jordan, who at 84 has retained all of her innovation and humor on stage. The NEA Jazz Master was in great form, particularly on her signature "Sheila's Blues," a song that is never repeated exactly the same way as she invents new lyrics to suit the moment and setting."[4]

In early October, Jordan was off to Santa Barbara to perform for the Santa Barbara Jazz Society as a special request from the longtime president of the organization, Kathryn Stockbridge. Sadly, Stockbridge passed away days before Jordan's arrival, allowing her to pay her respects during her concert. Longtime jazz critic and jazz radio DJ Stanley Naftaly comments about the October 6 concert:

> Last Sunday afternoon, at the Jazz Society's monthly concert, one of the two living legends of jazz still performing (Sonny Rollins is the other), delivered a consummate two-set, seminar on the history of jazz. Sheila Jordan, at 84 years of age, showed why she's always been one of the top vocalists in the world. It was particularly appropriate for this master to be here at this moment since Kathryn Stockbridge, the society's president for the last six years, had passed away suddenly earlier in the week.
>
> With the trio of Ian Bernard at the piano, Richard Simon on bass and Paul Kriebich on drums backing her, she immediately took charge of the proceedings in her relaxed, yet powerful way. Early on, she vocalized, "I've never met these cats, but they sure can play," in the midst of a tune and it only got cleaner and tastier from there on.
>
> Jordan started off with Oscar Brown Jr.'s tune, "Hum-Drum Blues," a tale of the vicissitudes of life, and followed with a swinging, scat-filled version of "Falling in Love With Love," Thus, from the beginning, she showed her inherent power and mastery of the music. The Lady knows it all.
>
> By any yardstick, it was a virtuosic performance from one end to the other. Next up was an Abby Lincoln song, "Bird Alone," a paean to emotional freedom. Jordan is known for her love of duets with the string bass and Richard Simon lit her up. "The Touch of Your Lips" became a love song between them.
>
> Jordan is one of only two jazz vocalists I know of, and the other is Ella Fitzgerald, who can leave a song in mid-stride and tell a story without missing a note or a beat, and she exhibited this ability on several occasions during the show.
>
> Vocalese is the art of singing lyrics to instrumental lines. Eddie Jefferson invented it and Lambert, Hendricks and Ross popularized it. Sheila used it often to insert stories into songs and thus make them willing vehicles for her thoughts and feelings.

> She taught the audience to scat and got each of the musicians to scat. It was wonderful. This is not only a living legend of jazz, but a beautiful human being. Everyone in the audience, your writer included of course, was profoundly in love with Jordan by the time we gave her two standing ovations. Congratulations to the Santa Barbara Jazz Society for bringing us this harmonious and exciting afternoon."[5]

That same month, on October 13, Jordan was given yet another honorary tribute in her hometown, this time with her Detroit friend and fellow musician, Barry Harris. It was a celebration of the forty-third anniversary of the All Nite Soul at the Jazz Ministry at Saint Peter's, better known as the Jazz Church. The event featured over eighty musicians paying tribute to both Jordan and Harris. There was an "exhibit wall" (the Legend Wall) in Saint Peter's Living Room that told the story of Jordan and Harris with memorabilia, including photograph collages organized by photo archivist Tad Hershorn of the Rutgers University Institute of Jazz Studies. Musicians who performed that evening included Gene Bertoncini, Alan Broadbent, Alex Brown, Cameron Brown, Don Byron, Valerie Capers, Sara Caswell, Jay Clayton, Connie Crothers, Harold Danko, Charles Davis, Billy Drummond, Ray Drummond, Peter Eldridge, John Ellis, Jeff Fairbanks, Carol Fredette, Ray Gallon, Lou Grassi, Barry Harris and Jazz Ensemble Choir, Ingrid Jensen, Dean Johnson, Howard Johnson and Gravity, Paul Knopf, Lee Konitz, Sarah McLawler, Jeff Newell, Harvie S, Kendra Shank, Tessa Souter, Ken Simon, Jerry Weldon, and Leroy Williams, among others. Souter shared her observations:

> Sheila stayed right to the very end to listen to everyone who performed. I couldn't see her when it was my turn to sing and I assumed she must have left, or maybe gone outside to get a drink of water or something to eat. No! Of course not. She was there the entire time and I sang "The Creator Has a Master Plan," partly because it was Pharoah Sanders's birthday that day and partly because it was the first song I ever sang for Sheila. But more importantly because the song speaks to the effect Sheila has had on my life.

Jordan's birthday celebrations had become somewhat of a tradition in November of each year. There was usually a celebration performance in New York and often another U.S. city or overseas. This time Jordan's New York celebration was at the Blue Note for her eighty-fifth birthday; she was joined by longtime friend and accompanist Steve Kuhn. Their relationship has endured over time and ripened into true artistry. Kuhn says,

> Sheila is always very easy to recognize. You hear her sing on a record and you know instantly it's her. That's Sheila Jordan. She was never blessed with the greatest set of pipes to begin with, but that really is not important.

> She was able to utilize what she had in terms of vocal equipment and bring a depth of feeling to the music that came from the heart. And that is the bottom line to all music as far as I'm concerned, to communicate on an emotional level with the audience. And she really did that from the very beginning, up to this day, and it will always be that way. I think that's her strongest quality in terms of the way she imparts what she's doing to an audience, that she reaches them on an emotional level.

Most singers have a special relationship with one or more accompanists that allows them to comfortably express the music in an artistic manner. There are infinite ways to interpret songs; therefore it's important for a singer to develop the kind of partnership and communication with an accompanist that results in producing mellifluous vocals as well as brilliant arrangements.

Jordan definitely has been known for her pairings, especially with pianist Steve Kuhn. According to Jordan:

> Singers were always after him to play for them and I can understand why. He knows how to accompany me and I feel very much at ease. I've had a couple of musical out-of-body experiences with Kuhn over the years. I don't get these very often but I've had them with the bass and voice and with Steve. I love singing Kuhn's tunes and I love the way he sings them. Besides being a great accompanist, Steve is like a brother to me. We remain friends to this day and on my birthday every year so far for the past four years we celebrate by performing our duo at the Blue Note in New York City and the Regatta Bar in Cambridge, Massachusetts.

One of her final performances of 2013 was on a stormy December evening just before the holidays. The gig was with bassist Cameron Brown, joined by special guest pianist Alan Broadbent, at one of Jordan's favorite clubs, the Cornelia Street Cafe. Jordan has often said how much she appreciates the intimacy of the room for doing bass and voice duets, and the constant support of the management through the years. Jordan's remarks on a Facebook post the following day read, "I want to thank all of you wonderful people for braving the terrible storm last night to come to Cornelia Street to hear me and Cameron and Alan keep jazz music alive. What a sacrifice all of you made. Neither wind, sleet, rain, snow, nor hail keeps beautiful friends from supporting jazz. I send you my love and gratitude and wish everyone a very happy holiday. You certainly made mine. I'll never forget it." With 2014 upon her, Jordan was once again booked through the year with performances at the Lionel Hampton Jazz Festival with Benny Golson and Eddie Palmieri, the Detroit Jazz Festival with Alan Broadbent and strings, a tour of Norway with the Bjorn Alterhaug Trio, another tour of Germany with vocalist Sabine Kühlich, and of course her regular teaching workshops: UMass Jazz in July, Vermont Jazz Center, and Interplay Jazz and

Arts. Although there will be many more offers and added performances, Jordan has been careful to pace herself accordingly—not an easy task for her because she always wants to be out sharing jazz and her stories.

"Sheila is inspiring," says Billy Drummond. "People love her all over the world. I've never seen her in front of an audience that she didn't have in the palm of her hands." Other musicians agree. Guitarist Stephan Kramer adds,

> Every time I see her perform, be it in a resort town in Vermont, in Stuttgart, Germany, at the Jazz Standard in New York, every time she takes the whole room with her and they feel it, if they want it or not, the diehard jazz buffs at the Unterfahrt, or the people who really don't know much about jazz, they trust her, follow her into the pain and the sorrow and the joy and love and exuberant celebration of life that she will include in her performance, and then come out the other side and feel great and uplifted from the experience. That is what she can do as a singer and performer, and she does it every time, no matter where, no matter what is going on in her life, no matter who she is playing with.

Longtime friend Carol Fredette agrees: "I think as she's become older she's even better. She sounds great but she's got something else going on too—she owns the stage."

Her friend Ra-Kalam (Moses) adds, "She had a lot of tough things in her life, a lot of heartbreak but always a positive person who always brought a positive energy. I don't remember hearing her complain about anything." Due to the many limitations she started out with coming into society and the music business, Jordan became proficient at knowing how to maneuver herself and her career to attain many of her accomplishments. Although she may claim that things just come to her, clearly she has been engineering her successes by being a quick study of human nature and orchestrating situations for the enhancement of herself and others. Just as great leaders guide us to our best achievements, Jordan has managed to apply these same concepts, consciously or unconsciously, to her life. As Coryelle Kramer recognizes, "She's incredibly strong. She's got a very quiet strength about her that comes out when she sings, when she laughs, and when she's fighting for things she believes in. But she doesn't have to push anybody over with it; it more like waves of strength that you feel coming off of her and that's what bowls you over."

It's interesting to observe that the most important inspirations for Jordan's tenacity and existence revolve around family, maternal instincts, the jazz community, and the expression and communication of jazz music. Jordan concludes,

> Tracey's been a wonderful happening in my life. She's like a very special song to me, and she's the other part of the music. In other words, I live for two things. I live for my daughter and I live to support jazz music. My

> relationship with my daughter is very special because she understands me and I understand her. We're great friends aside from being mother and daughter and I'm extremely grateful for that. Raising Tracey was scary in a sense, because I wasn't sure that I was a good mother or that I was doing things properly, but I did the best I could. I believe that deep in my daughter's heart she has a great love and respect for me. She understood my plight at various times and everything that I went through. And I've also had special moments with great musicians. Whenever I got uncomfortable or nervous or worried about whether everyone was going to like me, I just tried to remember how much I love the music. It's important for me to carry the message of this music. When I teach and when I sing, I feel like I'm a messenger of this music. And I want to see this music live. I don't want it to disappear after all the old-timers go. I hope it won't, and I don't think it will, but I want to be able to look down wherever I am and say, "Oh yeah, it's continuing. Isn't that wonderful." I first got the word from Bird, and from there I've been able to keep it alive. There are so many great players and singers and more coming up and that makes me feel good. When somebody says, "Jazz is dead," no, jazz isn't dead. It's just taking a little vacation sometimes, but it will always come back again.

It was difficult to select just a few testimonials in support of the incredible influence, inspiration, and positive effects Jordan has brought to other people's lives. Many people would stand in line to pay tribute to her, attesting to her magnificent spirit and ability to touch hearts in a deeply profound way. These are just a few that sum up her remarkable qualities.

Tessa Souter: "When she sings she is like an arrow heading straight to your core and it gets right to the heart of everyone—young and old—who cares to listen. Really listen. Listen even past the songs and the singing. Past technique, past all that, to the inner meaning and emotion. She really sings the heart of a song. And the effect on your heart is like a gong hitting a bell. And this is who she is as a person, too. She is the epitome of 'who you are is how you play.' And she is so generous. She shares so much. I don't think you can be a really beautiful musician unless you can share—even if it is only in your music. But she is one of those who shares in her music and her life. Her music is her gift to you."

Jay Clayton: "Sheila's a very caring person. She just likes to help people. I don't know how to explain it but you get to love her because you know she's a generous person."

Theo Bleckmann: "To me, Sheila is so much more than a singer or musician. Sheila is a spirit, a shaman, a healer. She is someone who channels love through music, through teaching, through her being completely in the moment in whatever she does and whomever she relates to. It always astonishes me how dedicated and present she is with anyone around her. She can spend hours talking on the phone with some stranger asking for her advice, giving it freely and generously.

"I have witnessed her healing touch in so many different circumstances, might it be in a concert, a rehearsal or while teaching. Sheila undeniably disarms and opens up those around her. She is funny and direct and doesn't take herself all too seriously and certainly does not perceive herself in the glowing light I am painting her in. She is real."

Steve Swallow: "Sheila's tough and determined. She's also modest to a fault, loyal and generous. She's a survivor. She's a reminder, to me, of a long-ago New York demimonde in which the arts flourished, and its denizens looked out for each other with great care and generosity."

Tierney Sutton: "Sheila's legacy will be of her great, courageous, and groundbreaking recordings and of the profound effect she's had on so many musicians, students, and friends."

Ra-Kalam (Bob Moses): "Sheila Jordan is a wild Indian, a warrior Spirit, bright like light, lighter than bright, intensely loving and fully juiced. As for the music, she's the truth of it, the heart of it, the love of it, the for real of it, a sonic alchemist turning sorrow and heartache into wings of joy, no doubt about it!"

Kenny Burrell: "She has a knowledge of the Jazz heritage, she has a knowledge of the Jazz repertoire which she can call on and not just the songs but the language that is there via recordings, via personal appearances and things that she's heard throughout her life."

Sonny Rollins: "I think Sheila is a great humanitarian. She didn't have to copy somebody. I mean, she lived during those days and they were very heavy days. She lived it. She was there. She was part of it. I have so much respect for her and admiration for her. What she went through, she had to go through a lot just like we all did. And she's come through it. So I have a huge admiration for Sheila, I really do."

Alan Pasqua: "She's an original. If they called jazz an original American art form, and then put a little asterisk there and the subset, Sheila's name would be there, because that's what she is, she's an original American art form. She's the essence of the music."

And, of course, Tracey shares what she feels is so important for people to know about her mother: "The struggle and strife that she went through for her art. I think that is a real testament to her love of what she does, her tenacity and her relentless pursuit of keeping the music pure and at the forefront."

And straight from Jordan, "I really can't say I regret anything in my life. I found out in my early teens after hearing Bird that this was the music I would dedicate my life to whether I sing it, teach it, or just support it—and that is what I am doing. I am very fortunate to have come as far as I have in my life. I survived and I'm still doing music and enjoying every note of it."

Appendix 1

Discography / Videography

AS LEADER/CO-LEADER

Portrait of Sheila

Blue Note, 1962
Recorded: Van Gelder Studio, Englewood Cliffs, NJ, September 19 and October 12, 1962
Performers: Barry Galbraith: guitar; Steve Swallow: bass; Denzil Best: drums; Sheila Jordan: vocals
Track list: (1) Falling in Love with Love; (2) If You Could See Me Now; (3) Am I Blue; (4) Dat Dere; (5) When the World Was Young; (6) Let's Face the Music and Dance; (7) Laugh, Clown, Laugh; (8) Who Can I Turn To?; (9) Baltimore Oriole; (10) I'm a Fool to Want You; (11) Hum Drum Blues; (12) Willow Weep for Me

Confirmation

East Wind, 1975 and Test of Time, reissued 2005
Recorded: Vanguard Studio, NYC, July 12 and 13, 1975
Performers: Norman Marnell: tenor saxophone; Alan Pasqua: piano; Cameron Brown: bass; Beaver Harris: drums; Sheila Jordan: vocals
Track list: (1) Introduction; (2) God Bless the Child; (3) My Favorite Things; (4) Inchworm; (5) Because We're Kids; (6) Confirmation; (7) By Myself; (8) Why Was I Born?; (9) Pearlie's Swine

Sheila Jordan and Arild Andersen: Sheila

SteepleChase, 1977
Recorded: Bendiksen Studio, Oslo, Norway, August 27 and 28, 1977
Performers: Arild Andersen: bass; Sheila Jordan: vocals
Track list: (1) Song of Joy; (2) Hold Out Your Hands; (3) Lush Life; (4) The Saga of Harrison Crabfeathers; (5) What Are You Doing the Rest of Your Life?; (6) On Green Dolphin Street; (7) It Never Entered My Mind; (8) Don't Explain; (9) Better than Anything; (10) The Lady; (11) Please Don't Talk About Me When I'm Gone; (12) Song of Joy

Playground

ECM, 1979
Recorded: Columbia Recording Studios, NYC, July 1979
Performers: Steve Kuhn: piano; Harvie Swartz: bass; Bob Moses: drums; Sheila Jordan: vocals
Track list: (1) Tomorrow's Son; (2) Gentle Thoughts; (3) Poem for No. 15; (4) The Zoo; (5) Deep Tango; (6) Life's Backward Glance

Steve Kuhn and Sheila Jordan: An Interview with Steve Kuhn and Sheila Jordan

ECM, 1980
Recorded: The Warner Bros. Music Show, 1980
Performers: Steve Kuhn: voice; Sheila Jordan: voice
Track list: (1) side 1, 21:21; (2) side 2, 26:56

Steve Kuhn Quartet

Private tape, 1980
Recorded: Kristianstad Jazz Festival, Sweden, July 5, 1980
Performers: Steve Kuhn: piano; Sheila Jordan: vocals; Harvie Swartz: bass; Bob Moses: drums
Track list: (unknown titles); Deep Tango; Little Willie Leaps

Steve Kuhn/Sheila Jordan Band: Last Year's Waltz

ECM, 1981
Recorded: Fat Tuesday's, NYC, April 1981
Performers: Steve Kuhn: piano; Harvie Swartz: bass; Bob Moses: drums; Sheila Jordan: vocals
Track list: (1) Turn to Gold; (2) The Drinking Song; (3) Last Year's Waltz; (4) I Remember You; (5) Mexico; (6) The Fruit Fly; (7) The

Feeling Within; (8) Old Folks/Well You Needn't; (9) Confirmation; (10) The City of Dallas

Sheila Jordan and Harvie Swartz: Old Time Feeling

Palo Alto/Muse, 1982
Recorded: Eurosound, NYC, October 15, 1982
Performers: Harvie Swartz: bass; Sheila Jordan: vocals.
Track list: (1) I Miss That Old Time Feeling; (2) A Sleepin' Bee; (3) How Deep Is the Ocean?; (4) The Thrill Is Gone; (5) Tribute (Quasimodo); (6) It Don't Mean a Thing (If It Ain't Got that Swing); (7) Lazy Afternoon; (8) Whose Little Angry Man Are You?; (9) Let's Face the Music and Dance; (10) Some Other Time; (11) Barbados

The Crossing

Blackhawk (original label; out of print), 1984
Recorded: Gramavision Studios, NYC, October 1 and 2, 1984
Performers: Tom Harrell: flügelhorn; Kenny Barron: piano; Harvie Swartz: bass; Ben Riley: drums; Sheila Jordan: vocals
Track list: (1) Inchworm; (2) Sheila's Blues; (3) Little Willie Leaps; (4) It Never Entered My Mind; (5) The Crossing; (6) You'd Be So Nice to Come Home To; (7) You Must Believe in Spring; (8) Suite for Lady and Prez; (9) Until Tomorrow

Body and Soul

CBS/Sony, 1986
Recorded: Sound Ideas Studio, NYC, September 16 and 17, 1986
Performers: Frank Wess: tenor saxophone; Kenny Barron: piano; Harvie Swartz: bass; Ben Riley: drums; Sheila Jordan: vocals
Track list: (1) Body and Soul; (2) Falling in Love with Love; (3) What Are You Doing the Rest of Your Life?; (4) A Sleepin' Bee; (5) I'm a Fool to Want You; (6) How Deep Is the Ocean?; (7) Lush Life; (8) Baltimore Oriole; (9) Mood Indigo; (10) When the World Was Young

Sheila Jordan and Harvie Swartz: The Very Thought of Two

MA, 1988
Recorded: Vario Hall, Tokyo, Japan, February 4, 1988
Performers: Harvie Swartz: bass; Sheila Jordan: vocals
Track list: (1) The Very Thought of You; (2) Lost in the Stars; (3) Honeysuckle Rose/Ain't Misbehavin'; (4) You Are My Sunshine; (5) Dat

Dere; (6) The Bird/Quasimodo; (7) Spirits Arise/Morning Song/The Water Is Wide; (8) Let's Face the Music and Dance/Cheek to Cheek/ Sheila's Blues; (9) You Must Believe in Spring (10) Once Upon a Time

Sheila Jordan and Harvie Swartz: Songs from Within

MA, 1989
Recorded: The Harmony Hall, Matsumoto, Japan, March 1989
Performers: Harvie Swartz: bass; Sheila Jordan: vocals
Track list: (1) Dedication; (2) If You Could See Me Now; (3) Waltz for Debby; (4) Good Morning Heartache; (5) St. Thomas; (6) You Don't Know What Love Is; (7) My Shining Hour; (8) We'll Be Together Again; (9) Alone Together; (10) A Child Is Born; (11) In a Sentimental Mood; (12) I Got Rhythm/Anthropology; (13) Birmingham Jail

Lost and Found

Muse, 1989
Recorded: Sound on Sound, NYC, September 28 and 29, 1989
Performers: Kenny Barron: piano; Harvie Swartz: bass; Ben Riley: drums; Sheila Jordan: vocals
Track list: (1) The Very Thought of You; (2) Good Morning Heartache; (3) Alone Together; (4) The Water Is Wide; (5) Anthropology; (6) Lost in the Stars; (7) I Concentrate on You; (8) My Shining Hour/ We'll Be Together Again

Sheila Jordan and Mark Murphy: One for Junior

Muse, 1991
Recorded: Sear Sound, NYC, September 24, 1991
Performers: Kenny Barron: piano; Bill Mays: synthesizer; Harvie Swartz: bass; Ben Riley: drums; Sheila Jordan, Mark Murphy: vocals
Track list: (1) Where You At?; (2) Round About/It All Goes Round; (3) One for Junior; (4) Trust in Me; (5) The Bird/Quasimodo/Embraceable You; (6) Aria 18; (7) The Best Thing for You; (8) Eastern Ballad; (9) Don't Like Goodbyes/Difficult to Say Goodbye

Heart Strings

Muse, 1993
Recorded: Clinton Recording Studios, NYC, March 5 and 6, 1993
Performers: Alan Broadbent: piano, arrangements; Harvie Swartz: bass; Marvin "Smitty" Smith: drums; Hiraga String Quartet with Amy

Hiraga, Laura Frautschi: violin; Maria Lambros Kannen: viola; Peter Wyrick: cello; Sheila Jordan: vocals

Track list: (1) Haunted Heart; (2) Out to Sea (Sail Away); (3) Japanese Dream/What'll I Do; (4) If I Had You; (5) Heart's Desire; (6) Inchworm/The Caterpillar Song; (7) Comes Love; (8) Look for the Silver Lining

Sheila Jordan and Cameron Brown: I've Grown Accustomed to the Bass

HighNote, 1997

Recorded: Live at De Werf Jazz'halo Music Days, Bruges, Belgium, November 11, 1997

Performers: Cameron Brown: bass; Sheila Jordan: vocals

Track list: (1) Introductory Remarks by Sheila Jordan; (2) The Very Thought of You; (3) Better than Anything; (4) Dat Dere; (5) Morning Song; (6) The Bird/Quasimodo/Embraceable You; (7) Goodbye Pork Pie Hat; (8) Good Morning Heartache; (9) I Got Rhythm/Listen to Monk (Rhythm-A-Ning); (10) Sheila's Blues; (11) I've Grown Accustomed to the Bass

Jazz Child

HighNote, 1998

Recorded: Sound on Sound, NYC, April 1 and 2, 1998

Performers: Steve Kuhn: piano; Dave Finck: bass; Billy Drummond: drums; Sheila Jordan, Theo Bleckmann: vocals

Track list: (1) Jazz Child; (2) The Moon Is a Harsh Mistress; (3) Reel Time; (4) Art Deco; (5) The Zoo; (6) My Ship; (7) Oh Henry; (8) Bird Alone; (9) Ballad for Miles/My Funny Valentine; (10) Buffalo Wings; (11) Everything Happens to Me; (12) Every Time We Say Goodbye / For All We Know; (13) Jazz Child—Reprise

Sheila Jordan and E.S.P. Trio: Sheila's Back in Town

Splasc(h), Italy, 1999

Live recording from a tour of Italy: Cremona, March 1; Koper, March 7; Busto Arsizio, March 10; Bologna, March 14; Alcamo, March 17; Forli, March 20; Ancona, March 21, 1998

Performers: Riccardo Parruci: flute; Roberto Cipelli: piano; Gloria Merani: violin; Alessandro Franconi: viola; Filippo Burchietti: cello; Attillio Zanchi: bass; Gianni Cazzola: drums; Sheila Jordan: vocals. String arrangements on track #3: Riccardo Parrucci, tracks #4, 8: Roberto Cipelli

Track list: (1) Art Deco; (2) The Bird/Quasimodo; (3) Prelude II; (4) Someone to Watch over Me; (5) Inchworm; (6) Look for the Silver Lining; (7) Sheila's Blues; (8) The Water Is Wide; (9) Morning Song/ Dat Dere; (10) I Got Rhythm/Rhythm-A-Ning; (11) Lazy Afternoon; (12) Where You At?

Sheila Jordan: From the Heart

32 Jazz, 2000

Compilation of tracks from Muse recordings: *Old Time Feeling, Lost and Found*, and *Heart Strings*

Performers: Harvie Swartz: bass; Kenny Barron: piano; Ben Riley: drums; Alan Broadbent: piano; Marvin "Smitty" Smith: drums; Hiraga String Quartet with Amy Hiraga, Laura Frautschi: violin; Maria Lambros Kannen: viola; Peter Wyrick: cello; Sheila Jordan: vocals

Track list: (1) Haunted Heart; (2) Out to Sea (Sail Away); (3) Japanese Dream/What'll I Do; (4) If I Had You; (5) Heart's Desire; (6) Medley: Inchworm/The Caterpillar Song; (7) Comes Love; (8) Look for the Silver Lining

Little Song

HighNote, 2002

Recorded: The Studio, NYC, June 3 and 4, 2002

Performers: Tom Harrell: trumpet, flügelhorn; Steve Kuhn: piano; David Finck: bass; Billy Drummond: drums; Sheila Jordan: vocals

Track list: (1) Little Song/Blackbird; (2) Autumn in New York; (3) Barbados; (4) On a Slow Boat to China; (5) Hello Young Lovers; (6) Fairweather; (7) Something's Gotta Give; (8) If I Should Lose You; (9) The Way He Captured Me; (10) Deep Tango; (11) The Touch of Your Lips; (12) When I Grow Too Old to Dream; (13) Little Song

Sheila Jordan Live with Serge Forté Trio: Believe in Jazz

Ella Productions, 2003

Recorded: Live at the Ferme-Asile, Sion, Switzerland, November 2003

Performers: Serge Forté: piano; Karl Jannuska: drums; Gary Brunton: bass; Sheila Jordan: vocals

Track list: (1) Comes Love; (2) Buffalo Wings; (3) Bird Alone; (4) Where You At?; (5) Little Song/Black Bird/Real Time; (6) Everything Happens to Me; (7) The Touch of Your Lips; (8) You Must Believe in Spring

Sheila Jordan and E.S.P. Trio: Straight Ahead

Splasc(h), 2004
Recorded: Obelix Studio (Uboldo VA) Italy, February 21 and 22, 2004
Performers: Paolo Fresu: trumpet, flügelhorn; Roberto Cipelli: piano; Attillio Zanchi: bass; Gianni Cazzola: drums; Sheila Jordan: vocals
Track list: (1) I Thought about You; (2) You Must Believe in Spring; (3) You Came (Vieste); (4) Straight Ahead; (5) Like Someone in Love; (6) The Meaning of the Blues; (7) The Thrill Is Gone; (8) The Promise of You; (9) I've Never Been in Love Before; (10) So Many Stars; (11) You

Sheila Jordan and Cameron Brown: Celebration

HighNote, 2004
Recorded: Live at the Triad, NYC, November 17 and 18, 2004
Performers: Cameron Brown: bass; Sheila Jordan, Jay Clayton: vocals
Track list: (1) Introductory Remarks; (2) Hum Drum Blues; (3) Mood Indigo; (4) It's You or No One; (5) Commentary; (6) Brother Where Are You?; (7) Blues Medley for Miles: Blue Skies/All Blues/Freddie Freeloader; (8) The Promise of You; (9) Commentary; (10) Astaire/Rodgers Medley: Let's Face the Music and Dance/Cheek to Cheek/I Won't Dance/I Could Have Danced All Night/Pick Yourself Up; (11) Commentary; (12) Straight Ahead; (13) Fats Meets Bird Medley: Honeysuckle Rose/Ain't Misbehavin'/Scrapple from the Apple; (14) Introducing Jay Clayton; (15) Birks Works; (16) Sheila's Blues; (17) Commentary; (18) The Crossing

Winter Sunshine

Justin Time, 2008
Recorded: Upstairs, Montreal, February 15 and 16, 2008, by Bill Szawlowski and Frank Marino. Produced by Jim West and Jean–Pierre Leduc. Engineered and mastered by Bill Szawlowski at Ventura Digital Audio, Brosard, Quebec
Performers: Sheila Jordan: vocals; Steve Amirault: piano; Kieran Overs: bass; André White: drums
Track list: (1) Comes Love; (2) I Remember You; (3) Dialogue (How 'Bout That); (4) Lady Be Good; (5) Medley: Whose Little Angry Man Are You?/St Thomas/Ode to Sonny Rollins; (6) Dialogue; (7) Dat Dere; (8) Ballad for Miles/It Never Entered My Mind; (9) All God's Chillun Got Rhythm/Little Willie Leaps; (10) Dialogue; (11) The Crossing; (12) Sheila's Blues

Sheila Jordan and Harvie S: Yesterdays

HighNote, 2012 (released)
Recorded: Live in concert, circa 1990
Performers: Sheila Jordan: vocals; Harvie S: bass
Track list: (1) Yesterdays; (2) Better than Anything; (3) The Very Thought of You; (4) You Don't Know What Love Is; (5) It Don't Mean a Thing If It Ain't Got that Swing; (6) Fats Waller Medley: Honeysuckle Rose/Ain't Misbehavin'; (7) Mood Indigo; (8) Waltz for Debby (Lazy Days); (9) I Concentrate on You; (10) Lazy Afternoon; (11) Blue Skies; (12) Fred Astaire Medley: Let's Face the Music and Dance/Cheek to Cheek/I Could Have Danced All Night

AS GUEST ARTIST

Peter Ind: Looking Out

Wave, 1960
Recorded: NYC, November 1960
Performers: Ronnie Ball: piano; Al Schackman: guitar; Peter Ind: bass; Sheila Jordan: vocals
Track: Yesterdays

George Russell: The Outer View

Riverside, 1962
Recorded: NYC, August 27, 1962
Performers: Don Ellis: trumpet; Garnett Brown: trombone; Paul Plummer: tenor saxophone; George Russell: piano; Steve Swallow: bass; Pete LaRoca: drums; Sheila Jordan: vocals
Track: You Are My Sunshine

Jack Reilly: Masks

Unichrom, 1968
Recorded: St. Peter's Lutheran Church, NYC, November 26, 1968
Performers: Norman Marnell: tenor saxophone; Jack Reilly: piano; Jack Six: bass; Joe Cocuzzo: drums; Sheila Jordan: vocals
Track: Benedictus

Carla Bley/Paul Haines: Escalator over the Hill

JCOA, 1968, 1970, 1971

Recorded: RCA Recording Studios, NYC, November 1968, November 1970–June 1971; the Cinematheque, NYC, March 1971; Public Theater, NYC, June 1971

Performers: Enrico Rava, Michael Snow: trumpet; Don Cherry: trumpet, vocals; Bob Carlisle: French horn; Sharon Freeman: French horn, vocals; Jimmy Knepper: trombone; Sam Burtis: trombone, vocals; Roswell Rudd, Jack Jeffers: trombone, vocals; John Buckingham: tuba; Howard Johnson: tuba, vocals; Perry Robinson, Souren Baronian: clarinet; Jimmy Lyons: alto saxophone; Gato Barbieri, Peggy Imig: tenor saxophone; Chris Woods: baritone saxophone; Don Preston: synthesizer, vocals; Carla Bley: organ, piano, vocals; Michael Mantler: trumpet, trombone, piano, keyboards, synthesizer, vocals; John McLaughlin, Sam Brown: guitar; Leroy Jenkins: violin; Nancy Newton: viola, vocals; Calo Scott: cello; Charlie Haden, Richard Youngstein, Ron McClure: bass; Jack Bruce: bass, vocals; Paul Motian: drums; Jeanne Lee, Jane Blackstone, Jonathan Cott, Steve Gebhardt, Tyrus Gerlach, Eileen Hale, Rosalind Hupp, Timothy Marquand, Tod Papageorge, Bob Stewart, Pat Stewart, Viva, Karen Mantler, Phyllis Schneider, Linda Ronstadt, Sheila Jordan: vocals

Track list: This Is Here; Escalator over the Hill; Ginger and David; Over Her Head; End of Animals; . . . And It's Again

Roswell Rudd and the Jazz Composer's Orchestra: Numatik Swing Band

JCOA, 1973

Recorded: Butterfly Mobile Sound Van, NYC, July 6, 1973

Performers: Enrico Rava, Mike Lawrence, Charles Sullivan, Michael Krasnov: trumpet; Art Baron, Gary Brocks: trombone; Janet Donaruma, Sharon Freeman, Jeffrey Schlegel: French horn; Roswell Rudd: French horn, tuba; Bob Stewart, Howard Johnson: tuba; Mike Bresler: piccolo, flute, soprano saxophone; Martin Alter: flute, oboe, alto saxophone; Carlos Ward: flute, alto saxophone; Perry Robinson: clarinet; Dewey Redman: clarinet, tenor saxophone; Charles Davis: soprano saxophone, baritone saxophone; Hod O'Brien: piano; Sirone, Charlie Haden: bass; Beaver Harris, Lou Grassi: drums; Sue Evans, Dan Johnson: percussion; Sheila Jordan: vocals

Track list: Vent; Breathahoward; Circulation; Lullaby for Greg; Aerosphere

Roswell Rudd: Flexible Flyer

Arista/Freedom, 1974
Recorded: Blue Rock Studio, NYC, March 1974
Performers: Roswell Rudd: trombone, French horn; Hod O'Brien: piano; Arild Andersen: bass; Barry Altschul: drums; Sheila Jordan: vocals
Track list: What Are You Doing the Rest of Your Life?; Maiden Voyage; Suh Blah Blah Buh Sibi; Waltzing in the Sagebrush; Moselle Variations: Whatever Turns You On Baby/Tuff Muffins/Moselle

Marcello Melis/Mario Schiano: Perdas De Fogu (Burning Stones)

RCA/Vista, 1974
Blue Rock Studio, NYC, June 13 and 14, 1974
Performers: Mario Schiano: alto saxophone; Don Pullen: piano; Bruce Johnson: guitar; Marcello Melis: bass; Jerome Cooper: drums; Ray Mantilla: percussion; Sheila Jordan: vocals
Track list: Sa Bruscia Narat; Italjazz; Rivvalta; Perdas De Fogu; Sulcis; Anghelu Ruju

Roswell Rudd: Blown-Bone

Phillips, 1976
Recorded: NYC, March 26 and 27, 1976
Performers: Enrico Rava: trumpet; Roswell Rudd: tuba, percussion; Kenny Davern: clarinet, soprano saxophone; Steve Lacy: soprano saxophone, percussion; Tyrone Washington: tenor saxophone; Patti Bown: piano; Wilbur Little: bass; Paul Motian: drums; Jordan Steckel: percussion; Sheila Jordan: vocals
Track list: Blues for the Planet Earth; You Blew It

Marcello Melis: Free to Dance

Black Saint, 1978
Recorded: Downtown Studio, NYC, May 1978
Performers: Lester Bowie, Enrico Rava: trumpet; George Lewis, Gary Valente: trombone; Don Pullen: piano; Fred Hopkins, Marcello Melis: bass; Nana Vasconcelos, Don Moye: percussion; Sheila Jordan, Jeanne Lee: vocals
Track list: Before the Lights Go On; Struggle to Be; Free to Dance

Various Artists: Lennie Tristano Memorial Concert

Jazz, 1979
Recorded: Town Hall, NYC, January 28, 1979
Performers: Harold Danko: piano; Cameron Brown: bass; Lou Grassi: drums; Sheila Jordan: vocals
Track list: You'd Be So Nice to Come Home To; Yesterdays; Confirmation

Steve Swallow: Home—Music by Steve Swallow to Poems by Robert Creeley

ECM, 1979
Recorded: Columbia Recording Studios, NYC, September 1979
Performers: David Liebman: soprano saxophone, tenor saxophone; Steve Kuhn: piano; Lyle Mays: synthesizer; Steve Swallow: bass; Bob Moses: drums; Sheila Jordan: vocals
Track list: Some Echoes; "She Was Young . . ."; "Nowhere One . . ."; Colors; Home; In the Fall; "You Didn't Think . . ."; Ice Cream; Echo; Midnight

Bob Moses: When Elephants Dream of Music

Gramavision, 1982
Recorded: Vanguard Studio, NYC, April 11 and 12, 1982
Performers: Chris Rogers: trumpet; Terumasa Hino: cornet; Barry Rogers: trombone; Howard Johnson: contrabass clarinet, tuba; David Gross: alto saxophone; Doc Halliday: tenor saxophone, soprano saxophone; Jim Pepper: tenor saxophone; Lyle Mays: synthesizer; David Friedman: vibraphone, marimba; Bill Frisell: guitar; Steve Swallow, Michael Formanek: bass; Bob Moses: drums, percussion, vocals; Joe Bonadio, Ayieb Dieng: percussion; Nana Vasconcelos: percussion, vocals; Sheila Jordan: vocals
Track: Happy to Be Here Today

Aki Takase: ABC

Union Jazz, 1982
Recorded: Vanguard Studios, NYC, May 20, 21, and 24, 1982
Performers: Aki Takase: piano; Cecil McBee: bass; Bob Moses: drums; Sheila Jordan: vocals
Track list: I Hear Your Music; Dohke

The George Gruntz Concert Jazz Band: Theatre

ECM, 1983
Recorded: Tonstudio Bauer, Ludwigsburg, Germany, July 1983
Performers: Bill Pussey, Marcus Belgrave, Tom Harrell, Palle Mikkelborg: trumpet, flügelhorn; Dave Bargeron: trombone, euphonium; Julian Priester, David Taylor: trombone; Peter Gordon, Tom Varner: French horn; Howard Johnson: tuba, bass clarinet; Ernst-Ludwig Petrowsky: alto saxophone, soprano saxophone, clarinet; Charlie Mariano: alto saxophone, soprano saxophone, flute; Seppo "Baron" Paakkunainen: tenor saxophone, flute; Dino Saluzzi: bandoneon; George Gruntz: keyboard, piano; Mark Egan: bass; Bob Moses: drums; Sheila Jordan: vocals
Track list: El Chancho; In the Tradition of Switzerland; No One Can Explain It; The Holy Grail of Jazz and Joy

Egil Kapstad: Epilog (Bill Evans in Memoriam)

NOPA, 1984
Recorded: Høvikodden Arts Centre, Oslo, Norway, 1984
Performers: Bjørn Johansen: tenor sax; Egil Kapstad: piano; Ørnulf Boye Hansen, Mette Steen: violin; Oddbjørn Bauer: viola; Merete Olsen: cello; Bjørn Alterhaug: bass; Egil "Bop" Johansen: drums; Sheila Jordan: vocals
Track list: Epilog, Part One; Epilog, Part Two

Various Artists: That's the Way I Feel Now: A Tribute to Thelonious Monk

A & M, 1984
Recorded: Mediasound Studios, NYC; Sound Suite, Detroit, 1984
Performers: Marcus Belgrave: trumpet; Jervonny Collier: trombone; David Was: flute; David McMurray: alto saxophone; Michael Ward: tenor saxophone; Don Was: guitar, synthesizer; Larry Fratangelo: percussion; Sheila Jordan, Sweet Pea Atkinson, Harry Bowens, Carol Hall, Donald Ray Mitchell: vocals
Track: Ba-Lue Bolivar Ba-Lues-Are

Various Artists: More Mistletoe Magic

Palo Alto, 1985
Recorded: Hollywood, CA, 1985
Performers: Harvie Swartz: bass; Sheila Jordan: vocals
Track list: God Rest Ye/We Three Kings

The George Gruntz Concert Jazz Band: Happening Now!

hat Art, 1987

Recorded: Caravan of Dreams, Fort Worth, TX, October 16 and 17, 1987

Performers: Marvin Stamm, Kenny Wheeler, Enrico Rava, Manfred Schoof, Franco Ambrosetti: trumpet, flügelhorn; Ray Anderson, Art Baron, David Taylor: trombone; Tom Varner, Sharon Freeman: French horn; Howard Johnson: baritone saxophone, tuba; Lee Konitz: alto saxophone, clarinet; Ernst Ludwig Petrowsky: alto saxophone, soprano saxophone, clarinet; Joe Henderson: tenor saxophone; Larry Schneider: soprano saxophone, tenor saxophone, clarinet; George Gruntz: keyboards, piano; Mike Richmond: bass; Bob Moses: drums; Sheila Jordan: vocals

Track: Happening Now?

The George Gruntz Concert Jazz Band: Sins 'N Wins 'N Funs: Left-Cores and Hard-Core En-Cores

TCOB, 1987, 1988

Recorded: Paladium, Geneva, Switzerland, April 12, 1987, and Berlin Jazz Festival, Berlin, Germany, November 2, 1988

Performers: Palle Mikkelborg, Arturo Sandoval: trumpet; Howard Johnson: tuba; Dino Saluzzi: bandoneon; Peter Erskine: drums; Sheila Jordan: vocals; others

Track list: Plainsong; The Berlin Tango

Bill Kirchner Nonet and Sheila Jordan: One Starry Night

Jazz Heads, 1987

Recorded: The Chicago Jazz Festival, Grant Park, Chicago, Illinois, September 4, 1987

Mastering engineer: Malcolm Addey; graphic design: Javier Chacin and Judy Kahn

Performers: Bill Kirchner: soprano saxophone, alto saxophone, flute, clarinet, piccolo; Ralph Lalama: tenor saxophone, flute, clarinet; Glenn Wilson: baritone saxophone, flute; Bill Warfield, Brian Lynch: trumpet, flügelhorn; Douglas Purviance: bass trombone; Marc Copland: piano; Mike Richmond: bass; Ron Vincent: drums; Sheila Jordan: vocals

Track list: (1) Opening Announcements; (2) So Many Stars; (3) Maximum Density; (4) Whose Little Angry Man?; (5) Quasimodo; (6) I Concentrate on You; (7) You'd Be So Nice to Come Home To; (8) Band Credits

Karlheinz Miklin: Looking Back

SOS Music, 1988
Recorded: Graz, Austria, April 1988
Performers: Karlheinz Miklin: alto flute, alto saxophone; Peter Mihelic: piano; Ewald Oberleitner: bass; Heimo Wiederhofer: drums; Sheila Jordan: vocals
Track list: Goodbye Pork Pie Hat; Don't Explain

Goetz Tangerding Trio: Jazztracks

Bhakti, 1989, 1990
Recorded: Studio Bauer, Ludwigsburg, Germany, October 25, 1989, and January 24, 1990
Performers: Goetz Tangerding: piano; Wolfgang Lackerschmid: vibraphone; Christian Stock: bass; Heimo Wiederhofer: drums; Sheila Jordan: vocals
Track list: Ballad of the Sad Young Men; Whose Little Angry Man?; Quasimodo

Various Artists: Songposts Vol. 1

Word of Mouth, 1991
Recorded: Current Sounds, NYC, August 27, 1991
Performers: Harvie Swartz: bass; Sheila Jordan: vocals
Track list: Waltz for Debby; I've Grown Accustomed to the Bass

George Gruntz / Allen Ginsberg: Cosmopolitan Greetings

Musikszene Schwiez MGB, 1992
Recorded: Philharmonie, Köln (Cologne), Germany, May 26, 1992
Performers: Don Cherry: trumpet, ethno-instruments; Andy Haderer, Rob Bruynen, Klaus Osterloh, John Marshall: trumpet; Ray Anderson: trombone, vocals; Dave Horler, Ludwig Nuss, Bernt Laukamp, Roy Deuvall: trombone; Howard Johnson: tuba, baritone saxophone, vocals; Heiner Wilberny, Harald Rosenstein, Olivier Peters, Rolf Römer, Steffen Schorn: reeds; George Gruntz: piano; Mike Richmond: bass; Danny Gottlieb: drums; Christoph Eidens, Freddie Santiago: percussion; Renee Manning, Sheila Jordan, Mark Murphy: vocals
Track list: Happening Now?; Those Two and Maturity; 7th Avenue Express Blues; FUN (NY DEATH); Prophecy

Lee Konitz: Rhapsody II

Paddle Wheel, 1993
Recorded: The Studio, NYC, July 7, 1993
Performers: Lee Konitz: soprano saxophone; Harvie Swartz: bass; Sheila Jordan: vocals
Track: You Don't Know What Love Is

Jane Bunnett: The Water Is Wide

Evidence, 1993
Recorded: Reaction Sound, August 18 and 19, 1993
Performers: Larry Cramer: trumpet; Jane Bunnett: soprano saxophone; Don Pullen: piano; Kieran Overs: bass; Billy Hart: drums; Sheila Jordan, Jeanne Lee: vocals
Track list: You Must Believe in Spring; The Water Is Wide

Various Artists: Spirits—Live at Vartan Jazz

Vartan Jazz, 1994
Recorded: Vartan Jazz, Denver, CO, September 30 and October 1, 1994
Performers: Mark Soskin: piano; Harvie Swartz: bass; Joe LaBarbera: drums; Sheila Jordan: vocals
Track list: Danny Boy; Quasimodo

Cameron Brown: Here and Now! Vol. 1

OmniTone, 1997
Recorded: Gouvy, Belgium, and Brussels, Belgium, November 1997
Performers: Dave Ballou: trumpet, flügelhorn; Dewey Redman: tenor saxophone; Cameron Brown: bass; Leon Parker: drums; Sheila Jordan: vocals
Track list: Art Deco; For All We Know; Rylie's Bounce; Remembrance; What Reason Could I Give?/For Dad and Dannie; Double Arc Jake

Roswell Rudd: Broad Strokes

KFW, 1999
Recorded: Nevessa Studio, Saugerties, NY, September 22, 1999
Performers: Roswell Rudd, Steve Swell, Josh Roseman: trombone; Ron Finck, Harvey Kaiser, Steve Lacy, Elton Dean: saxophones;

Bobby Johnson Jr., Greg Glassman: trumpet; David Winograd: tuba; Matthew Finck, Duke Baker, Eddie Diehl, Thurston Moore, Kim Gordon, Lee Ranaldo: guitar; Mike Kull: piano; Christopher Rudd, Steve Riddick, Roswell Rudd, Sheila Jordan: vocals; Ken Filiano, Bill Dotts, Jean-Jacques Avenel, Allan Murphy: bass; Lou Grassi, John Betsch, Eugene Randolph, Steve Shelley: drums; Carlos Gomez: percussion

Track: The Light

Christian Stock Trio: Straight Ahead

YVP Music, 1999

Recorded: Augsburg, Germany, November 10, 1999

Performers: Karel Ruzicka: piano; Christian Stock: bass; Walter Bittner: drums; Sheila Jordan: vocals

Track list: Autumn in New York; Barbados; Sail Away; Song of Joy

The Aardvark Jazz Orchestra: Bethlehem Counterpoint

Aardmuse, 2002

Recorded: 2002

Performers: K. C. Dunbar, Jeanne Snodgrass, Taylor Ho Bynum, Greg Kelley, Mike Peipman: trumpet; Bob Pilkington, Jay Keyser: trombone; Jeff Marsanskis, Bill Lowe: trombone, tuba; Arni Cheatham, Peter Bloom, Phil Scarff, Daniel Ian Smith, Mark Messier, Dan Zupan, Brad Jones, Dan Bosshardt: reeds; Richard Nelson: guitar; Jesse Williams, Ken Filiano, Jane Wang: bass; Jerry Edwards: bass, vocals; Harry Wellott: drums; Craig Ellis: percussion; Donna Hewitt-Didham, Sheila Jordan: vocals

Track list: God Rest Ye Merry, Gentlemen/We Three Kings/Bethlehem Counterpoint; Begats; Celestial Light; Who Is the Prophet?; Sweet Child

Frank Mantooth: Ladies Sing for Lovers

MCG Jazz, 2003, 2004

Recorded: 2003–2004

Performers: Tom DeLibero, Kevin Lawson, Bruce Gates, Stacy Rowles: trumpet; Sonny Hernandez, Kevin Stout, Nathan Tanouye: trombone; Marty Erickson: tuba; Daniel Culpepper, Paul Riggio: French horn; Colin Skinner: bassoon, woodwind; Juliette Lewis: oboe, woodwind; Victor Ash: clarinet, woodwind, vocals; Jerry DiMuzio: flute; Howard McGill, Andy Panayi: flute, alto flute, piccolo, woodwind; Kim Park:

flute, alto saxophone, soprano saxophone, tenor saxophone; Jay Craig: bass clarinet, baritone saxophone; Frank Mantooth: piano; Danny Embrey: guitar; Helen Chytrova: violin; Pavel Horejsi: viola; Ondrej Cibulka: cello; Bob Bowman: bass; Todd Strait: drums; Sheila Jordan: vocals
Track: Ballad of the Sad Young Men

Sabine Kühlich and Crisp featuring Sheila Jordan: Fly Away

Acoustic Music, 2006
Recorded: March 2006
Performers: Tine Schneider: piano; Hubert Winter: saxophones; Rudi Engel: bass; Bill Elgart: drums; Sabine Kühlich, Sheila Jordan: vocals
Track list: Ornithology; Beautiful Love/Delicious and Lovely; How Deep Is the Ocean

Sheila Jordan and Sabine Kühlich: Two Generations of Singers

Digiland Records, 2006
Recorded: Live at Stadtgarten, Köln, March 25, 2006
Performers: Olaf Schneider, Stefan Michalke: piano; Stefan Werni: bass; Sabine Kühlich, Sheila Jordan: vocals
Track list: Je m'assois; Walzer der heimlichen Hoffnung; How Deep Is the Ocean; Autumn in New York; Beautiful Love/Delicious and Lovely; Sheila's Blues; I Got Rhythm; If I Should Lose You

Ellen Johnson: These Days

Vocal Visions, 2006
Recorded: April–August 2006
Performers: Larry Koonse: guitar; Darek Oles: bass; Roy McCurdy: drums; Ana Gazzola: percussion; Ellen Johnson, Sheila Jordan: vocals.
Track list: The Crossing; Little Messenger.

Peter Yellin: How Long Has This Been Going On?

Jazzed Media, 2007
Recorded: East Side Sound, NYC, November 20 and 22, 2007
Performers: Peter Yellin: alto saxophone, soprano saxophone; Bob Mintzer: tenor saxophone; Renee Rosnes: piano; Michael Wolfe: piano; Dwayne Burno: bass; Peter Leitch: guitar; Harvie S: bass; Billy Hart: drums; Winard Harper: drums; Sheila Jordan: vocals
Track: Everything Happens to Me

VIDEOS/YOUTUBE

Sheila Jordan: In the Voice of a Woman

1995
Documentary
Filmmaker: Cade Bursell

"Sheila Jordan and Mike Nock—Billie Holiday Tribute"

Australian TV, Sunday
Recorded: 1980?
Performers: Sheila Jordan: vocals; Mike Nock: piano; bassist: unknown
Track list: Billie Holiday Tribute
You Tube: http://www.youtube.com/watch?feature=player_embedded&v=NSe3Vf_UGrI

"Phil Woods & Sheila Jordan: Guinevere's Garden/Body and Soul"

Recorded: Twenty-fifth Berlin Jazz Festival, October 1988
Performers: George Gruntz Big Band, with George Gruntz: piano; Mike Richmond: bass; Peter Erskin: drums; Sharon Freeman, Tom Varner: French horn; Ray Anderson, Art Baron, David Taylor: trombones; Manfred Schoof, Marvin Stamm, Arturo Sandoval, Kenny Wheeler: trumpets; Bob Malach, Larry Schneider, Chris Hunter, Ernst-Ludwig Petrovsky: saxes; Howard Johnson: tuba and baritone sax; Sheila Jordan: vocals
http://www.youtube.com/watch?v=IZpnMI_rhY4

"Sheila Jordan and Steve Kuhn Trio—Hum Drum Blues—Chivas Jazz"

Recorded: Live at the Chivas Jazz Festival, Directv Music Hall, São Paulo, Brasil, 2004
Performers: Steve Kuhn Trio (Steve Kuhn: piano; David Finck: bass; Billy Drummond: drums; Sheila Jordan: vocals) performs "Hum Drum Blues" in SP/Brasil, part of the LPC Projetos Culturais (Toy Lima, Artistic Director), aired on TV Cultura de Sao Paulo
http://www.youtube.com/watch?feature=player_embedded&v=zGEHMy_lfR4

"Sheila Jordan Being Awarded the IAJE Humanitarian Award"

At the Hilton ballroom in NYC, 2007
http://www.youtube.com/watch?feature=player_embedded&v=f8zayr-H7f4#t=17

"Sheila Jordan: Jazz Child Interview"

Recorded: TDC (Technology Development Center), Ventura, CA, 2008
Video Production: Sound Visions Media (Jeff Foster, producer; Ellen Johnson, interviewer)

"My Life Is Dedicated to Jazz—Sheila Jordan Interview"

Recorded: Jazz in July: UMass Thirtieth Anniversary, Bret Primack, 2011
http://www.youtube.com/watch?v=agLYvah6vxk&list=PLBC34F8544FD21400&index=2

"Una ragazzina di 83 anni"

Interview and concert clips with Sheila Jordan, July 11, 2011
http://www.youtube.com/watch?v=o5z0-aAl_Q4

Appendix 2

Awards and Honors

2012	National Endowment for the Arts (NEA) Jazz Masters Award—Lifetime Honors Award
2010	New York Nightlife Award—Outstanding Jazz Vocalist
2008	Mary Lou Williams Women in Jazz Award for Lifetime of Service
2007	International Association of Jazz Educators (IAJE) Humanitarian Award
2006	Manhattan Association of Cabarets and Clubs (MAC) Lifetime Achievement Award
2004	Lil Hardin Armstrong Jazz Heritage Award
2004	Jazz Vocal Coalition Honorary Jazz Mentor Award
1995	The Societie of the Culturally Concerned—Detroit's Lifetime Achievement Award in Jazz
1991	*The Wire*—Best Album of the Year for *Lost and Found* (Muse)
1975	*Swing Journal*—Vocal Album of the Year for *Confirmation* (reissue 2005)
1963	*DownBeat* Critics Poll: "Talent Deserving Wider Recognition"—first place (went on to win nine more times)

Appendix 3

Music Examples

* Letters in circles indicate bass notes. The rhythmic placement of the Cm harmony should vary. In performance, Ms. Jordan often combines this composition with a ballad played by Miles Davis. On her CD "Jazz Child," the rhythm section modulates to "My Funny Valentine" in measure 35.

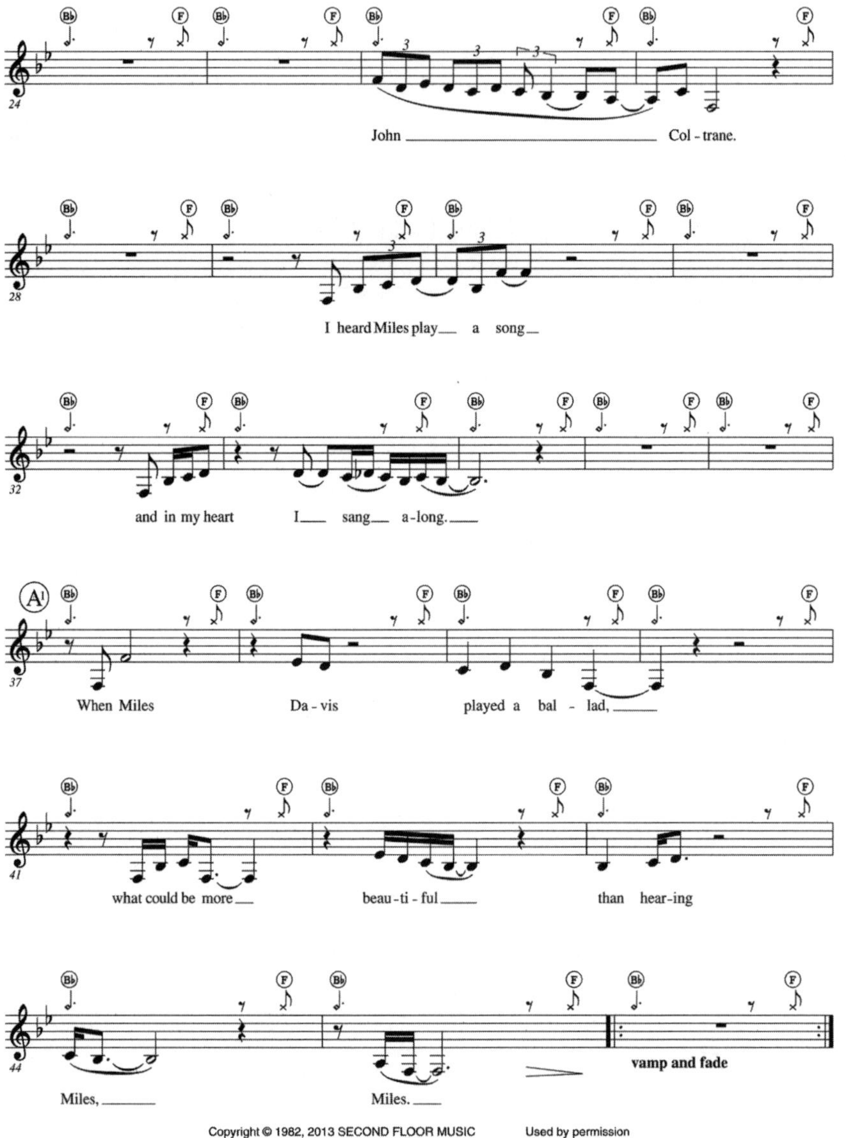
John ___ Col - trane.
I heard Miles play ___ a song ___
and in my heart I ___ sang ___ a-long. ___
When Miles Da - vis played a bal - lad, ___
what could be more ___ beau - ti - ful ___ than hear-ing
Miles, ___ Miles. ___
vamp and fade

Sung by Sheila Jordan on One For Junior / Sheila Jordan and Mark Murphy (Muse 5489-32Jazz 32063)

* When Sheila sings this piece, she often sings four bars of George & Ira Gershwin's "Embraceable You" here.

This composition was first recorded on The Crossing / Sheila Jordan (Black Hawk BKH 50501)
vocal lead sheet
D
The Crossing
Folk song style
Music and Lyric by
SHEILA JORDAN
Rubato
There are mo - ments in your life - time when the
whole world seems in - sane. If you search be - yond the
mad - ness there is peace of mind to gain, where there
is no time or sea - son and there is no fear or
strain. Take your trou - bles to the cross - ing, it's where
joy out - weighs the pain. Oh! The
tempo (♩ = ca. 116)
1. cross - ing, oh, the cross - ing. It's been known by man - y
2. cross - ing, oh, the cross - ing. What a bless - ing it can

A7 D G
names. Some have found it through re - li - gion, put - ting
be. When you're feel - ing down and lone - ly there's an
Em7 A7 B D
faith in God each day. When your world seems lost and
an - swer, there's a key. And for those of you who
G E/G# 1. A7
shat - tered and your dreams have gone a - stray, nev - er
won - der what the cross - ing means to
D G
seek out self de - struc - tion, there's a
E A7 D to solos (17-32)
cross - ing that can help you find your way. Oh! The
2. last time A7 rubato D
me, it's the love I feel when I'm
G E A7 D
sing - ing for you, oh, the spir - it of the mu - sic sets me free.

Recorded on Little Song / Sheila Jordan (HighNote HCD 7096)

vocal lead sheet
D♭

Little Song

C lead sheet

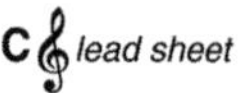

Workshop Blues

Medium swing

SHEILA JORDAN

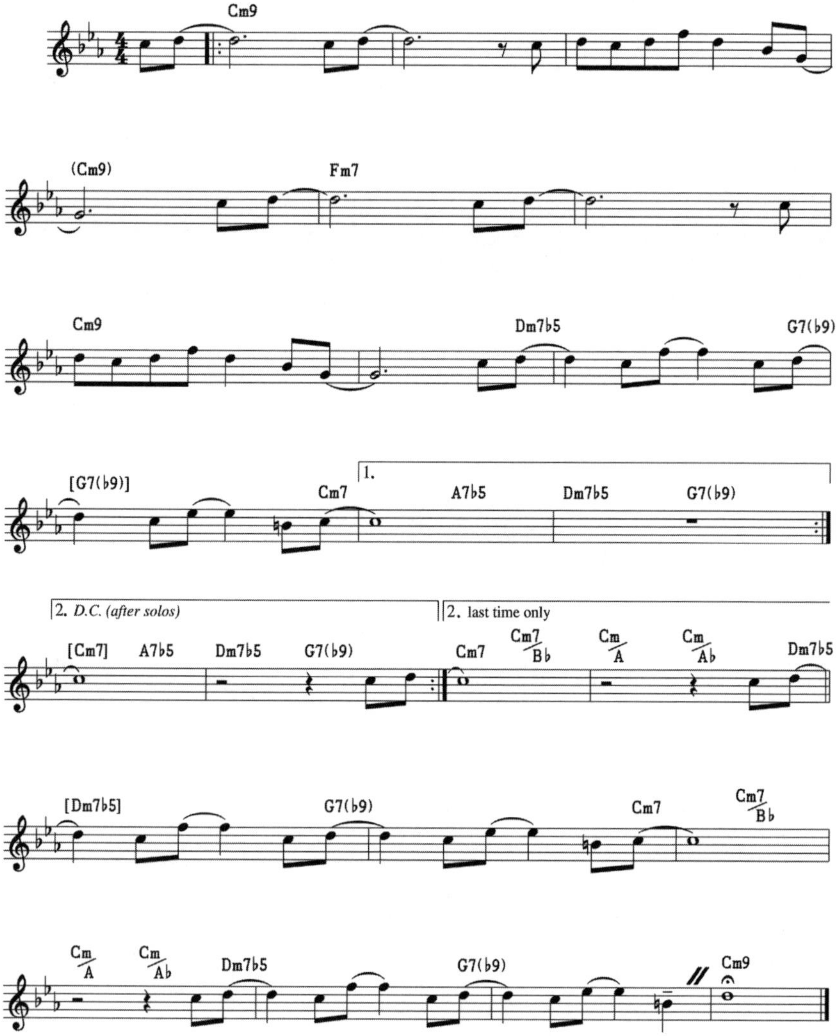

Cm9
(Cm9)
Fm7
Cm9
Dm7b5
G7(b9)
[G7(b9)]
Cm7
1.
A7b5
Dm7b5
G7(b9)
2. D.C. (after solos)
[Cm7]
A7b5
Dm7b5
G7(b9)
2. last time only
Cm7
Cm7/Bb
Cm/A
Cm/Ab
Dm7b5
[Dm7b5]
G7(b9)
Cm7
Cm7/Bb
Cm/A
Cm/Ab
Dm7b5
G7(b9)
Cm9

Sheila's Blues

by Sheila Jordan

1. It started with the blues, yeah.
I know you all are gonna pay some dues.
Hey, singers! Hey, swingers! It started with the blues.
Yeah, yeah, yeah, yeah, yeah, yeah, yeah.
You gotta sing your song.
Lemme tell ya, I'm here to help ya, as you go along.

2. Well, you can talk about what you did last night,
whether you had a good time, or whether you got in a fight.
Talk about the day. Hey, hey, waddaya say?
Tell me how you feel, yeah, but you gotta make sure that you're really real.
Make it up as you go along, that's how you sing a blues song.
I'm gonna show you what I mean:

3. Well, I was born in Detroit, Michigan, back in 1928.
Yeah, I was born in Detroit, Michigan,
November the eighteenth, 1928, Mickey Mouse's birthday.
But my mother she was only sixteen years old and she couldn't raise me.
So she sent me to live with my grandparents in a small coal mining town in Pennsylvania State.

4. You see what I mean? All you gotta do is sing.
Sing about where you came from, and maybe about your birthday.
But it really doesn't always have to be that way.
Just tell me what you feel, as long as you make it real. Hey, singers, singers, singers, singers, singers, singers sing your song,
and the band will play, and groove as you sing along.

5. Well, getting back to me,
I used to sing with the miners in the beer garden up the street every Saturday night.
The miners used to sit around and drink their beer and whiskey
and sing their songs, "You are my sunshine, my only sunshine."
Rarely, rarely, rarely, rarely, rarely, rarely, rarely, rarely, rarely, rarely, rarely, rarely, rarely, rarely, rarely, rarely, rarely, rarely, rarely, rarely,

6. Rarely, rarely, rarely did they ever fight.
Do you know what I mean, singers?
You gotta do your thing, do your thing and make it swing.
Yeah, yeah, yeah, it's all up to you, I think you'll know what to do.
Just tell everybody how you feel, 'cause, hey, that's the real deal.

Sheila's Blues (Sheila Jordan) - page 2

7. Getting back to me, well, I moved back to Detroit, Michigan, when I was about fourteen.
Hangin' down at the "Club Sudan," well, that was everybody's scene.
You didn't have to be twenty-one years old to get in there.
It was just a place for kids to play and sing.

8. Well, we were always chasin' Charlie Parker.
I think he wrote that song for us— "Chasin' the Bird," "Chasin' the Bird," "Chasin' the Bird."
When he used to play at the "Club El Cino," where you had to be twenty-one years old to get in,
I used to forge my mother's birth certificate.
All I had was a veil, high-heeled shoes that were killing my feet.
I was gonna get in the door to hear the Bird, but the man said,
"Hey, kid! Hey kid! Hey kid! Hey, little white girl,

9. Go home and do your homework!"
So we went round in the alley and we were sitting on the garbage cans.
Bird! Bird! Bird! Bird! Bird knew we were there, and he opened up the door, and he played his heart out for me.
Oh, what a treat, what a treat, what a treat, what a treat, what a treat, what a treat, what a treat, what a treat, what a treat for a fourteen-year-old kid that loved jazz.

10. Now I'm gonna let Jeanfrançois play, and he'll make, make, make your day.
Tell us about it!

11. (Jeanfrançois Prins guitar solo)

12. Oh yeah, singers, I forgot to tell you,
when the instrumentalists play, don't forget to listen!
Don't let your mind wander off.
You know what I mean, you gotta be on the list'nin' scene.
I know you can do what I say. Hey!

13. Well, if it wasn't for jazz music, I wouldn't be alive today. Oh, no!
If it wasn't for jazz music, I wouldn't be alive today.
Because back when I was just a skinny little teenager by the nickname of Jeannie Dawson, runnin' down on John R. in Detroit, Michigan, to buy all those fantastic bebop records, so I could hear Thelonious Monk and Miles Davis and Max Roach and Ray Brown and Dizzy Gillespie and Miles Davis and Fats Navarro and Kenny Dorham and Billie Holiday and Sarah Vaughan and Ella Fitzgerald and Count Basie and Duke Ellington, and of course, Lester Young, the "Prez" (You can do it kids, I'm tellin' you!)—
I wouldn't be up here singing, and tellin' you that you should do the blues today!

Music Is the Answer
(lyrics to "Remembrance" by Don Cherry)
by Sheila Jordan (used by permission)

I remember days from years gone by
When my family and friends would laugh and sing and cry
Life was never easy
Living took its toll
Music was the answer
It kept me strong and it saved my soul.

Times have changed most loving friends have passed
But the memories I keep alive will always last
Music was the answer
Singing songs of strife
Helped me find the reason
To carry on the rest of my life.

Live your life and start each day anew
Put your heart and your soul in everything you do
Face each waking moment
Hope will see you through
Music is the answer
Keep it alive and your dreams will come true.

The Art of Don
(lyrics to "Art Deco" by Don Cherry)
by Sheila Jordan (used by permission)

Ev'ry time I hear you,
There's something deep inside me
Will not go away,
Stays with me ev'ry day,
I'm walking along and singing this song,
With visions of you in my head.
Maybe tomorrow I'll face new sorrow,
But for today I'll smile instead.
Waltzing on air,
I haven't a care,
Since you told my heart it could sing.
With ev'ry minute,
Your music's in it,
The sound goes through me,
Your spirit moves me,
In ways that words cannot explain.

Appendix 4

List of Interviews

Sheila Jordan interviews, transcripts, recordings, e-mail, phone calls: August 2008 to February 2014

Other interviewees:

Andersen, Arild (October 2013)
Antonioli, Laurie (February 2014)
Bleckmann, Theo (February 2010)
Bolar, Willie (September 2013)
Brown, Cameron (February 2012)
Burrell, Kenny (November 2013)
Clayton, Jay (June 2010 and November 2013)
Dobbins, Len (March 2009)
Drummond, Billy (October 2013)
Elling, Kurt (April 2009)
Finck, David (April 2009)
Foster, Frank (March 2011)
Fredette, Carol (March 2013)
Gallon, Ray (February 2014)
Gruntz, George (June 2011)
Jordan, Tracey (February 2009)
King (Devries), Jenny (March 2011)
Kramer, Coryelle (February 2013)
Kramer, Stephan (October 2010)
Kuhn, Steve (July 2009)
Leduc, Jean-Pierre (January 2014)
Luparello, Andy (May 2009)
Mitchell, Leroy (November 2009)
Moses, Bob (Ra-Kalam) (March 2013)
Murphy, Mark (January 2013)
Pasqua, Alan (November 2009)
Rollins, Sonny (October 2013)
Rudd, Roswell (April 2009)
S, Harvie (April 2009 and October 2013)
Souter, Tessa (October 2013)
Sutton, Tierney (October 2008)
Swallow, Steve (April 2009)
Tillis, Dr. Fred (January 2013)
Uman, Eugene (February 2013)
Zanchi, Attilio (February 2013)

Notes

CHAPTER 1: GOD BLESSED THE CHILD

1. Lara Pellegrinelli, "Sheila Jordan: Jazz Child," *JazzTimes*, March 2001.
2. John Fordham, "Sheila Jordan: Ronnie Scott's London," *Guardian*, July 2001.

CHAPTER 3: DETROIT DAYS

1. Anthony Macias, "Detroit Was Heavy: Modern Jazz, Bebop, and African American Expressive Culture," *Journal of African American History* 95, no. 1 (Winter 2010).
2. Stanley Dance, "Tommy Flanagan: Out of the Background," *DownBeat* 33 (January 13, 1966).
3. Lars Bjorn, *Before Motown: A History of Jazz in Detroit 1920–1960* (University of Michigan Press, 2001). The tunes were "Bird Gets the Worm," "Klaunstance," "Another Hair Do," and "Bluebird." Ira Gitler, *Swing to Bop* (Oxford University Press, 1987).
4. Christopher Gair, *The Beat Generation* (Oxford: Oneworld Publications, 2006), 16–17.

CHAPTER 4: A HELLUVA TOWN

1. Eunmi Shim, *Lennie Tristano: His Life in Music* (University of Michigan Press, 2007).
2. Brian Priestley, *Mingus: A Critical Biography* (Da Capo Press, 1982).
3. Shim, *Lennie Tristano*.
4. Dave Frishberg, *Written Word*, davefrishberg.net/memoirs.php, 2013.
5. Ibid.

6. Suzanne Lorge, "Mark Murphy: Inside the Mystery," *All About Jazz*, July 31, 2009, http://www.allaboutjazz.com/php/article.php?id=33361&pg=1#.UugxaWTTlGE.

7. Corinna Ludwig, "Doyle Dane Bernbach," *Transatlantic Perspectives*, May 20, 2011, http://www.transatlanticperspectives.org/entry.php?rec=35, retrieved December 12, 2013.

8. Duncan Heining, *George Russell: The Story of an American Composer* (Scarecrow Press, 2010).

9. Ibid.

10. Don Heckman, "Sheila Jordan: Improvising Singer," *DownBeat*, May 9, 1963.

11. Scott Yanow, review of the recording *Portrait of Sheila*, *All Music*, http://www.allmusic.com/album/portrait-of-sheila-jordan-mw0000202415.

12. Heining, *George Russell.*

13. Andrew Rowan, "Sheila Jordan, *Confirmation* (1975)," *All About Jazz*, June 15, 2005.

14. Scott Yanow, review of the recording *Sheila*, *All Music*, http://www.allmusic.com/album/sheila-mw0000188372.

15. Ted Gioia, *The History of Jazz* (Oxford University Press, 2011).

16. "Robert Creeley & Steve Swallow: Poetic Collaborations," Poets.org, from the Academy of American Poets, http://www.poets.org/viewmedia.php/prmMID/5798, 1997–2013.

CHAPTER 5: AUTUMN IN NEW YORK

1. Tyran Grillo, "Steve Kuhn Quartet: Last Year's Waltz (ECM 1213)," *between sound and space* (an ECM Records resource and beyond), November 6, 2011.

2. Michael Kydonieus, "When Elephants Dream of Music—Bob Moses," review, *Jazzbo Notes*, April 23, 2009, http://www.jazzbonotes.com/reviews/when-elephants-dream-of-music-bob-moses.

3. Robin D. G. Kelley, *Thelonious Monk: The Life and Times of an American Original* (Free Press, 2009).

4. Ted Joans, "The Funeral of Thelonious Monk," *Coda Magazine*, April 1982.

5. Peter Sleight, "Swinging, Crooning and Scat: Sheila Jordan, *The Crossing*. Blackhawk Records," review, *Sun Sentinel*, Fort Lauderdale, FL, August 3, 1986.

6. A. James Liska, "Jazz Review: George Gruntz Band: Journey of Contrasts," *Los Angeles Times*, October 16, 1987.

7. Scott Yanow, *Bebop: Third Ear—The Essential Listening Companion* (Backbeat Books, 2000).

8. Howard Reich, "For Her Birthday, Sheila Jordan Shares Freely of Her Vocal Gifts," live performance review, *Chicago Tribune*, November 24, 1992.

9. Lara Pellegrinelli, "Sheila Jordan: Jazz Child," *JazzTimes*, March 2001.

10. David Royko, "Sheila Jordan and Mark Murphy: One for Junior," *Chicago Tribune*, Sunday, January 16, 1994.

11. Yanow, *Bebop*.

12. Michael G. Nastos, review of *Jazz Child* in *All Music Guide to Jazz: The Definitive Guide to Jazz Music*, ed. Vladimir Bogdanov, Chris Woodstra, and Stephen Thomas Erlewine (Backbeat Books, 2002).

13. Thom Jurek, review of *Sheila's Back in Town* in *All Music Guide to Jazz: The Definitive Guide to Jazz Music*, ed. Vladimir Bogdanov, Chris Woodstra, and Stephen Thomas Erlewine (Backbeat Books, 2002).

14. Harvey Pekar, "Roswell Rudd, Broad Strokes," review, *JazzTimes*, December 2000.

CHAPTER 6: BETTER THAN ANYTHING

1. Mathew Bahl, "Sheila Jordan: From the Heart," review, *All About Jazz*, October 1, 2000.

2. Scott Albin, "Sheila Jordan: The Very Thought of You," review, jazz.com, October 2008, http://www.jazz.com/music/2008/10/29/sheila-jordan-the-very-thought-of-you.

3. Joel Roberts, "Sheila Jordan: Little Song," review, *All About Jazz*, December 3, 2003.

4. Christopher Louden, "Sheila Jordan: Little Song," review, *JazzTimes*, June 2003.

5. Len Dobbins, unedited notes from *Winter Sunshine*, Justin Time, 2008.

6. Lara Pellegrinelli, "Sheila Jordan: Jazz Child," *JazzTimes*, March 2001.

7. David Dupont, "Sheila Jordan," *One Final Note*, webzine, March 2005, http://www.onefinalnote.com/features/2005/jordan-sheila.

8. Don Heckman, "Sheila Jordan's Voice Shines in Santa Monica," *Los Angeles Times*, April 23, 2005.

9. Howard Reich, "Voices of Jazz Are Alive and Well," *Chicago Tribune*, July 23, 2005.

10. Michael P. Gladstone, "Sabine Kühlich & Crisp featuring Sheila Jordan: Fly Away (2006)," *All About Jazz*, July 15, 2006.

11. Don Heckman, "Singer Ellen Johnson's Straightforward Crossing," *Los Angeles Times*, April 11, 2007.

12. Tessa Souter, "Sheila Jordan," *London Jazz News*, November 16, 2009.

13. Jerry D'Souza, "Sheila Jordan: Winter Sunshine (2008)," *All About Jazz*, December 19, 2008.

14. Georgia Mancio, review of Sheila Jordan at the Bull's Head, London Jazz Festival, *London Jazz News*, November 20, 2009.

15. Nicolas Dauplay, "Sheila Jordan: with the Ambassadors of Light Jazz Trio & the Brattleboro Music Center String Quartet," review, bluesandjazzsounds.com, http://www.bluesandjazzsounds.com/reviews/sjordondauplay.htm.

16. Gary Graff, "Sound Check: Don Was Honors Detroit Jazz at Concert of Colors," *Oakland Press*, http://www.theoaklandpress.com/general-news/20120712/sound-check-don-was-honors-detroit-jazz-at-concert-of-colors.

17. John Birchard, "Women in Jazz Festival: Second Night," *Rifftides*, an *artsjournal* blog, May 17, 2008, http://www.artsjournal.com/rifftides/2008/05/women_in_jazz_festival_second.html.

18. David R. Adler, "NEA Jazz Masters Concert 2012: A Parade of Jazz Giants Salutes the Newest Recipients of Jazz's Highest Honor," *JazzTimes*, January 12, 2012.

19. Brian Pace, "The 2012 NEA Jazz Masters Induction Ceremony Highlights," *The Pace Report*, January 2012, http://vimeo.com/35398529.

20. Howard Mandel, "NEA Jazz Masters @ Jazz at Lincoln Center Live and Webcast Smash," *Jazz Beyond Jazz*, an *artsjournal* blog, January 11, 2012, https://www.artsjournal.com/jazzbeyondjazz/2012/01/nea-jazz-masters-jazz-at-lincoln-center-live-and-webcast-smash.html.

21. Leslie Gourse, *Madame Jazz: Contemporary Women Instrumentalists* (Oxford University Press, 1995).

22. Ibid.

23. Vickie Willis, "Be-in-Tween the Spa[ ]Ces: The Location of Women and Subversion in Jazz," *Journal of American Culture* 31, no. 3 (August 2008).

CHAPTER 7: THE BIRD

1. Patrick Burke, *Come In and Hear the Truth: Jazz and Race on 52nd Street* (University of Chicago Press, 2008); Bill Gottlieb, "Posin'," and "Weird Wizard," *DownBeat* 14, no.19 (September 10, 1947).

CHAPTER 8: I'VE GROWN ACCUSTOMED TO THE BASS

1. "Sheila Jordan & Harvie Swartz (Vine St. Bar & Grill)," review, *Variety*, July 1981.

2. Andrew Gilbert, "Sheila Goes Soaring Without a Net," review, *Santa Cruz Sentinel*, 1990.

3. Kevin Whitehead, review of *Songs from Within*, National Public Radio (*Fresh Air*), September 1993.

4. Kirk Silsbee, liner notes for *Yesterdays*, HighNote, November 2011.

5. Paul de Barros, "Sheila Jordan's 'Yesterdays' a Treasure," review, *Seattle Times*, January 2012.

6. Lloyd Sachs, review, *Jazzespress*, January 26, 2012.

7. Ken Dryden, review, www.jazzhalo.be, November 1997.

8. Mathew Bahl, "Sheila Jordan: I've Grown Accustomed to the Bass," review, *All About Jazz*, September 2000.

9. James Muretich, review, *Calgary Herald*, 1999.

10. Libby Graham, "Jazzvox Concert: Sheila Jordan and Cameron Brown," review, *The Listening Room*, http://jazzfox9.blogspot.com, February 2012.

11. Lara Pelligrinelli, "Sheila's Dream," poem, n.d.

CHAPTER 9: WHITE IN A BLACK WORLD

1. Anthony Macias, "Detroit Was Heavy: Modern Jazz, Bebop, and African American Expressive Culture," *Journal of African American History* 95, no. 1 (Winter 2010).
2. Ibid.
3. Ibid.
4. Lars Bjorn and Jim Gallert, article quoted from "Police Relationship with Negroes Still Detroit's Sore Spot," *Michigan Chronicle*, March 21, 1953, in *Before Motown: A History of Jazz in Detroit, 1920–60* (University of Michigan Press), 2001.
5. Patrick Burke, *Come In and Hear the Truth: Jazz and Race on 52nd Street* (University of Chicago Press, 2008).
6. Ibid.

CHAPTER 10: THE CROSSING

1. Geoffrey I. Wills, "Forty Lives In the Bebop Business: Mental Health in a Group of Eminent Jazz Musicians," *British Journal of Psychiatry*, March 2003.

CHAPTER 11: REEL TIME MENTOR

1. Suzanne Lorge, "Mark Murphy: Inside the Mystery," *All About Jazz*, July 31, 2009, http://www.allaboutjazz.com/php/article.php?id=33361&pg=2#.UugvN2TTlGE.

CHAPTER 12: WHERE YOU AT?

1. Francine Schwartz, live performance review, *DC Metro Theater Arts*, May 17, 2013.
2. Mike Joyce, "At Kennedy Center, a Heartfelt Tribute to Shirley Horn," *Washington Post*, December 13, 2004.
3. Mark Stryker, "Swing of Styles Highlights the Detroit Jazz Festival," *Detroit Free Press*, September 3, 2013.
4. Andrea Canter, "The Spirit and Sound of Motor City: The 2013 Detroit Jazz Festival," *Jazz Police*, September 16, 2013, http://www.jazzpolice.com/content/view/10863/79.
5. Stanley Naftaly, "Sheila Jordan at Soho," review, October 2013, http://www.sbjazz.org/past-events-reviews/review-sheila-jordan-soho-oct-2013.

Bibliography

Adler, David R. "NEA Jazz Masters Concert 2012: A Parade of Jazz Giants Salutes the Newest Recipients of Jazz's Highest Honor." *JazzTimes*, January 12, 2012.

Albin, Scott. "Sheila Jordan: The Very Thought of You." Review, jazz.com, October 2008. http://www.jazz.com/music/2008/10/29/sheila-jordan-the-very-thought-of-you.

Bahl, Matthew. "Sheila Jordan: I've Grown Accustomed to the Bass." Review, *All About Jazz*, September 2000.

Birchard, John. "13th Annual Women in Jazz Festival: Second Night." *Rifftides Arts Journal*, May 17, 2008. http://www.artsjournal.com/rifftides/2008/05/women_in_jazz_festival_second.html.

Bjorn, Lars. *Before Motown: A History of Jazz in Detroit 1920–1960*. University of Michigan Press, 2001.

Burke, Patrick. *Come In and Hear the Truth: Jazz and Race on 52nd Street*. University of Chicago Press, 2008.

Burton, Clarence Monroe, William Stocking, and Gordon K. Miller. *The City of Detroit, Michigan 1701–1922*. S. J. Clarke Publishing Company, 1922.

Canter, Andrea. "The Spirit and Sound of Motor City: The 2013 Detroit Jazz Festival," Jazz Police, September 16, 2013. http://www.jazzpolice.com/content/view/10863/79.

Dance, Stanley. "Tommy Flanagan: Out of the Background." *DownBeat*, January 13, 1966.

Dauplay, Nicolas. "Sheila Jordan: with the Ambassadors of Light Jazz Trio & the Brattleboro Music Center String Quartet." Review, bluesandjazzsounds.com, http://www.bluesandjazzsounds.com/reviews/sjordondauplay.htm.

Davis, Miles, with Quincy Troupe. *Miles: The Autobiography*. Simon and Schuster, 1989.

de Barros, Paul. "Sheila Jordan's 'Yesterdays' a Treasure." Review, *Seattle Times*, January 2012.

Dobbins, Len. Unedited notes from *Winter Sunshine*, Justin Time, 2008.

Dryden, Ken. Review online at www.jazzhalo.be, November 1997.

D'Souza, Jerry. "Sheila Jordan: Winter Sunshine (2008)," *All About Jazz*, December 19, 2008.

Dupont, David. "Sheila Jordan." *One Final Note*, webzine, March 2005, http://www.onefinalnote.com/features/2005/jordan-sheila.

Fordham, John. "Sheila Jordan: Ronnie Scott's London." *Guardian*, July 2001.

Frishberg, Dave. "Written Word: Memoirs." davefirshberg.net/memoirs.php, 2013.

Gair, Christopher. *The Beat Generation*. Oxford: Oneworld Publications, 2006, 16–17.

Gilbert, Andrew. "Sheila Goes Soaring Without A Net." Review, *Santa Cruz Sentinel*, 1990.

Gioia, Ted. *The History of Jazz*. Oxford University Press, 2011.

Gladstone, Michael P. "Sabine Kühlich & Crisp featuring Sheila Jordan: Fly Away." *All About Jazz*, July 15, 2006.

Graham, Libby. "Jazzvox Concert: Sheila Jordan and Cameron Brown." Review, *The Listening Room*, http://jazzfox9.blogspot.com, February 2012.

Grillo, Tyran. "Steve Kuhn Quartet: Last Year's Waltz (ECM 1213)." between sound and space an ECM Records resource (and beyond), November 6, 2011.

Gourse, Leslie. *Madame Jazz: Contemporary Women Instrumentalists*. Oxford University Press, 1995.

Heckman, Don. "Sheila Jordan: Improvising Singer." *Down Beat*, May 9, 1963.

———. "Sheila Jordan's Voice Shines in Santa Monica." *Los Angeles Times*, April 23, 2005.

———. "Singer Ellen Johnson's Straightforward Crossing." *Los Angeles Times*, April 11, 2007.

Heining, Duncan. *George Russell: The Story of an American Composer*. Scarecrow Press, 2010.

Joans, Ted. "The Funeral of Thelonious Monk." *Coda Magazine*, April 1982.

Johnson, Ellen. "Sheila Jordan Messenger of Jazz," *Singer Magazine*, August 2004.

Joyce, Mike. "At Kennedy Center, a Heartfelt Tribute to Shirley Horn." *Washington Post*, December 13, 2004.

Kahn, Ashley. "After Hours: New York's Jazz Joints through the Ages." *JazzTimes*, September 2006.

Kelley, Robin D. G. *Thelonious Monk: The Life and Times of an American Original*. Free Press, 2009.

Kydonieus, Michael. "When Elephants Dream of Music—Bob Moses." Review, *Jazzbo Notes*, April 23, 2009, http://www.jazzbonotes.com/reviews/when-elephants-dream-of-music-bob-moses.

Latimer, Charles L. "Bebop and Beyond: Sheila Jordan Speaks." *Detroit Music History*, September 29, 2013, detroitmusichistory.com/Sheila-jordan.html.

Liska, A. James. "Jazz Review: George Gruntz Band: Journey of Contrasts." *Los Angeles Times*, October 16, 1987.

Lorge, Suzanne. "Mark Murphy: Inside the Mystery." *All About Jazz*, July 31, 2009, http://www.allaboutjazz.com/php/article.php?id=33361&pg=1#.UugxaWTTIGE.

Louden, Christopher. "Sheila Jordan: Little Song." Review, *JazzTimes*, June 2003.

Ludwig, Corinna. "Doyle Dane Bernbach." *Transatlantic Perspectives*, May 20, 2011, http://www.transatlanticperspectives.org/entry.php?rec=35.

Macias, Anthony. "Detroit Was Heavy: Modern Jazz, Bebop, and African American Expressive Culture." *Journal of African American History* 95, no. 1 (Winter 2010).

Mancio, Georgia. Review of Sheila Jordan at the Bull's Head, London Jazz Festival. *London Jazz News*, November 20, 2009.

Mandel, Howard. "NEA Jazz Masters @ Jazz at Lincoln Center Live and Webcast Smash." *Jazz Beyond Jazz*, an *artsjournal* blog, January 11, 2012, https://www.artsjournal.com/jazzbeyondjazz/2012/01/nea-jazz-masters-jazz-at-lincoln-centerlive-and-webcast-smash.html.

Mathieson, Kenny. "Sheila Jordan: The Last Jazz Singer." *The Wire*, May 1992.

Muretich, James. Review, *Calgary Herald*, 1999.

Naftaly, Stanley. "Sheila Jordan at Soho." Santa Barbara Jazz Society, October 2013.

Nastos, Michael G. Review of *Jazz Child*. In *All Music Guide to Jazz: The Definitive Guide to Jazz Music*, edited by Vladimir Bogdanov, Chris Woodstra, and Stephen Thomas Erlewine. Backbeat Books, 2002.

Pace, Brian. "The 2012 NEA Jazz Master's Induction Ceremony Highlights." *Pace Report*, January 2012, http://vimeo.com/3539852952.

Pekar, Harvey. "Roswell Rudd, Broad Strokes." Review, *JazzTimes*, December 2000.

Pellegrinelli, Lara. "Sheila Jordan: Jazz Child." *JazzTimes*, March 2001.

———. "Sheila's Dream," poem, n.d.

Priestley, Brian. *Mingus: A Critical Biography*. Da Capo Press, 1982.

Reich, Howard. "For Her Birthday, Sheila Jordan Shares Freely of Her Vocal Gifts." Live performance review, *Chicago Tribune*, November 24, 1992.

———. "Voices of Jazz Are Alive and Well." *Chicago Tribune*, July 23, 2005.

"Robert Creeley & Steve Swallow: Poetic Collaborations." poets.org, from the Academy of American Poets, http://www.poets.org/viewmedia.php/prmMID/5798, 1997–2013.

Roberts, Joel. "Sheila Jordan: Little Song." Review, *All About Jazz*, December 3, 2003.

Rowan, Andrew. "Sheila Jordan, Confirmation (1975)." Review, *All About Jazz*, June 15, 2005.

Royko, David. "Sheila Jordan and Mark Murphy: One for Junior." *Chicago Tribune*, January 16, 1994.

Sachs, Lloyd. Review, *Jazzespress*, January 26, 2012.

Schwartz, Francine. Live performance review, *DC Metro Theater Arts*, May 17, 2013.

"Sheila Jordan & Harvie Swartz (Vine St. Bar & Grill)." Review, *Variety*, July 1981.

Shim, Eunmi. *Lennie Tristano: His Life in Music*. University of Michigan Press, 2007.

Silsbee, Kirk. Liner notes to *Yesterdays*. HighNote, November 2011.

Sleight, Peter. "Swinging, Crooning and Scat: Sheila Jordan, *The Crossing*, Blackhawk Records," Review, Fort Lauderdale *Sun Sentinel*, August 3, 1986.

Souter, Tessa. "Sheila Jordan." *London Jazz News*, November 16, 2009.

Stryker, Mark. "Swing of Styles Highlights the Detroit Jazz Festival." *Detroit Free Press*, September 3, 2013.

Tafuri, Frank. Liner notes for *Here and How!*, vol. 2, OmniTone, no date available.

Whitehead, Kevin. Review of *Songs from Within*, National Public Radio (*Fresh Air*), September 1993.

Willis, Vickie. "Be-in-tween the Spa[ ]ces: The Location of Women and Subversion in Jazz." *Journal of American Culture*, August 12, 2008.

Wills, Geoffrey I. "Forty Lives in the Bebop Business: Mental Health in a Group of Eminent Jazz Musicians." *British Journal of Psychiatry*, March 2003.

Yanow, Scott. *Bebop: Third Ear—The Essential Listening Companion*. Backbeat Books, August 2000.

———. *The Jazz Singers: The Ultimate Guide*. Backbeat Books, 2008.

———. Review of "Sheila, All Music," no date, http://www.allmusic.com/album/sheila-mw0000188372.

Index

About the Author

As someone who has acquired a proficiency in a range of fields, **Ellen Johnson** uses her devotion to the arts to inspire others. Growing up in the cultural atmosphere of Chicago, Johnson first discovered her love for music and theater, eventually leading her to become a professional vocalist, lyricist, actress, writer, and educator. Even as a child she was a voracious reader, with a penchant for writing poetry and short stories—anticipating her future work as a music publicist and jazz editor for *Singer and Musician Magazine*.

Her intensive knowledge of the jazz world began in the late 1970s under the guidance of respected pianist and educator Willie Pickens and hands-on professional appearances in concerts and festivals. As a vocalist Johnson has recorded, performed, or studied with Charles McPherson, Louie Bellson, Bobby McFerrin, Sheila Jordan, Jay Clayton, John Clayton, Roy McCurdy, John Stowell, Hugh Martin, and Rick Helzer, among many other accomplished musicians. Through her own companies, Vocal Visions and Sound Visions Media, she has promoted and produced jazz recordings and music instructional products, including her own releases *Form and Formless*, *These Days*, *Chinchilla Serenade*, *Too Good to Title*, and *Cups of the Heart* and educational releases *The Warm Up CD*, *Vocal Builders*, and *You Sing Jazz*. Besides her own songs, Johnson has published lyrics to the Sonny Rollins composition "St. Thomas" and three Charles Mingus compositions, "Peggy's Blue Skylight," "Nostalgia in Times Square," and "Noddin Ya Head Blues."

Johnson's education includes a master's in vocal performance from San Diego State University, a bachelor's in music in vocal performance from the American Conservatory of Music, coursework toward a PhD from the University of Humanistic Studies, UCLA extension courses in their Music Business Certificate Program, the Opera Audition Program at the American Institute of Musical Studies (AIMS) in Graz, Austria, and being the first vocalist at the Birch Creek Summer Jazz Program (with Gene Aiken and Harold J. Jones). Her research, studies on music healing, creativity, and a certification in expressive arts therapy encouraged her to complete training in creativity coaching with Eric Maisel.

Johnson has taught for or been on the voice faculties of the University of San Diego, the Old Globe Theatre's MFA program, California Polytechnic University Pomona, Portland Community College, Southwestern College, the Rubicon Theater Summer Youth Program, and the Jefferson School of Performing Arts. She has given master classes at various colleges throughout the United States, including the University of Southern California, Bradley University, and Portland State University. Johnson was past president of the San Diego chapter of the National Association of Teachers of Singing (NATS), past California chapter vocal representative for the International Association of Jazz Educators (IAJE), and cofounder and past president of the Jazz Vocal Coalition (JZVOC). She currently resides in the San Francisco area, where she continues as a freelance musician, writer, and creativity consultant and serves on the voice faculty of the Jazzschool at the California Jazz Conservatory (CJC).